THE DIEPPE RAID

THE COMBINED OPERATIONS ASSAULT ON HITLER'S
EUROPEAN FORTRESS, AUGUST 1942

THE DIEPPE RAID

THE COMBINED OPERATIONS ASSAULT ON HITLER'S EUROPEAN FORTRESS, AUGUST 1942

An Official History

Frontline Books

THE DIEPPE RAID
The Combined Operations Assault on Hitler's European Fortress, August 1942

This edition published in 2019
and reprinted in this format in 2025
by Frontline Books
an imprint of
Pen & Sword Books Ltd,
Yorkshire - Philadelphia

This book is based on the revised version of Battle Summary No.33, which is located under the file reference ADM 205/174, from a series of records from the Admiralty, which is held at The National Archives, Kew, and is licensed under the Open Government Licence v3.0. A number of additional appendices are based on file reference ADM 234/447, which is also which is held at The National Archives, Kew, and is also and is licensed under the Open Government Licence v3.0.

Text alterations and additions © Frontline Books

ISBN: 978 1 399022 354

All rights reserved. No part of this book may be reproduced, transmitted, downloaded, decompiled or reverse engineered in any form or by any means, electronic or mechanical including photocopying, recording or by any information storage and retrieval system, without permission from the Publisher in writing. NO AI TRAINING: Without in any way limiting the Author's and Publisher's exclusive rights under copyright, any use of this publication to "train" generative artificial intelligence (AI) technologies to generate text is expressly prohibited. The Author and Publisher reserve all rights to license uses of this work for generative AI training and development of machine learning language models

Printed and bound in the UK by CPI Group (UK) Ltd, Croydon, CR0 4YY.

The Publisher's authorised representative in the EU for product safety is Authorised Rep Compliance Ltd., Ground Floor, 71 Lower Baggot Street, Dublin D02 P593, Ireland. | www.arccompliance.com

For a complete list of Pen & Sword titles please contact

PEN & SWORD BOOKS LIMITED
47 Church Street, Barnsley, South Yorkshire, S70 2AS, England
E-mail: enquiries@pen-and-sword.co.uk
Website: www.pen-and-sword.co.uk
or
PEN AND SWORD BOOKS
1950 Lawrence Road, Havertown, PA 19083, USA
E-mail: uspen-and-sword@casematepublishers.com
Website: www.penandswordbooks.com

Contents

List of Plans	viii
Foreword	ix
Publisher's Note	xi
Abbreviations	xii

Part I
Preparations

Section
1. Introduction	1
2. Dieppe: Defences	2
3. Origins of the Plan	3
4. Adoption of Plan "Rutter"	5
5. Objectives	6
6. Confirmation of the Original Plan	7
7. Modification of Plan	8
8. Abandonment of "Rutter"	9
9. Operation "Jubilee"	10

Part II
The Passage

10. The Embarkation and Minesweeping	13
11. The Passage	14
12. The Approach	15
13. Situation 0340 hours, 19th August	16
14. Action with Enemy Forces	17
15. The Destroyers	18
16. Radar Warnings	19
17. Results of the Action	21

Part III
The Assault

18. General remarks	22
19. The Eastern Outer Flank (Yellow beaches)	22
20. The Western Outer Flank (Orange beaches)	25
21. The Eastern Inner Flank (Blue beach)	26
22. Naval attempts to evacuate Blue beach	28

23. The Western Inner Flank (Green Beach – Pourville)		29
24. The Main Assault (Red and White Beaches) – Dieppe		30
25. Landing the Tanks		32
26. Naval Support		33
27. The Floating Reserve and R.M. Commando		35

Part IV
The Withdrawal

28. Situation at 0900 hours	38
29. Evacuation of Green Beach (Pourville)	39
30. Evacuation of Red and White Beaches	41
31. Decision to abandon operation	43
32. Loss of H.M.S. *Berkeley*	45
33. Remarks on the Evacuation	45
34. The Return to England	47

Part V
The Air Battle

35. Air Forces	48
36. Enemy Air Opposition	49

Part VI
The Aftermath

37. Conclusion	51

Part VII
Appendices

A	List of H.M. Ships on Operation "Jubilee"	55
B	Organization of H.M. Ships on Operation "Jubilee"	62
C	Military and Air Forces on Operation "Jubilee"	65
D	Casualties	67
E	Types of Landing Craft	71
F	Analysis of Bombing Attacks in Support of Operation "Jubilee"	72
G	Summary of the Lessons learnt	74
H	Extracts from German Reports on Dieppe Raid	77

Additional Appendices from Initial Version of Battle Summary No.33

I	Naval Operational Order No.I	126
J	List of Ships, Groups and Senior Officers	132
K	Operation "Jubilee" – Instructions to L.S.I.	137
L	Operation "Jubilee" – Instructions to Destroyers	141
M	Orders for Naval A.A. Fire	146
N	Operation "Jubilee" – Orders for Coastal Craft	148
O	Table of Movements of Coastal Craft After the Assault	153
P	Operation "Jubilee" – Instructions to Cutting Out Force	156
Q	Orders for Withdrawal of Troops and Return Passage	163
R	Orders for Naval Beach Parties	168
S	Detailed Military Plan	172
T	Information – Enemy	178

U	Assault and Occupation	182
V	Schedule of Timings	185
W	Detailed Air Plan	200
X	Officers in Command	221
Y	Report by Naval Force Commander	231
Z	Report by Military Force Commander	242
AA	Report by the Air Force Commander	250
BB	Order of Battle of the Royal Air Force	265
CC	Analysis of Bombing Attacks	268
DD	An Estimate of Enemy Aircraft Seen over Dieppe During the Action	270
EE	Reactions of the German Air Force	271
FF	Medical Arrangements for Casualty Evacuation	276
GG	Medical Evacuation at a Dockyard	282
HH	Security Arrangements	284
II	Security Lapses and Action Taken	291
JJ	German State of Readiness	293
KK	Enemy Defences and Weapons	294
LL	Enemy Defences Summarised	298
MM	Sections of German Defence Plans	301

Notes and references	305
Notes on Sources	313

List of Plans

Plan 1: Dieppe, 19 August 1942 — 116
Showing Principal Batteries, Landing Places and Troops Engaged

Plan 2: Dieppe Operation Jubilee — 118
19 August 1942: Diagram to Illustrate Tracks of Units on Passage

Plan 3: Disposition of Naval Force During the Passage — 120

Plan 4: Dieppe Action with Enemy Forces — 122

Plan 5: Plot of Enemy Convoy 18 – 19 August 1942 — 123

Plan 6: Dieppe After the Raid August 19th 1942 — 124

Appendix MM: Sections Of German Defence Plans — 301

Foreword

Battle Summary No.33, *Raid on Dieppe* was originally written in 1944. The events of the Raid had been carefully analysed at Combined Operations Headquarters as soon as it was over, and a combined report was issued in October 1942, (under reference B.R. 1887), which, together with the contemporary reports of Force Commanders etc., was largely used in the compilation of the Battle Summary.

Since then information from returned Prisoners of War and other sources, notably the Official History of the Canadian Army by Colonel C.P. Stacey, have become available. The ensuing revision, which is the basis of this book, contains additions and amendments in the light of this information.

The real interest of the Raid lies in the lessons drawn from it, which in their application provided the key to the success of the remarkable series of Allied landings carried out from November 1942 onwards, culminating in Normandy in June 1944.

Admiralty, London,
November 1958

Publishers Note

This 'official history' is reproduced in the form that it was originally written. Aside from correcting obvious spelling mistakes or typographical errors, we have strived to keep the edits and alterations to the absolute minimum. As a result of this policy, a number of inconsistencies remain. For example, Hughes-Hallett is often included without the hyphen. The format and style of some of the appendices has been adjusted to assist in easier reference by the modern reader.

Abbreviations

A.A.   Anti-aircraft

C.C.O.   Chief of Combined Operations
C.-in-C.   Commander-in-Chief
C.O.   Commanding Officer

E-boat   German armed motorboat. (British Term)
E.T.O.U.S.A.   European Theatre of Operations US Army

F.O.O.   Forward Observation Officer

G.O.C.   General Officer Commanding

H.Q.   Headquarters

L.C.A.   Landing Craft Assault
L.C.F.   Landing Craft Flak
L.C.M.   Landing Craft Mechanized
L.C.P.   Landing Craft Personnel
L.C.S.   Landing Craft Support
L.C.T.   Landing Craft Tank
L.S.I.   Landing Ship Infantry*

M.F.C.   Military Force Commander
M.G.B.   Motor Gunboat
M.L.   Motor Launch
M.T.B.   Motor Torpedo Boat (British)

N.F.C.   Naval Force Commander

ABBREVIATIONS

R-Boat	Motor Boat used for Minesweeping (German Term)
R.M.	Royal Marines
S-Boat	German M.T.B. (German Term)
S.G.B.	Steam Gunboat
S.O.	Senior Officer
T.O.O.	Time of Origin (of Signals)
U.J.	Anti-Submarine Trawler (German Term)
U.S.A.A.C.	United States Army Air Corps

* *Note*: The letters L, M, S, often found in brackets after landing craft mean Large, Medium and Small

Part 1

Preparations

1. Introduction.
The month of April 1942, when the raid on Dieppe was first considered, marked in almost every theatre of war, the nadir of Allied fortunes since the capitulation of France in 1940. In the Far East, the Japanese had so far carried all before them; Singapore fell on 15th February, Java surrendered on 9th March; Rangoon had been occupied and the fate of Burma and north-east India was in the balance. Some four thousand miles further east, Japanese landings had taken place in East New Guinea; Australia felt herself gravely menaced. In the Middle East a German advance of some 300 miles in Cyrenaica took place in the first week of February; Admiral Sir Andrew Cunningham's Mediterranean Fleet, gravely weakened by recent casualties was hard put to it to protect the vital convoys to Malta, then undergoing savage air attack.

Serious losses had been suffered recently by the British Navy[1] and at the same time a new fleet had to be formed for service in the Far East. True, the enforced entry of the United States in the previous December guaranteed <u>ultimate</u> success, but some critical months must yet elapse before the damage inflicted on the American Fleet at Pearl Harbour could be made good. The Battle of the Atlantic had entered its grimmest phase; U-boats sank a higher tonnage of merchant shipping in the quarter ending March 1942 than in any previous period, and this was on the increase. Only in Russia had the Axis received a check, where their armies, having failed to achieve a knock-out blow in the autumn, had been caught unprepared for the rigours of a winter campaign and had suffered heavy punishment at the hands of the Russians. The Spring break-up, however, imposed a lull on the Russian front in March.

The British and American Governments had for some time been much concerned about the best way of relieving the intense strain on the Russians. By this time, industry in both the United Kingdom and the

United States was getting geared to war. Munitions and equipment, so desperately lacking in the earlier stages, were being produced in ever greater quantities; increasing shipments against increasing opposition were being sent to Murmansk. But agitation for a "Second Front" in the west was growing in intensity; and troops stationed in the United Kingdom, notably the Canadians, were becoming more and more doubtful whether "they also serve who only stand and wait". Investigation, however had proved that a large-scale cross-channel operation would not be feasible in 1942. The best that could be devised was a series of raids on an increasing scale. These had culminated in the fine exploit at St. Nazaire[2] on 28th March 1942.

It was against this background that the raid on Dieppe, first known as Operation "Rutter" and later re-named "Jubilee", was undertaken. This was the largest raid actually carried out, and the only one in which the landing of tanks was attempted and in which more than an hour or two was allowed for military operations on shore; it was also the last, because the available landing craft were soon afterwards required for use in the North African expedition, and subsequently the strategic policy regarding raids underwent a change.

2. **Dieppe: Defences.**
The town and port of Dieppe contained several military objectives such as stores, docks, shipping, railway yards, a radar station at Caude-Cote and the fighter airfield of St. Aubin on the western outskirts of the town. It was estimated that the defences were comparatively weak and manned by second rate troops. The port was also well within range of English shore-based fighters. In other respects, Dieppe was not altogether an easy target for a surprise landing. It lies in a stretch of chalk cliffs which extend from Cap d'Antifer to the town of Ault, 56 miles to the north-east. In the vicinity of the port they are fairly high and present an almost unbroken front to the sea. The only considerable gap is at Dieppe itself, where the river d'Arques enters the channel. Other openings in the neighbourhood are few and confined. The beaches are narrow and rocky with occasional ledges which render landings almost impracticable at or near low water. Smooth water was essential for any undertaking and wind in excess of force 3 was said to cause a swell. Under these circumstances in the opinion of Combined Operations Headquarters, opportunities for landing were limited to "about two days a month on an average during the summer".[3] Dieppe however was regarded as the only objective which was a "worth while" target and yet a practicable one from the point of view of distance, defences and beaches.

PREPARATIONS

So far as was known the defences of Dieppe consisted of a battery of six 5.9-in. naval guns at Varengeville ("Hess" Battery) and a battery of four 5.9-in. naval guns at Berneval ("Goebbels" Battery). Three field batteries each of four guns either 4-in. or 5.9-in., were thought to be situated on the east headland commanding the harbour, behind the town near Arques la Bataille, where divisional H.Q. was believed to be located, and near Appeville, not far from the fortified position "Quatre Vents" Farm. Besides these there were a number of A.A. batteries both light and heavy, some being dual purpose guns, and of course included in the defences were machine guns in pill-boxes, and small guns behind concrete defences.[4]

In estimating the suitability of Dieppe as a target, the question of naval and aerial covering bombardment had also to be considered. Very powerful bomber and fighter forces were within easy flying distance of the French coast and it was possible for cruisers or even battleships to manoeuvre off the town in comparative safety. The possibility of effective support in such cases depends partly on the nature of the terrain. If the coast line is fairly low with more or less open country extending some distance inland, the enemy's defences can be bombarded and his lines of supply and reinforcement disrupted during the critical initial disembarkation. The conditions however were not altogether favourable in this respect. Pill-boxes and light gun positions round the harbour entrance, enfilading the coast line to the westward, could be engaged by direct fire but the built-up area near the main landing beaches constituted a serious obstacle to naval or aerial bombardment during an actual landing. The shell bursts from heavy naval guns would probably have endangered the landing parties whilst the distance between the sea and the houses was much too narrow for aerial bombardment. There was of course the alternative of heavy protracted bombing to flatten the houses along the sea front prior to the raid but it was considered that such action would probably warn the enemy of the impending assault and kill a large number of Frenchmen.

3. Origins of the Plan.

The possibilities of an attack were first investigated by the Target Committee of Combined Operations Headquarters early in April 1942,[5] and about the middle of that month the Planning Staff of that Headquarters, – under the general direction of Captain J. Hughes Hallett R.N. – began to prepare an outline plan.

A frontal assault was not contemplated, landings on each flank being proposed – at Quiberville, some six miles to the west of Dieppe, and at

Oriel-sur-Mer, about double the distance to the east. These flank landings were to be roughly Brigade strength, and a third Brigade was to be held as a floating reserve prepared to reinforce either of the flank landings or to synchronise a frontal attack on Dieppe with the approach of the other Brigades to the city.

On 30th March, 1942, the Chiefs of Staff had made their approval for the military part of the plans for large raids contingent upon their being agreed by a senior officer nominated by the Commander-in-Chief, Home Forces.[6] In this instance Lieutenant General B.L. Montgomery was chosen. He was, at the time, C.-in-C. South Eastern Command in which the 2nd Canadian Division was stationed. He at once criticised the military plan, on the ground that the distances to be covered by the troops landed on the flanks were such that the city could not possibly be captured within the period dictated by Naval and Air considerations. He therefore proposed that a dawn frontal assault should be made instead, synchronised with two smaller landings either side to seize the cliffs which overlooked Dieppe.

Under this decision of the Chiefs of Staff, H.Q. Home Forces became closely associated with the preparation of the outline plan, and on 14th April their representatives joined the planning syndicate, General Montgomery being kept in broad touch with progress.

In the course of the discussions that took place during April, certain disadvantages which might derive from the C.O.H.Q. proposals for converging attacks on Dieppe were examined. Chief of these was held to be the possible loss of surprise which could occur before the main assaults on the city had time to develop from the flank landings, six and twelve miles away. In this connection, some of the intervening country – particularly to the west – was enclosed and lent itself to delaying action. Further, if time was to be lost in bringing our strength to bear against Dieppe itself, it would not only make re-embarkation within the time limit dictated by Naval and Air considerations very difficult but would also increase the risk of German reserves being enabled to intervene in the battle.

These considerations, among others, led to the preparation of two schemes. One (Scheme A) envisaged a frontal assault precede by flank attacks at Puits and Pourville whilst parachute and glider borne troops were simultaneously to capture the batteries at Berneval and Varengeville-sur-Mer. The second (Scheme B), which was in principle a modified version of the original C.O.H.Q. plan, was to dispense with an initial frontal assault and to land two battalions at Puits and two at Pourville, with two more as a floating reserve, whilst a seventh battalion and a battalion of tanks landed at Quiberville.

When these two plans of attack had been prepared they were considered at a conference held on 18th April, at which the Commander-in-Chief, Home Forces, was represented by his Deputy Chief of the General Staff and Brigadier, General Staff, (Plans). In the course of the discussion which then took place, it became apparent that the weight of Army opinion favoured Scheme A. The Naval view was that though a frontal assault was hazardous it was feasible from the naval aspect, subject to a short interval being accepted between the main frontal attack and the subsidiary flank landings, in order to give the L.S.(I) sufficient sea room; it was immaterial whether the main attack precede or followed the flank attacks. All were agreed that the landings should take place in darkness, that they should follow as closely as possible after a heavy air bombardment of Dieppe, and that low flying attacks against targets should take place as soon as there was sufficient light.

Thus it was that an outline plan on the lines of Scheme A was prepared for the approval of the Chiefs of Staff.

4. Adoption of Plan "Rutter".

On 25th April the first formal meeting to consider the plans for the operation (to which the code-name "Rutter" had been given) was held, Vice Admiral the Lord Louis Mountbatten, Chief of Combined Operations being in the chair. The question of a frontal assault on Dieppe was discussed.

The Army representatives explained the reasons which led them to favour this form of attack. In the first place to land any force as far west as Quibervillle would make a surprise attack on Dieppe more difficult to achieve. In the second place tanks landed on that beach would have to cross two streams which might prove to be considerable obstacles. The bridges over them would have to be seized at a very early stage in order to make sure they were not demolished by the enemy. Lastly, all available intelligence at that time showed that Dieppe was lightly held by a single low category battalion, and that the troops in the town, numbering no more than 1,400 all told, could not be heavily reinforced for some time and not by more than 2,500 men within four hours. As the operation was a raid, the time on shore was limited by the anticipated rate of reinforcement of the enemy and governed by the distance of the landing from the objective. The Naval Planners still expressed doubts as to the expediency of the frontal assault basing the opinion on general and not on naval grounds.[7] It was again emphasised that the landing would be preceded by a bombing attack on the town just before the craft carrying the assaulting troops touched down. This air bombardment would be of maximum intensity, and it was thought that the defence would be too confused by it and by subsequent attacks by low-flying aircraft to offer stout or prolonged resistance.

The bombing was to be carried out from both high and low level, the high altitude attack being against the town generally, the low-level attack against the sea front and beach defences. The question of fighter cover and air support for the land forces was debated at some length for it was realised that support from the air would be of paramount importance. It was agreed that the system of Command should be a Joint Command exercised by Naval, Military and R.A.F. Force Commanders.

5. **Objectives.**
The Outline Plan, including the principle of a frontal assault, preceded by bombing was then adopted and on 9th May was submitted to the Chiefs of Staff Committee.[8]
The objectives[9] were defined as:

1. Invasion craft consisting of converted barges and tank landing craft.
2. German Headquarters located in various hotels.
3. Gambetta Barracks, and also barracks and coast guard station on the cliff at Puits.
4. The Casino, used as an ammunition dump.
5. Railways, marshalling yards, and tunnels.
6. Gas works and power station.
7. Pharmaceutical factory; the destruction of this was desirable in view of the shortage of these products in Germany.
8. Petrol tanks or dumps.
9. Bridges and locks.
10. Food stores at Bassin de Paris, used for German Army.
11. St. Aubin Fighter Airfield.
12. Town Hall.
13. Radar station at Caude-Cote.
14. Post office in which was located the main telephone exchange.
15. E and R-Boats and Siebel Ferries.
16. Area of town occupied by Germans.

But the main purpose of the raid was not these minor objectives. A large scale amphibious invasion of France would eventually be necessary and before serious planning for this operation could be undertaken, it was essential to mount a raid on a divisional scale so as to decide whether a direct attack on a defended port was a reasonable operation of war,[10] or whether invading forces should be landed on open beaches at a distance from the objective. It was also necessary to test the different types of landing craft under fire and to obtain experience of an opposed landing of tanks. Though the raid was to all appearances a compete and costly failure, the lessons learnt were invaluable and were the basis of planning for all subsequent landing operations.

6. **Confirmation of the Original Plan.**
On 13th May the Chiefs of Staff Committee approved the Preliminary Plan as the basis for detailed planning by the Force Commanders. It approved also the employment of Canadian troops and appointed as Military and Air Force Commanders respectively, Major-General J.H. Roberts, and Air Vice-Marshal T. Leigh-Mallory. The Naval Force Commander – Rear-Admiral H.T. Baillie-Grohman – was not appointed till 1st June as he was then serving in the Middle East, but his place on the planning committee was taken by Commodore T.H. Back. It had also been decided on a previous occasion that the naval Commander-in-Chief, Portsmouth, Admiral Sir William James would be responsible for certain aspects of the raid. He was to settle all administrative questions, decide the time of sailing, make arrangements for the passage to and fro' and provide the necessary naval cover. Operations between the time of landing and re-embarkation were however, outside his sphere of control. The meeting also agreed to seek from the Cabinet approval for the bombing of the town should the Force Commanders deem that this was desirable. A minute was accordingly sent to the Prime Minister on 19th May pointing out that, under the then Cabinet ruling, targets in France could only be bombed when weather conditions permitted of accurate attacks, a restriction which had proved a handicap at St. Nazaire. On that occasion aircraft of Bomber Command arriving over the town stirred up the defences but the diversionary attack which was an important part of the plan was rendered abortive by cloud conditions hiding the dock area which was their objective.

It was hoped that this ruling might be relaxed in cases of Combined Operations. This permission was obtained. On 1st June the Chiefs of Staff were informed that though the Prime Minister was still against the indiscriminate bombing of French towns at night, an exception would be made in the case of coastal raids.

The plan now provided for a frontal assault by two infantry battalions and up to 30 Army tanks with support from sea and air. The main assault was to be preceded by high level bombing and by flank attacks delivered half an hour previously, by comparatively small forces. One battalion was to capture the A.A. coast defence and mobile batteries in the area east of Dieppe, and then aid in taking the town. Two other battalions were to perform a similar role to the west and also capture the airfield of St. Aubin. Simultaneously, parachute troops were to attack coastal and A.A. batteries and the divisional headquarters 4 miles southeast of Dieppe. The whole operation was to be carried out on two tides, the rear parties being withdrawn under cover of darkness.

It was at this stage that Rear-Admiral Baillie-Grohman arrived in England to take over the detailed naval planning and training for the operation, with his Headquarters in the Isle of Wight (H.M.S. *Vectis*). He was handed the plan by Lord Louis Mountbatten, and a day or so later attended a meeting under the chairmanship of the Chief of Combined Operations, at which were present amongst others General Sir Bernard Paget (C.-in-C., Home Forces), Lieut. General B.L. Montgomery, (South Eastern Command) and the Force Commanders. Admiral Baillie-Grohman was concerned at the weakness of the naval supporting fire[11] as proposed (4 "Hunt" class destroyers mounting 4-in. guns) but the Army Officers considered that the air attack as planned could take the place of naval gunfire.

7. **Modification of Plan.**

On 5th June a modification to the plan was introduced. It was decided to abandon the high-level bombing of Dieppe on air and military grounds. "The Air Force Commander was of the opinion that the bombing of the port itself during the night prior to the assault would not be the most profitable way to use bombers and might only result in putting the enemy on alert". The Military Commander took the view that the destruction of large numbers of houses and the setting of a considerable portion of the town on fire, would probably prevent the tanks from operating in streets chocked with debris.[12] As an alternative to high-level bombing the Air Force Commander proposed that diversionary bombing attacks should be made on Boulogne and the airfields at Abbeville-Drucat and Crécy. In view of the above opinions high-level bombing was abandoned in favour of diversionary air attacks which, it was considered, would occupy the attention of the German radar organization and might put out of action for some hours two airfields which the enemy would certainly wish to use during the operation. It was also agreed that cannon-fighters should attack the beach defences and the high ground on either side of Dieppe and that the German Divisional Headquarters at Arques-la-Bataille should be bombed.[13] These decisions represented an important modification of the original plan. The bombardment was now to be limited to the 4-in. guns of six destroyers and the 250-lb. bombs of the Hurricanes.[14] A force of M.G.B.'s was to operate off Boulogne in the early stages of the raid to give the impression that the assault would take place there instead of at Dieppe.

A period of intensive training followed with the idea of carrying out the operation at the first favourable date after 24th June. The period when astronomical and tidal conditions were favourable was limited to some 5 or 6 days twice a month[15]; and it had been accepted that settled fair weather for a period of at least 48 hours was necessary for the operation. Unfortunately, the weather proved uniformly unfavourable for the airborne troops though not consistently so for the beach landings, and on 5th July the operation was further postponed and the plan again altered. Owing to the changed states of the tides, troops would now have to be re-embarked three hours later than originally arranged. This necessitated three hours longer air cover and, in the opinion of the Military Commander, might give the enemy the opportunity to organize infantry and artillery opposition on a scale which might prejudice the re-embarkation. The Force Commanders therefore informed the Chief of Combined Operations that in their view the operation had a diminishing chance of success as each day passed and should not be carried out in its original form on the date proposed (7th July). They were accordingly instructed to consider a modified plan whereby the operation would take place on one tide only. The landing was now to be made as near low water as possible and to be completed or nearly completed by the next high water. Though on the one hand this "one tide" plan had the advantage of increasing the intensity of air support by shortening the time during which cover would have to be given, on the other hand, it tended to complicate the task of removing the German barges in Dieppe harbour, which was one of the objects of the raid.

8. **Abandonment of "Rutter"**.

These modifications were accepted, but the weather continued unfavourable and as the prospects of improvement were poor, the operation was cancelled on 7th July. Early that morning the project had received a setback. Four German fighter bombers, probably F.W.190S, dropped four 500K.g. bombs on two L.S.I. (H.M.S. *Princess Astrid* and H.M.S. *Princess Josephine Charlotte*) then lying in Yarmouth Roads, Isle of Wight, with troops embarked ready for the operation. Both ships were hit, the *Josephine Charlotte* being severely damaged. Large adjustments in the operation orders were rapidly made by the Naval and Military Force Commanders' Staffs, and despatched the same day to all ships concerned; and the expedition could have sailed at any time had the weather permitted, albeit the operation would have been somewhat handicapped.[16] This episode probably influenced the decision to cancel the expedition and disperse the forces.

9. Operation "Jubilee".

Subsequently it was decided to remount the operation under the name "Jubilee" as a "one tide" plan. General Montgomery strongly deprecated the revival of the operation, on the grounds that once the fully briefed forces had been dispersed, all hope of secrecy would be lost and he recommended that the raid on Dieppe should be cancelled "for all time". The Chiefs of Staff, however, after careful consideration approved the operation, and in the event, it actually achieved surprise.[17]

In essentials the actual plan of attack was the same as for "Rutter", but there were some modifications, the most important of which was the substitution of Commandos for airborne troops for the attacks on the extreme flanks to capture the batteries at Berneval and Varengeville, since the use of paratroops demanded ideal weather conditions, [18] and also a considerable time would be required for briefing. It had originally been intended to use ten drifters to create a smoke-walled "sanctuary", in which the landing and other craft would lie while the troops were ashore; in the final plan these were dispensed with, as it was considered that the same result could be produced by smoke screens laid by destroyers, landing craft and from the air. Smoke carrying aircraft, too, were to mask the defences on the east cliff at the moment the main landing touched down.

Before Operation "Jubilee" could take place, there were changes in the Command. In the Army chain of command, in view of the preponderant part to be taken by the Canadians, Lieut. General H.G.D. Crerar, G.O.C., 1st Canadian Corps took the place of Lieut. General Montgomery[19], who thereafter took no part in the operation.[20] On the naval side, Rear-Admiral Baillie-Grohman, and his Chief of Staff, Commodore Back, were no longer available, and at the suggestion of Lord Louis Mountbatten two members of the naval staff of Combined Operations Headquarters, – Captain J. Hughes Hallett and Commander (acting – Captain) J.D. Luce – were appointed as Naval Force Commander and Chief of Staff on 17th July.

By early August the plan had assumed its final shape. There were to be four flank attacks launched at nautical twilight, followed half an hour later by the assault on Dieppe. The landing places were to be:

East of Dieppe
Beach at Berneval   Yellow 1
Beach at Belleville sur Mer   Yellow 2
Beach at Puits   Blue

PREPARATIONS

Dieppe
East   Red
West   White

West of Dieppe

Beach at Pourville   Green
Beach near Varengeville   Orange 1
Beach ¼ mile east of River Saane   Orange 2

The Naval Force[21] consisted of 237 vessels, vis:

Destroyers   8
Gunboat   1
Sloop   1
Landing Ship, Infantry   9
Steam Gunboats   4
Motor Gunboats   12
Motor Launches   16
Chasseurs   7
Landing Craft, Tank   24
Landing Craft, Flak (Large)   6
Landing Craft, Support   8
Landing Craft, Mechanised   7
Landing Craft, Personnel   74
Landing Craft, Assault   60

They carried 6088 troops,

Canadian Army   305 Officers, 4,658 O.R. = 4,963
Commandos
Nos. 3, 4, 6 and R.M 65   65 Officers, 992 O.R. = 1,057
Inter Allied Commando   18
U.S. 1st Ranger   50
                                                                6,088

Air Forces consisted of:

Fighters   60 squadrons
Fighter Bombers   2 squadrons
Bombers   5 squadrons
Total   67 squadrons

11

The attack from Yellow beaches aimed at the capture of the "Goebbels" battery near Berneval, and that from Orange beaches at the corresponding one – "Hess" – near Varengeville. Of the inner flank attacks, that from Blue beach was designed to take another battery – "Rommel" – and attack in the rear the east headland above Dieppe. From Green beach, troops were to capture the fortified position at "Quatre Vents" Farm and take the western headland overlooking the town in the rear. Other troops were to move up the Scie Valley against the airfield of St. Aubin and the German divisional headquarters, which was believed to be at Arques-la-Bataille.[22] Supported by tanks the troops landed on the main (Red and White) beaches were to take and hold the town. The east and west headlands were to be heavily bombed by Bostons as were also the battery on the east cliff and the two batteries behind the town, and immediately after aircraft were to throw smoke screens over the two headlands. Fighters armed with cannon were to co-operate with the attacks on the Berneval and Varengeville batteries and were also to shoot-up the defences along the front at Dieppe.

Destroyers would provide covering bombardment from seaward while L.C.F. and L.C.S. would give close support during the landings. Once the defences were mastered and our troops were established in the town, the gunboat *Locust* and the "Chasseurs" carrying the Royal Marine Commando were to enter Dieppe harbour, cut out the landing barges, trawlers and any other naval vessels and demolish naval installations and harbour works.

Unfavourable weather and tides caused some delay but on 17th August the forecast for the next two days, though not very good was better than that expected later, and at 1000[23] the necessary preliminary order was issued for the expedition to sail on the night of 18/19th August. The flank landings were timed for 0450, the main assault for 0520.[24] At a final conference between C.C.O. and the Force Commanders, "the question of air bombardment by heavy bombers was again discussed, but the decision not to use them was confirmed, the Military Force Commander remaining of the opinion that the destruction wrought by such bombardments would make the passage of tanks through Dieppe very difficult if not impossible."[25] All was set for what the Naval Commander, in a signal made before landing, termed "an unusually complex and hazardous operation."[26]

Part II

The Passage

10. The Embarkation, Minesweeping.
The preliminary order for operation "Jubilee" was issued at 1000 on 17th August and the executive order by Commander-in-Chief, Portsmouth's signal, 1002A/18th August, 1942. Embarkation of the tanks sailing from Portsmouth began on the night of 17th, though a smoke screen at Gosport delayed the completion of the loading there until 0330 of 18th. The loading hards at Newhaven had been found unsuitable, so the tanks sailing from that port had been embarked at Gosport and sent round there during the previous ten days.[27] Troops were taken on board during the afternoon and evening of 18th August, everything going according to plan.

As a large area off Dieppe was believed to have been mined by the enemy, proceedings were opened by our minesweepers. During the afternoon of the 18th, the 9th and 13th Minesweeping Flotilla sailed separately from Portsmouth for the vicinity of Beach Head, so as to give the impression that one flotilla was carrying out a clearance sweep in the area and the other proceeding on passage up Channel. At 2130, as arranged, they were joined at NN[28] by the four M.L.'s which were to act as their mark boats and rescue craft. In their preliminary manoeuvres here a difficulty arose, as L.C.P. of Group 5, had reached the scene before schedule, having been granted permission to sail 15 minutes early because of the southerly wind. But no delay resulted, and from this point the 9th and 13th Flotillas set course for DD and LL[29] respectively, to seep channels through the enemy minefield to FF and QQ[30]. The 9th Flotilla which consisted of the *Sidmouth, Bangor, Blackpool, Bridlington, Bridport, Bude, Rhyl* and *Tenby*, commenced sweeping at 0003 and at 0105 turned to port and got in sweeps; the 13th Flotilla which comprised the *Blyth, Clacton, Eastbourne, Felixstowe, Ilfracombe, Polruan, Stornaway* and *Rothsay*, began eight minutes earlier and passed QQ at 0051. Everything went without a hitch: the channels were about four cables wide, clearly marked on each side and at the ends; only one mine was seen.[31] The flotillas then manoeuvred to keep clear of the approaching expedition, and soon after 0500 turned for home setting flag dan buoys to mark the channels in daylight on the way back. They returned in company to Portsmouth, having carried out their work "with efficiency and precision".

11. **The Passage.**
The passage was to be made in darkness. The moon (in its first quarter) set at 2316.[32]

The size of the expedition, the necessity for dispersal and the existence of the enemy minefield necessitated an elaborate time-table for its passage. With one or two minor exceptions this was faithfully adhered to up to its closing stages.

The Force was organised in 13 groups.[33] Groups 1 and 3 consisted of the L.S.I.s bound for Orange, Green and Blue beaches respectively, and Group 4 of those for Red and White beaches.

Groups 5 and 6, bound for Yellow and Green beaches, and Group 7 carrying the floating reserve were comprised of L.C.P. Flotillas.

Groups 8 to 12 consisted of the tank landing craft and Group 13 the Chasseurs carrying the R.M. Commandos and the *Alresford*. Each group included its coastal forces and close support craft, M.G.B.s, L.C.F. etc.

Groups 1, 2, 3, 4, 12, 13 and part of 10 sailed from Portsmouth and Southampton, the rest from Newhaven and Shoreham. Those from Southampton had to leave before dark; in order to baffle the routine German evening photographic air reconnaissance, they were elaborately disguised to resemble a coastal convoy.

At 2125, 18th August, the *Queen Emma*, (Landing Ship, Infantry), passed the East Solent Gate leading Groups 3, 2, 1 and 4 followed by destroyers, all in single line ahead with the escorting S.G.B's and M.G.B's disposed on either beam.[34] The speed of the *Queen Emma* being slightly in excess of that intended, the Naval Force Commander in H.M.S. *Calpe* made a signal to her at 0016, 19th August, to reduce speed to 18 knots. The *Calpe* led the destroyers to take station ahead of her, and at 0045 and again at 0106 altered course to enter the western passage through the minefield which she did at 0110. The *Queen Emma* should have followed, but failed to observe the destroyers' alterations of course and, with the L.S.I. of Groups 1, 2 and 3, entered the eastern passage instead. Here at 0140 they overtook the *Fernie*, which had joined Groups 5 and 8 off Newhaven and was leading them down the far channel according to plan. The minefield had been crossed by 0155 and the L.S.I. had disappeared from sight to starboard. On reaching QQ[35] the *Calpe* hauled out to the eastward and stopped. At 0145 she sighted the L.S.I. of Groups 1, 2 and 3 and signalled her position by flashing lamp. Twenty-five minutes later the *Glengyle*,[36] leading Group 4, emerged from the western channel exactly according to schedule and the *Calpe* proceeded to accompany them to their "lowering position"[37](RR), 10 miles from Dieppe. Group 4 was escorted by the *Slazak* and *Brocklesby*. The *Locust* failed to keep up with the rest of Group 4 and, with M.L. 291, crossed the minefield by an unswept route and was at QQ[38] by 0245. The first swarms of small craft were then emerging from the eastern channel with Groups 5 and 8 leading.

12. The Approach.

As soon as they had cleared the minefield, the leading forces formed up for the opening attack. In the van with their escorting craft were the *Prince Albert*[39] of Group 1 carrying No.4 Commando, the *Princess Beatrix*[40] and *Invicta*[41] of Group 2 carrying the South Saskatchewan Regiment, the *Queen Emma*[42] and *Princess Astrid*[43] of Group 3 with the Royal Regiment of Canada and Group 5 with No.3 Commando. These were intended to carry out the flank landings at 0450 at Orange, Green, Blue and Yellow beaches, respectively. They were followed by the *Glengyle*,[44] *Prince Charles*[45] and *Prince Leopold*[46] of Group 4 with the Royal Hamilton Light Infantry and the Essex Scottish who were to make the initial assault on the beaches of Dieppe itself at 0520, and the *Duke of Wellington*[47] with reinforcements for Blue beach. Next came the *Calpe* (the headquarters ship), *Fernie* (the standby headquarters ship) with the *Locust* and Group 8. Behind were Group 6 with the Camerons of Canada who were to land on Green beach at 0520, and Group 7 with the Fusiliers Mont-Royal who constituted the floating reserve: then followed Group 9, with Groups 10 and 11 far astern, all three carrying tanks for Red and White beaches. The destroyers acted as screening forces, the second division (*Garth*, *Berkeley*, *Albrighton* and *Bleasdale*) being to starboard, and the third division (*Slazak* and *Brocklesby*) to port.

The L.S.I. now made for their respective lowering positions (SS, GG, BB and RR[48] for Groups 1, 2, 3 and 4, respectively) and all craft were safely in the water within three minutes of schedule – 0300 for Groups 1, 2 and 3, 0320 for Group 4. The distance from the lowering positions to the beaches was about ten miles. This long run in was accepted because it was desired to keep the landing ships outside the range of the enemy radar. The L.S.I. turned somewhat unwillingly for home, the monotony of their return passage being broken only by a minor collision between the *Princess Beatrix* and *Invicta*. The landing craft formed up. The *Princess Astrid's* flotilla lost precious minutes through some of their number forming up on an M.G.B. which, having got out of station, had appeared near the spot where M.G.B. 316 was expected.

13. **Situation 0340 hours 19th August.**
By 0340 it was possible to view the progress made with considerable satisfaction. There had been some inevitable deviations from programme, but they had been neither numerous nor important. The L.S.I. were steaming homeward after accomplishing their task successfully and the first waves of landing craft had formed up and were being led in to their respective beaches as follows:

Orange Beach (Varengeville)	M.G.B. 312, the *Prince Albert's* Flotilla, S.G.B. 9.
Green Beach (Pourville)	M.G.B. 317, the *Princess Beatrix* and *Invicta's* flotillas S.G.B.6.
White Beach (Dieppe, West)	M.G.B. 326, the *Glengyle's* flotilla.
Red Beach (Dieppe, East)	M.L. 291, the *Prince Charles* and *Prince Albert's* flotillas.
Blue Beach (Puits)	M.G.B. 316, the *Queen Emma's* and *Princess Astrid's* flotilla, S.G.B.8.
Yellow Beach (Berneval)	Group 5 (S.G.B. 5, 26 L.C.P. M.L. 346 L.C.F (L) 1).

In the rear was the *Duke of Wellington's* flotilla bound for Blue beach. On either wing the six destroyers were carrying out protective patrols and beyond them lay outer screens of coastal craft. To the northward spread over several miles stretched the remaining groups. Firstly Groups 8 and 6 with the *Fernie* ahead and the *Calpe* astern of the former, then Groups 7, 9, 10 and 11. In the rear, due to clear the minefield by 0355, were the *Alresford* and her Chasseurs whilst well on the far side of the passages was Group 12 and its spare L.C.T., not due on the scene for some hours.

Meanwhile from 0330 to 0450 M.G.B.s 6, 7 and 9 were making the small-scale diversion off Boulogne according to plan. Depth charges and smoke floats were dropped but the enemy seemed unimpressed. No hostile ships were sighted nor was there any sign of activity ashore.

It had been thought possible that the convoy might be attacked by enemy E-Boats, but none were sighted. They were otherwise engaged.

The fifth German S-Boat (M.T.B.) flotilla was laying mines during the night in Lyme Bay; the fourth S-Boat flotilla was at Boulogne, and after the attack commenced the German Naval Command decided that it was useless to employ E-Boats against a force protected by destroyers.[49]

Just when all was going so smoothly there occurred an unfortunate mischance.

14. **Action with Enemy Forces.**
During the passage Group 5 had become somewhat disorganized, a slight delay outside the harbour necessitating a rather greater speed than the L.C.P. could comfortably maintain. Group 5 consisted of 23 L.C.P. (L) carrying No.3 Commando which was to land on Yellow beaches to the eastward. The group was escorted by S.G.B. 5., M.L. 346 and L.C.F. (L) 1, the whole under the command of Commander D.G. Wyburd, R.N., while the troops were commanded by Lieutenant-Colonel J.F. Durnford-Slater.

At 0340 the *Slazak* and *Brocklesby* crossed the bows of Group 5 from starboard to port.[50] Then came a critical interlude. At 0347 Group 5 suddenly encountered an enemy convoy consisting of five small motor coasters escorted by three escort vessels. Three patrol vessels off Dieppe apparently supported this convoy later.[51] About 7 miles from the shore S.G.B. 5 sighted a ship on her port bow and immediately the group was lit up by enemy star shell. It was at first thought that the *Slazak* and *Brocklesby* had mistaken Group 5 for the enemy, but it was soon seen that this was not the case; in fact, the destroyers at this time were about 4 miles to the N.N.E.[52]

The enemy opened a heavy fire on our ships mainly with light A.A. guns but also with guns up to 3- or 4-in. calibre.[53] Commander Wyburd had "decided beforehand that should the enemy be encountered, he would continue his course and speed, and endeavour to fight his way through". He had issued orders to this effect, being convinced that any general alteration of course and speed would so disorganize the formation of Group 5 as to render an organized landing impossible.[54] S.G.B. 5 accordingly continued on her course at 9½ knots for about 10 minutes. She was the enemy's main target and was hit many times. Five hits were scored on her boiler, all her guns were put out of action, her wireless was disabled and 40 per cent. of those on board became casualties, though, surprisingly enough, only one man was killed.

Owing to lack of illuminant our ships were not able to see the enemy and could only fire at the points from which tracer seemed to come.

Commander Wyburd remained on the bridge under heavy fire and showed great gallantry and determination, but at 0407 S.G.B. 5 was silenced and partially disabled and it became evident that the plan to fight a way through had failed. By this time the L.C.P. had scattered and S.G.B. 5 turned away at 6 knots.

M.L. 346, leading Group 5, had been hit several times. At 0412, having lost contact with the group she set course for Yellow beaches. She called up S.G.B. 5 continually so as to report the position but "all waves appeared to be jammed, no messages could be sent."[55]

L.C.F. (L) 1 armed with two twin 4-in. guns continued the action and although her fire control was soon disabled she fought with great energy and determination and succeeded in setting one of the enemy on fire and claims to have sunk another.[56]

15. **The Destroyers.**

The *Slazak* and *Brocklesby* took no part in the action, as the captain of the *Slazak* who was senior officer, of 3rd Destroyer Division thought that the firing was from the shore. As the special function of the destroyers was to protect the convoy it is unfortunate that the situation was not realised. At 0530 the *Brocklesby* parted company with the *Slazak* to investigate a burning ship 4 miles 340° from Berneval. This was UJ. 1404 abandoned by her crew who were in the water. Survivors to the number of 25 were rescued but the commanding officer had been killed early in the action. The *Brocklesby* shelled the enemy craft which finally blew up at about 0645.

The *Garth* (senior officer of 2nd Destroyer Division), had sighted star shell at 0351 followed by tracer fire, and thought that the 3rd Division was firing at enemy shipping. Increasing speed, he steered towards the firing but, before reaching the scene of the action, decided that it was necessary to alter course to the southward to get into station astern of the landing craft at the proper time, so as to cover the main assault with their bombarding fire. By this time only five L.C.P. were in sight from S.G.B. 5. Some time was spent in trying to repair the S.G.B.'s wireless so as to report the situation to the Naval Force Commander but this proved impossible and soon afterwards the S.G.B.'s engines broke down completely.

Commander Wyburd and Colonel Durnford-Slater then decided that the landing of the troops on Yellow beach could not be effected according to plan, and at 0455 they transferred to an L.C.P. with the intention of finding a ship in another group to pass a signal to Naval Force Commander, failing which they intended to report in person on board the *Calpe*. The other four L.C.P. were ordered to tow and escort the S.G.B. back to Newhaven; three of these, however, misunderstood their orders and followed Commander Wyburd's

L.C.P. at a distance. Commander Wyburd proceeded towards Dieppe, boarding an M.L. on the way to try to pass a signal, but owing to traffic congestion he was unable to do so in spite of using the priority "Most Immediate."

Of the 23 L.C.P. in Group 5, four had broken down before the action and eventually returned to Newhaven, four were damaged in the action but succeeded in making their way home, [57] one accompanied S.G.B. 5 four proceeded with Commander Wyburd to look for the *Calpe*, three closed L.C.F. (L) 1, and the other seven, accompanied by M.L. 346, went in and landed their troops on Yellow beaches.

L.C.F. (L) 1 continued the action until 0450 by which time many of her crew, including all her officers, were killed or wounded. As it was then zero hour she broke off the action and, considering it was useless to land the troops at Yellow beaches, proceeded towards Dieppe in company with three L.C.P.[58] on the way this party met four L.C.P. with Commander Wyburd and all proceeded in company towards the H.Q. ship.

16. Radar Warnings.

The presence of these enemy craft does not appear to have been detected by radar[59] by any vessel of the expedition. The enemy was, however, located by shore radar stations, and was plotted by Portsmouth at 0040, 0100 and 0226. A warning signal was made by Commander-in-Chief, Portsmouth, at 0127A: "Small craft apparently patrolling approximately 350° Treport 15 miles at 0100". There was so far nothing to show that these craft were likely to enter the operational area, but fresh reports showed that this was very possible, so at 0244A a further message was sent to the Naval Force Commander: "Two craft 302° Treport 10 miles, course 190° 13 knots at 0226".

Thus, a full hour before the encounter, warning had been given of the presence of unidentified craft, which were then but 4 miles from the projected track of Group 5 and were almost bound to intercept it, if course and speed were maintained. At 0300 the enemy was apparently not more than 2 miles from the line of advance of Group 5.

Judging from information given in M[60] the only ship that realised the association between the enemy ships reported by Portsmouth and the subsequent encounter was the *Fernie*, the stand-by H.Q. ship. In her Captain's report it is stated: "0350 engagement between surface ships 100° 5 to 6 miles. Thought at the time to have been *Brocklesby* and *Slazak* engaging enemy convoy previously reported by Commander-in-Chief, Portsmouth. Two medium sized vessels were observed silhouetted against star shell at a long range."[61]

The *Locust*, between entries of 0212 and 0245, notes: "Signals were received during passage indicating the movements of certain small craft on the French coast."[62] The only mention by the *Calpe* is: "0348 observed engagement between surface craft."[63] The destroyers most concerned were the *Slazak* and *Brocklesby*, who were acting as screening force to the eastward. It is clear that to both of them the encounter came as a complete surprise, and to judge from the information available neither had any idea that unidentified craft were in the vicinity. Even after the action had started the importance of immediate support was not realised. Nor apparently had it been possible to discern the proximity of a force whose approach had been indicated in the signal from Portsmouth. The Naval Force Commander says: "At about 0350 gunfire was observed to E.S.E. which it was realised must be in the immediate vicinity of Group 5. At the time I considered that this might be caused by an E-boat attack but with the knowledge that the *Slazak* and *Brocklesby* were within about 4 miles of Group 5 and that *Calpe* was the only ship in the immediate vicinity of the *Glengyle* and Group 4, it was decided to keep Group 4 in sight."[64]

The unexpectedness of the encounter is confirmed by the fact that the destroyers continued to patrol on a pre-determined course[65] incompatible with any intention of intercepting the force reported by Commander-in-Chief, Portsmouth. To prevent enemy contact with Group 5 the destroyers would have had to make a large alteration of course. This they did not do. They maintained their original patrol and, when the enemy opened fire, were about 4 miles astern of Group 5.[66]

Nor did the action taken by Group 5 conform with the Operation orders. According to Operation order No.1[67] senior officers of Groups were to take drastic avoiding action if enemy forces were encountered during passage. These orders were complied with by Commanding Officer of Group 1 who successfully evaded an enemy force shortly before the landing.[68] C.C.O. says: "Commander Wyburd had decided beforehand that should the enemy be met with at sea, he would continue his course and endeavour to fight a way through." He had issued orders to this effect before the operation began.[69] The Naval Force Commander does not comment on this point beyond stating that he considers that Commander Wyburd should have made more use of the speed and smoke-laying capabilities of his S.G.B.[70] Commander Wyburd in his report[71] does not mention either of these points. It is clear, however, that no support was received from the destroyers and though there is considerable conflict of evidence as to their precise position relative to Group 5 when the action opened, the distance between them was evidently not more than 4 miles (see Plan 4) at 0347.

17. Results of the Action.

The effect of this action must not, however, be overestimated. The German report shows that the enemy Naval H.Q.s at first regarded the gunfire out to sea as being merely another of the numerous night actions between coastal forces[72] and not as the precursor of an immediate landing attack. By 0500, however, an alarm had been given to the coastal sector concerned, though the immunity which attended some of the first landings and the fact that Point D'Ailly lighthouse continued to flash, indicates that it was not very quickly acted upon.[73] It appears that the effect of the naval action was to alert the German coast defence system, that is to say the "Goebbels" and "Hess" batteries and the radar stations, whose role was to engage hostile shipping rather than to repel a landing. The other defences and the infantry were not alerted until out troops landed at Pourville. It can thus be said that the naval encounter did not compromise the effect of surprise.

The result of the action was to cripple our eastern flank attack, for the small number of troops which eventually landed on Yellow beaches could entertain no hope of capturing the 5.9-inch battery which was their objective.

On the other hand, even if the Berneval battery had been captured it does not necessarily follow that the main landings would have been successful. In fact, the sniping and harassing fire maintained on the battery by the very small party of troops which succeeded in landing on Yellow II beach effectively kept down the battery's fire until they re-embarked at 0810. Even then its fire had no effect on the main landing, probably because the whole inshore area was shrouded by a dense pall of smoke. The German report implies that the battery was firing shortly after 0900,[74] but the first time it was observed by the British to open fire was when the force was 3 or 4 miles from the coast during the withdrawal.

Part III

The Assault[75]

18. General remarks.
The assault and actions ashore will be described beach by beach, first the outer flank landings (on Yellow 1 and Yellow 2 beaches to the east and Orange 1 and Orange 2 beaches to the west), then the inner flank landings (on Blue beach to the east and Green beach to the west), and finally the main assault at Red and White beaches; but it must be remembered that these various operations were taking place almost simultaneously.

In the event, things went much better on the western flank than on the eastern, complete success being achieved on both Orange beaches, and partial success on Green beach. But to the east though there was a measure of success at Yellow 2, the landing party was wiped out at Yellow 1; and the assault at Blue beach, on the success of which the frontal assault hinged, was a costly failure. In consequence of this the batteries and machine gun posts of the east cliff were able to dominate the approaches to Dieppe and to bring a heavy fire on the Red and White beaches, where the main assault, despite great gallantry and tragic losses, likewise came to grief.

For the sake of convenience, the air battle will be described separately; but it must be understood that it was taking place at the same time as the Naval and Military action, and that the air cover provided endured from dawn to dusk.

19. The Eastern Outer Flank. (Yellow beaches)
This attack was to be made from the beaches at Berneval and Belleville-sur-Mer with the "Goebbels" battery of four 5.9-in. guns as the principal objective. The troops – of No. 3 Commando – were transported in landing craft of Group 5, and we have already seen how, as a result of the clash with the enemy escort, only a small proportion of them were put ashore.

THE ASSAULT

The landing at Yellow 1 (Berneval) was a complete failure, and of those who got ashore, none either reached their objective or returned.

At Yellow 2 (Belleville), only one landing craft reached the shore, but the twenty officers and men whom she landed succeeded in exercising an effect quite disproportionate to their numbers, and after remaining on shore for over three hours, re-embarked with only one casualty.

Yellow I (Berneval).

At 0425 M.L. 346 sighted four L.C.P. which were soon joined by another. They knew nothing of what had happened to the rest of Group 5 but were prepared to go in on their own under the flotilla officer. They touched down at about 0510 some 20 minutes behind schedule. Save for some slight opposition from a pill-box during the approach[76] the enemy seems to have held the weight of his fire until our craft had beached. During the final approach enemy movements had been observed on the top of the cliff and our troops ashore were heavily attacked with grenades and small arms fire as they attempted to leave the beach.

Whilst the landing was in progress an armed trawler approached, fired at our aircraft in the vicinity and laid a smoke screen off Yellow 1 beach. She was attacked by M.L. 346 and disappeared into the smoke. At 0535 another ship, later found to be armed tanker *Franz*, of 200 tons, approached from the southwest. M.L. 346 at once engaged her with gunfire and prepared to use depth charges but before this could be done the enemy abandoned the ship which drifted towards the rocks on fire and in a sinking condition. At 0545 L.C.P. (L) 85 arrived on the scene and touched down at 0600 putting her troops ashore amid heavy fire.

By that time enemy opposition was considerable; the "Goebbels" battery had opened up on the beach and the L.C.P. lying off shore. Lt.-Cdr. Corke the flotilla officer in L.C.P. (L) 42, had been mortally wounded, most of his crew were casualties and his craft and L.C.P. (L) 81 had both to be abandoned in a sinking condition. At considerable risk M.L. 346 gave all possible supporting fire which here, as elsewhere, proved quite inadequate for the task. None of the troops succeeded in reaching their objective and the entire force was killed or captured.

At 0615 a Very's light was fired from the beach, and L.C.P. (L) 1, 85, 157 and 41 went in to endeavour to carry out evacuation while M.L. 346 approached to within half a mile to give covering fire. The first three beached; no troops could be seen but the naval beachmaster and his party were embarked under very heavy fire in L.C.P. (L) 157; the beach party had seen nothing of the troops after the landing. The L.C.P. then endeavoured to withdraw but L.C.P. (L) 157 was hard on the rocks and in attempting to assist her L.C.P. (L) 1 also went aground. The crew and the beach party from L.C.P. (L) 157 were taken off by L.C.P. (L) 85 and L.C.P. (L) 1 eventually got clear. By this time M.L. 230 had arrived from Dieppe and the three surviving craft accompanied her to the "Boat Pool" at about 0730 by which time it was clear that there was no hope of bringing off the troops. These totally unarmoured L.C.P., which held on to the last under heavy fire, performed a remarkable feat.

In a final attempt to evacuate Yellow 1 beach some L.C.P. (L) from the "Boat Pool" were sent in at about 0950. They appear, however, to have gone by error to Blue beach instead, for under heavy fire they picked up from a capsized boat nine soldiers, who turned out to be Canadians and not Commandos.

Yellow 2 (Belleville).

Here L.C.P. (L) 15, commanded by Lt. H.T. Buckee, R.N.V.R., enjoyed the distinction of making a solitary landing. She carried three officers and 17 other ranks, the headquarters party of No. 6 Troop, under Major P. Young, Bedfordshire and Hertfordshire Regiment, and put them ashore quietly and unopposed at 0445, five minutes before zero. The reports do not mention any immediate opposition. Despite inadequate equipment, the party succeeded in getting through the wire and by 0530 had reached the top of the cliff, just as our aircraft attacked the battery. Our men succeeded in getting to within 200 yards of their target and then settled down to intensive sniping. They were highly successful and drove the Germans to pay them the compliment of turning one of the heavy guns against them, after rifle fire had proved ineffective. Fortunately, it could not be depressed enough, and the black and yellow fumes, accompanying its discharge provided a tempting target, which was exploited to the full. After carrying out these tactics for about an hour and a half our men made an orderly withdrawal at 0800 to L.C.P. (L) 15 which had meanwhile been lying off the beaches under spasmodic fire, and now in spite of intense opposition came into the beach and, covered by M.L. 346, withdrew the troops, whose only casualty was one wounded. M.L. 346 escorted L.C.P. (L) 15 back to Newhaven where they arrived at 1231. On the way back, they were attacked by a Junker 88 but all the bombs missed.

While Major Young's small force could of course entertain no hope of capturing the battery, the sniping tactics employed greatly interfered with its handling and materially kept down its rate of fire during the period of the main landing. In fact, it was not till 0900 that the battery was again firing.[77]

The Germans assumed that a Commando of about 250 men had landed at Yellow beaches,[78] and as they must have known the total number at Yellow 1, it follows that they conceived a greatly exaggerated idea of the forces landed at Yellow 2, which is much to the credit of Major Young and his party.

20. **The Western Outer Flank (Orange beaches).**
The force to be landed here consisted of 250 officers and men from No. 4 Commando, under Lt.-Colonel the Lord Lovat, M.C. and was brought in by the landing craft of the *Prince Albert* under the command of Lt.-Cdr. H.H.H. Mulleneux, R.N., who was in M.G.B. 312 supported by an L.C.S. and S.G.B. 9. Their chief objective was the capture of the "Hess" battery of six 5.9-in. guns behind the village of Varengeville. On the way in – at about 0350 – three darkened vessels, eastward bound, were sighted on the port bow. As the Point d'Ailly light was showing, it was assumed that this was an enemy convoy and contact was successfully avoided by a sharp alteration of course to starboard. The enemy headed towards the tracer now splashing the sky round Group 5.[79] At 0430 the flotilla divided according to plan. The landing was made almost exactly to schedule at 0450 and encountered no opposition; the troops achieved complete success and afterwards withdrew according to plan.
Orange 1 Beach (Vasterival).
Attention from the landing here had been at first diverted by the well-timed attack on the battery by British cannon fighters, but, when the aircraft had passed and the troops were ashore, a heavy though inaccurate fire was directed on the withdrawing landing craft. Our troops were under the command of Major D. Mills Roberts, Irish Guards, and got ashore without much opposition, considerate bi-lingual notices drawing their attention to land mine-fields. Houses in Varengeville were searched and the Mortar party closed the battery through a thick wood. At 0550 brisk small arms fire was opened on the battery. The 2-in. mortar was set up and with its third shot scored a hit on the ready-use ammunition, stacked alongside the guns. There was a blinding flash and a heavy explosion silenced the guns while "the screams and cries of the wounded Germans could plainly be heard." The battery did not fire again, though it had already got off a few salvos which fell near the force moving up towards the main beaches.

Enemy attempts to fight the flames were heavily sniped and Bren gunners fired bursts into the flames at frequent intervals; the enemy machine gun positions were silenced and the battery shelled by our mortar up to the moment when Lord Lovat's party made their assault after which Major Mills Roberts party returned to the beach.
Orange 2 Beach (Mouth of the Saane).
Lord Lovat's party helped by Spitfires which caused a diversion, landed successfully on Orange 2 beach, which with few casualties they crossed,

and made their way inland to approach the battery from the rear. Meanwhile the L.C.S. and S.G.B. 9. had engaged enemy coastal defences. As they pushed forward Lord Lovat's men heard the roar of the explosion at the battery, and one troop, coming on about 35 German assault troops forming up behind a farmhouse, evidently to counter-attack Major Mills Roberts' party, wiped them out by Tommy-gun fire. At 0625, with the aid of a low-level air attack, an assault was made on the battery. Despite heavy opposition this was completely successful. The battery with two strong points enfilading it, was captured at the point of the bayonet.

Lord Lovat claimed that the guns in the battery were demolished and the crews wiped out except for four who were captured.[80] The German Report, however, says that their casualties were 30 killed, 21 wounded and 10 missing out of a total of 112 and that the battery had been re-occupied and was firing again with two guns at 0903.[81] Our troops then withdrew to Orange 1 beach under desultory sniping fire. Meanwhile the landing craft had withdrawn seawards but coming under fairly heavy fire, again approached the beach and lay close inshore, where the enemy's fire could not reach them and where they were unmolested except for occasional sniping.

The re-embarkation started at 0730, three extra L.C.A. having been sent from the Boat Pool to assist, and was carried out from Orange 1 beach, which was free of enemy fire, though shells were falling on Orange 2 beach. The withdrawal of the troops was not easy; owing to the flatness of the beach and the ebbing tide, troops had to wade out up to their necks in water, but all including the wounded were brought off, and the operation was completed by 0815. The wounded were transferred to the *Fernie* and the flotilla returned to Newhaven arriving at 1745. The casualties sustained by No. 4 Commando were two officers and nine men killed, three officers and 19 men wounded, and 13 men missing believed killed. The C.C.O. remarks[82] "This hazardous assault on "Hess" battery was carried out strictly according to plan and may well become a model for future operations of this kind."

21. **The Eastern Inner Flank (Blue Beach, Puits).**
Great importance was attached to the landing at Puits; unfortunately, it was doomed to failure. "It had always been realised that unless the east headland which overlooks the town and port of Dieppe was captured, the frontal assault on the town, on which the whole operation chiefly depended, would probably fail."[83] Near this eastern headland there were numerous objectives, notably the "Rommel" four-gun battery, barracks, gas works and various gun sites. They were to be attacked by

troops of the Royal Regiment of Canada, transported in landing craft of the *Queen Emma, Princess Astrid* and *Duke of Wellington*, supported by M.G.B. 316 and S.G.B. 8, with Lt.-Cdr. H.W. Goulding, D.S.O., R.N.R., as the Senior Landing Officer. No covering bombardment was planned. "Surprise is the element upon which reliance is placed for the success of the landing on Green and Blue beaches and they will not be supported by gunfire from destroyers."[84]

By making his landfall on the harbour entrance, Lt.-Cdr. Goulding succeeded in picking out this "narrow and difficult beach" but this dog-legged course further delayed his force which, it will be remembered, had been delayed in forming up,[85] and it only touched down at 0506,[86] 16 minutes late, when it was already getting light. The landing did not meet with very severe opposition which indicates that a fair measure of surprise was achieved. The effect of this delay must not, therefore, be over-estimated. At the less important Green beach, where the landing was made almost exactly to schedule, the troops encountered very heavy opposition as soon as they got ashore. In the opinion of the Naval Force Commander, "the main difficulty seems to have been that the troops under-estimated the height of the sea wall (10 to 12 feet) and were consequently insufficiently prepared for surmounting it. The ensuring delay gave the enemy time to recover from his first surprise and to bring down heavy and accurate fire."

Be this as it may, there can be no doubt that the Blue beach assault never came within measurable distance of success. The landing craft which advanced under cover of smoke laid by aircraft were not fired on until they were about 100 yards off the beach but the troops lost heavily as they left the landing craft and still more heavily when they reached the lofty sea wall which ran along the beach some 50 yards from the water's edge: here they were pinned down by enfilading fire from well-concealed positions on the flanks. L.C.S. 25 and L.C.S. 8 maintained spirited supporting fire from almost point-blank range and continued in action until most of their guns were silenced but "were almost completely ineffective against strengthened houses and pill-boxes",[87] and could not even be sure of their targets.[88] A second wave of landing craft which had been unable to keep up with the others touched down at 0525 but the troops they landed suffered just as heavily, their mortar detachment being quickly wiped out. At 0545 some L.C.A. from the *Duke of Wellington* which constituted the third wave though heavily shelled, succeeded in putting their troops ashore. L.C.M. 99 was heavily hit and suffered a number of casualties. The beachmaster and his staff, who were on board her were transferred to L.C.A. 208 and an attempt was made to land them, but the enemy's fire had increased so much that the L.C.A. could not make the beach.

Unfortunately, the troops could effect little in the face of such intense opposition on so difficult a beach. A small party led by Lt.-Col. D.E. Catto, Commanding Officer of the Battalion, succeeded in cutting a path through the wire, and reaching the top of the cliff cleared the houses there, but their retreat was cut off; they were unable to join up with Essex Scottish from Red beach and ultimately, at 1620, were forced to surrender. Apart from a solitary corporal they were probably the only men to get beyond the beach. The rest were pinned down by accurate and increasingly vicious fire including hand grenades hurled from the cliff top and 3-in. mortar fire. The "Rommel" battery despite several bombing and machine gunning attacks by the R.A.F. only checked its fire for a few minutes. In such a situation there could be but one result "The troops never succeeded in getting beyond the sea wall where they were pinned down by steadily increasing fire, until all but a few men who escaped by swimming were either killed or captured."[89] The casualties were crushing – 24 officers and 459 other ranks killed, wounded and missing, out of an embarkation strength of 27 officers and 516 other ranks.[90]

The dismal results expected from failure in this sector were fully realised. The batteries and machine gun posts of the east cliff were able to dominate the approaches to Dieppe and bring heavy fire to bear on Red and White beaches.

22. **Naval attempts to evacuate Blue Beach.**

While the troops had been facing this ordeal ashore, the landing craft had been withdrawn and were lying about 8 cables off shore; those which were badly damaged or had severe casualties were ordered to join the Boat Pool to the westward off Red and White beaches.

Shortly before 0600 an L.C.A. endeavoured to approach the beach but was hit and sunk. Soon after 0700 a message sent by someone unknown[91] was received in the *Calpe* by Naval Force Commander asking for all Landing Craft to return to the beach to evacuate the beach party. Only two craft picked it up – L.C.S. 8 and L.C.A. 209, which were patrolling off the beach.

L.C.A. 209 went in and was half swamped by the rush of soldiers; she left the beach but when 50 yards out was hit by a heavy shell and sank; only two of the crew and one soldier survived. Soon after 0700 the rest of the landing craft proceeded to join the Boat Pool, while Lt.-Cdr. Goulding, having been unable to get his signal through to the Naval Force Commander went on board *Calpe* to report at about 0745.

At about 1005 some L.C.P. (L) which were trying to evacuate Yellow I beach, closed Blue beach by error and in spite of heavy fire rescued nine soldiers from an upturned boat.

The *Garth* was bombarding batteries on the east cliff and though in touch with the Forward Observation Officer was not able to effect much as she was frequently straddled by the enemy and had to turn away. While Lt.-Cdr. Goulding was still on board the *Calpe*, a signal was received from the *Garth* saying that Blue beach was asking for help and evacuation.[92] The Naval Force Commander ordered Lt.-Cdr. Goulding to take an M.L. for support and to attempt an evacuation. Lt.-Cdr. Goulding accordingly boarded M.L. 291 at 1100, and as none of his own landing craft were in the vicinity he collected some L.C.A. and one L.C.S. and proceeded towards the beach. Lt.-Cdr. McMullen was sent to assist him. Very heavy fire was opened as the craft approached and they were forced to retire; on one was seen on the beach, and Lt.-Cdr Goulding made a signal to the *Calpe* reporting failure to evacuate. Another attempt to evacuate the beach was made shortly afterwards by some of the *Princess Astrid's* craft. They saw no one on the beach and retired under heavy fire losing one craft. After this all craft were required for the main evacuation.

23. **The Western Inner Flank (Green Beach – Pourville).**
Here the combined flotillas of the *Princess Beatrix* and *Invicta* were to land officers and men of the South Saskatchewan Regiment. They were to take Pourville with the German defence headquarters there, the radar station nearby and other targets and also to aid the Royal Hamilton Light Infantry against the "Quatre Vents" Farm, the capture of which was regarded as essential, if the withdrawal was to be accomplished without severe casualties. They were also to cover the western flank of the outer perimeter of Dieppe. The Queen's Own Camerons of Canada were to land half an hour later and pass through to attack the airfield of St. Aubin, and link up with the tanks to take the Divisional Headquarters at Arques-la-Bataille and a heavy gun position not far away.

The South Saskatchewan Regiment touched down unopposed at 0452 but as the troops went ashore they came under concentrated fire from machine guns and A.A. guns.[93] This, however, was overcome. "A" company scaled the sea wall, silenced two pillboxes and moved against the radar station, which their strenuous efforts failed to take, through lack of adequate artillery and mortar support. "C" company meanwhile established themselves in Pourville and captured the German headquarters there. "B" and "D" companies under Lt.-Col. C.C.I.

Merritt made a most determined attack on "Quatre Vents." Strong opposition was encountered in this area and during the morning a reserve enemy battalion appeared on the west side of the River Scie, while the Saskatchewan's were later reinforced by part of the Cameron battalion. The river was crossed but heavy and accurate fire to which our men could make no sufficient reply, prevented them from capturing the place before the order to withdraw was received.

The landing was covered by L.C.S. 9 and L.C.S. 31. The enemy opened fire soon after the troops were ashore and L.C.S. 9 in attempting to land Lt.-Cdr. Prior, senior officer, Green beach landings, was heavily hit and later sank. Lt.-Cdr. Prior was eventually landed by L.C.S. 31. L.C.A. 170 also came under heavy fire while attempting to land the beach party and had to withdraw suffering several casualties including the beachmaster, who was severely wounded. The landing craft then withdrew under cover of smoke and joined the Boat Pool.

The Queen's Own Cameron Highlanders in L.C.P. of Group 6 under Commander H.V.P. McClintock, owing partly to the anxiety of the Senior Military Officer not to be landed ahead of time and partly to navigational difficulties occasioned by smoke during the final approach landed at 0550, half an hour late.[94] The enemy fire encountered by the landing craft was not very heavy and having put their troops ashore they withdrew to the Boat Pool. Despite this delay, the troops crossed the beach with few casualties, though the Commanding Officer, Lt.-Colonel A.C. Gostling, was killed as he set foot on shore: our craft found that there was still enemy opposition commanding the beach though it was only moderate and mostly mortar fire. After a hurried conference at the South Saskatchewan headquarters it was decided that, as the area to the east was still untaken, the Highlanders should advance against the airfield along the west bank of the Scie. But they were unable to take a vital bridge and soon after 0845, as the tanks which should have joined them at about 0630 had not appeared, the withdrawal was begun. Thus, it had not been possible to maintain their initial success.

24. **The Main Assault (Red and White Beaches) – Dieppe.**
The main assault was to be delivered against the sea front of Dieppe itself: this was some 1,700 yards long backed by a sea wall,[95] boulevards and gardens. The western end (White beach) was to be attacked by the Royal Hamilton Light Infantry, the eastern (Red beach) by the Essex Scottish Regiment, supported by the 14th Canadian Tank Battalion (the Calgary Regiment) and some small subsidiary units. Immediate success in this sector was a cardinal feature of the plan. The Royal Hamilton Light Infantry were to attack gun positions, notably the "Goering"

heavy battery, assist the South Saskatchewan Regiment in the attack on "Quatre Vents" and join the Essex Scottish Regiment in controlling Dieppe. The latter was to concentrate on the dock area and eastern side of the town, attack various gun sites, capture two emergency landing grounds and join up with the Royal Regiment of Canada. The landings were to be supported by tanks landed at White beach: detachments of the Royal Canadian Engineers were to land with the first wave, and demolish portions of the sea wall to enable the tanks to get on to the esplanade and thence to enter the town and co-operate with the Highlanders from Green beach against St. Aubin and Arques-la-Bataille. Men of the Royal Hamilton Light Infantry were transported in the *Glengyle*, the Essex Scottish Regiment in the *Prince Charles* and *Prince Leopold*. The 2nd Destroyer Division (*Berkeley*, *Bleasdale*, *Garth*, *Albrighton*) and the *Locust* were to support the initial landing by bombarding the sea front and then the flanks whilst the R.A.F. delivered a cannon fire attack and laid a smoke screen over the eastern headland.

At 0502 the 2nd Destroyer Division spread to take up bombarding positions astern of the landing craft and ten minutes later opened fire. Three buildings on the front were set on fire and others damaged. The R.A.F. attacked the defences according to plan. The assault craft under Lt.-Cdr. C.W. McMullen, S.O. Landings for White beach and with Commander G.T. Lambert, in general command were led in by M.G.B. 326 and M.L. 291. They were given close support by the L.C.S. and L.C.F. and were screened by smoke laid by the L.C.M.

The enemy's fire was not heavy and the landing craft beached at 0523 only three minutes late, in spite of delay in forming up. The troops landed with little loss but their troubles then developed rapidly, because instead of advancing quickly while the enemy was still taking cover from the bombardment they remained under the shelter of the sea wall, thus losing precious moments. When they started to advance the Germans had recovered and opened a heavy fire. The landing craft withdrew under fire and joined the Boat Pool off the main beaches; a few were hit but none was lost. The Support Craft remined close inshore.

The preliminary naval and air attacks over, the enemy opened an intense and well-directed fire which caused heavy casualties on both Red and White beaches. Very much greater than had been anticipated was the murderous enfilade fire from guns concealed in the east cliff face. These guns were "impossible to detect even at close range until they fired and could not easily be silenced by our own fire. This enfilade fire made the capture and retention of the beaches almost impossible and was therefore the main cause of the failure to press on through

Dieppe and attain objectives laid down in the plan."[96] The situation was made much worse by barbed wire defences which proved more formidable than had been expected, and by the ill success which attended our tanks.

25. **Landing the Tanks.**

These were to have been landed in four waves, on Red and White beaches. The first flight consisting of the L.C.T. of Group 8 guided by H.M.S. *Fernie*, with Lt.-Cdr. Lord Beatty the senior officer of Groups 8 and 9 of L.C.T., in M.L. 343 arrived about ten minutes late – at 0535 – owing to navigational difficulties.[97] The Infantry was thus deprived of the valuable covering fire which the tanks might have given in the first crucial minutes. The L.C.T. met with tremendous fire as soon as they cleared the smoke. L.C.T. 145 beached successfully and landed her three tanks "but on withdrawing she was heavily hit, disabled and had to be sunk." L.C.T. 127 sustained very heavy damage and most of her crew were killed or wounded but she got her tanks ashore and withdrew from the beach. L.C.T. 159 was hit approaching the shore and she came in with the ramp half down; she was disabled and could not get off the beach. L.C.T. 126 was also heavily hit and set on fire, but she landed her tanks and subsequently sank in deep water off the shore. L.C.T. 121 beached and probably landed her tanks but was disabled and remained on the beach. L.C.T. 163 "was hit in the engine room when close in shore: a fire was started and before it could be extinguished, the fumes overcame the helmsman so that the L.C.T. swung to port and failed to make a landing. Another rating took the wheel and brought the craft in again; when 70 yards from the beach the helmsman was killed by a direct hit and the steering damaged with the result that the ship swung once more to port. A third attempt was made with the same result, the helmsman again being killed, but at the fourth attempt L.C.T. 163 crept in, using as cover L.C.T.145 which was then 60 yards from the beach and sinking. This time the landing was successful."[98] But the heavy fire encountered and to some extent the original delay, had most unfortunate effects, as the assault demolition parties of engineers, who were to break the sea wall to enable the tanks to penetrate through the crust of the enemy's defences were unable to carry out their task owing to heavy casualties. Many of their stores were set on fire before landing. This resulted in all prospects of successful penetration being foredoomed to failure.[99]

The four L.C.T. of Group 9 made up the second flight. They were L.C.T. 124, 125, 165 and 166, and arrived at 0605. The enemy fire was intense. L.C.T. 124 landed her tanks and withdrew but was sunk later.

L.C.T. 125 landed one tank and was then ordered to withdraw by the beachmaster for what reason does not appear.[100] About 45 minutes later she beached again; but all her officers and crew were killed or wounded; a second tank left the craft. The L.C.T. was heavily damaged but her wounded first lieutenant managed to get her away from the beach and she was taken in tow by the *Alresford*. L.C.T. 165 landed her tanks, her steering gear was hit, she was out of control and received considerable damage but got away from the beach and repaired her steering gear. L.C.T. 166 landed her tanks without difficulty and withdrew.

There are discrepancies in the total number of tanks disembarked but the probable number is 28 out of 30, a result highly creditable to the L.C.T. The number "drowned" seems to have been one or two. Unfortunately, once ashore the tanks were unable to accomplish much. Apart from the obstacle presented by the sea wall the tanks had trouble in moving across the shingle and came up against unexpected opposition from unmapped anti-tank guns, as well as the fire from the eastern headland. In consequence of these difficulties the tanks could give little aid. Of the 28 disembarked, 13 and probably 15, crossed the sea wall and reached the promenade, but all the exits were blocked and most of the tanks eventually returned to the beach.[101] The ten L.C.T. of Groups 10 and 11 were to have formed the third and fourth waves, but in view of the rapid deterioration in the situation it was decided that no useful purpose could be served by sending them in, so they were finally sent home.

26. **Naval Support.**
All this time covering fire was being vigorously given by support craft. L.C.F. (L) 2 fought with great gallantry. Closing to point-blank range she gave close support until she was disabled, her captain killed, her guns put out of action one by one and she finally sank. The *Locust* also attempted to give aid. She was to have taken part in the initial bombardment but had been unable to keep up with the main forces and in the darkness had formed up on the wrong group. However, she arrived off Red and White beaches about 0530. "Owing to the obscure situation on shore she was unable to provide much useful or effective bombardment."[102] She approached the harbour entrance and at 0607 opened fire with her 4-in. gun on the cliff to east of the harbour but came under accurate fire from the heavy batteries on the cliff and also from a new battery near the east side of the harbour. At 0611 she received a direct hit on the bridge superstructure starboard side, causing casualties; she withdrew and was instructed not to enter till the situation to the east of the harbour had improved.

The destroyers also were heavily engaged but their guns were too light to have much effect on the strong and well concealed enemy gun positions. It had been intended to control the destroyers' fire by means of F.O.Os., who were to land with the troops, but most of them became casualties or could not establish communication. Nevertheless, they achieved some success. The *Albrighton* silenced an A.A. battery above Pourville and heavily shelled the Tobacco Factory near the main beaches with partial success.

The *Bleasdale* engaged a battery about 100 yards along the cliffs to the east of Dieppe but was unable to silence it. The *Garth* also bombarded positions on the east cliff. The C.C.O. in his report says[103] "At no time was the support which the ships were able to give sufficient for the purpose and this was one of the main reasons why the landing at Blue, Red and White beaches was unsuccessful." The Germans were surprised at the weakness of our supporting gunfire during the landings.[104] Our ships were frequently subjected to air attack in spite of the very efficient protection given by our fighters. Naval A.A. guns were claimed to have shot down 24 enemy aircraft,[105] the *Slazak* claiming four of them, and unfortunately, also five of our own, which contrary to orders were flying low towards our ships.

S.G.B. 8 and 9 made a sweep for enemy surface craft at 0600 but sighted nothing. They were attacked by a formation of Focker-Wolf 190, one of which was shot down. S.G.B. 9 was disabled but carried out repairs and both boats returned towards Dieppe at 0830. While they were away, owing to a false report at 0750 of E-Boats approaching from Boulogne,[106] the *Slazak*, *Brocklesby* and *Bleasdale* were sent to the north-east to intercept. The destroyers had to leave the fighter screen to carry out their mission and were subjected to numerous air attacks, the *Slazak* receiving some damage from near misses. The landing craft by that time were mostly in the Boat Pool screened from the enemy's fire by a most efficient smoke screen.

"Throughout the period which followed" wrote Captain Hughes Hallett,[107] "enemy fire from the shore steadily increased, and the destroyers were forced constantly to shift their positions in order to avoid damage and keep under cover of smoke ..... H.M.S. *Calpe's* appearance during most of this period must have resembled that of a Fleet Flagship on regatta day as there were seldom less than six to ten craft alongside. They came to transfer wounded, bring reports, or seek instructions, and their presence was rather an embarrassment to the Commanding Officer, when he wished to manoeuvre to avoid gunfire ..... My general impression during this phase .... was a feeling of inability to give the troops effective support. The military situation was completely obscure, and the large quantities of smoke drifting inshore made it impossible to see what was happening ….."».

27. The Floating Reserve and R.M. Commando.

Meanwhile the enemy opposition had proved much too intense to be overcome by our military forces who were able to attain only an insignificant part of their objectives. Seldom had great gallantry been so ill-rewarded. "In fact, the main beach was never properly secured, and the main force never succeeded in getting clear of it …. A steadily increasing volume of fire was brought to bear on the foreshore in the main landing area, which had the effect of pinning down the troops throughout the whole operation."[108] Some of the Royal Hamilton Light Infantry aided by the Royal Canadian Engineers eventually succeeded in attacking the Casino – the prominent building at the western end of the beach – and at 0712 reported its capture, and some small parties infiltrated into the town but were not powerful enough to effect much. A small body which made an attack on the west headland, was killed to a man. The Essex Scottish Regiment was soon under very severe fire from field artillery and heavy mortars and sustained serious losses. A small party crossed the esplanade and occupied two buildings nearby, from which the enemy was engaged with success, but the vast majority of the forces were pinned down to the beach area by sheets of enemy fire, and as already related the tanks were quite unable to afford any effective support.

In an attempt to secure the vital eastern headland, the Military Force Commander who apparently did not fully know of the critical position ashore, decided to send in his floating reserve – the Fusiliers Mont Royal – to Red beach. With the aid of smoke, and in the face of very heavy firing, part of them were successfully put ashore at 0704 under the direction of Lt.-Cdr. J.H. Dathan, R.N., Senior Officer of Group 7 in M.L. 214. He took in 26 L.C.P. losing two when beached and a third during the withdrawal. So intense was the enemy's fire that the Fusiliers achieved little or no success and suffered serious losses as soon as they landed. Two small parties succeeded in penetrating into the town and dock area but few returned. Meanwhile, owing to failure to allow for the then strong westerly set of the tide and the superabundance of smoke, some 300 officers and men of the Fusiliers had to be landed, not according to plan, but on the very constricted beach below the western headland. No frontal advance was practicable and attempts to move out on either flank proved unsuccessful. About noon 288 of them, of whom some 100 wounded, surrendered.

Meanwhile at a conference in the *Calpe* it had been decided that, as the harbour was still in enemy hands it would be necessary to abandon the idea of an attack on shipping there by a naval cutting-out party from the Royal Marine Commando and the latter was put at the disposal of the Military Force Commander. Knowledge of events ashore was far from complete, but it seemed to General Roberts that if White beach was promptly reinforced, there was a fair chance that the infantry would be able to capture the western headland and still break into the town and that it would be possible to carry out many of the demolition tasks before the hour of withdrawal. He therefore decided to use the Royal Marine Commando consisting of 18 officers and 352 other ranks under Lt.-Col. J.P. Phillipps, R.M., to reinforce White beach. Commander Ryder was instructed to tranship the commando from the *Locust* and six Chasseurs into seven L.C.A. and L.C.M. from the Boat Pool.

The Chasseurs (French patrol craft) constituted the body of Group 13 which had been led across by the *Alresford*. One fell out during the passage through mechanical trouble; the rest were approaching Dieppe by 0600 after an uneventful crossing, and with the *Locust* had been lying off the beaches.

The landing craft moved in, with three Chasseurs on each flank to screen them from the fire of the shore batteries and to provide smoke. At 0830 the group went into land and the gravity of the situation became only too apparent. "It was not long before I realised that this landing was to be a sea parallel of the Charge of the Light Brigade" wrote the senior officer, Chasseurs.[109] Shellfire was opened on the craft almost immediately at about 4,000 yards, increasing in intensity as the range shortened. The fire was mostly coming from the eastern cliff and the end and base of the mole, and, as the range decreased, rifle and machine gun fire opened, the Chasseurs being no longer able to support the force owing to the shallow water.[110] As the leading craft emerged from the smoke they came under a most devastating fire and Col. Phillipps' craft went aground. It was obvious that no useful purpose could be served by attempting to continue, and at the cost of his life Col. Phillipps at once signalled to those behind him to retire. "Putting on a pair of white gloves so that his hands could be more easily seen, he jumped on to the forward deck of his landing craft and signalled to the remainder to put about and head for the shelter of the smoke screen. He had scarcely sent this signal when he fell mortally wounded, but by his action he undoubtedly saved some 200 of his men from landing on a beach swept by murderous and concentrated fire."[111] Despite severe damage and casualties, most craft succeeded in obeying this instruction though by the time the action was over Royal Marine Commando casualties killed and missing amounted to six officers and 60 other ranks.[112] In view of these events at White beach, the senior officer,

Chasseurs made a situation report to the Naval Force Commander in the *Calpe* saying that the position on Red and White beaches was out of control; this was passed shortly after 0915. It was clear that nothing more could be done and soon afterwards arrangements were in progress for the final withdrawal.

Part IV

The Withdrawal

28. Situation at 0900 hours.
As has already been related, the troops who landed in the west on Orange beaches had successfully completed their task and were on their way home. The small party which landed in the east on Yellow II beach had also been safely withdrawn and was on its way back to England. The troops who had landed on Yellow I beach had been killed or captured and the naval beach party had been withdrawn.

At Blue beach all hope of evacuating any survivors from the Royal Regiment of Canada had been abandoned. At Green beach the South Saskatchewan Regiment held Pourville and was still trying to capture "Quatre Vents" Farm, while the Camerons of Canada were about to assault the bridge of the Scie prior to advancing on the airfield at St. Aubin. It now became evident to the Commanding Officers of the two battalions that they would not be able to accomplish their task as the enemy was stronger than was expected and the tanks which should have pushed through from Dieppe to support them had not appeared. A fighting retirement was accordingly commenced at 0930 and by about 1000 was successfully accomplished under heavy fire. Up to this time the casualties suffered by the two battalions amounted to about 20 per cent. of their strength, but later their losses were far heavier. It was known that the troops would have to wait for three-quarters of an hour until the arrival of the landing craft and so positions were taken up to defend the beach.

On Red and White beaches the Essex, Scottish and Royal Hamilton Light Infantry were barely able to maintain themselves but were holding the Casino, and a few men had penetrated into the town of Dieppe. The tanks had mostly been disabled. The reserve battalion, the Fusiliers Mont Royal, had suffered too heavily on landing to have any influence on the situation, while of the Marines, constituting the last reserve, those who landed had been almost completely wiped out.

The landing craft after putting their troops ashore had joined the Boat Pool which had been established off Red and White beaches and was protected by an almost continuous smoke screen. The Boat Pool was under the orders of Commander H.V.P. McClintock. The destroyers and support craft were giving the troops ashore what support they could, but the enemy fire was increasing.

At 0900 the Military Force Commander came to the conclusion that the troops were unlikely to capture the headlands east and west of Dieppe and that the main assault had failed. He therefore decided not to land the remaining tanks, and Groups 10 and 11 were ordered to return to England escorted by the *Garth*, which was running short of ammunition, and the *Alresford*, which was towing a damaged L.C.T. Operation orders had laid down 1100 as the hour for commencing the withdrawal. The Force Commanders would have liked to advance this to 1030, but the R.A.F. adviser pointed out that this alteration would upset the time-table and might make it impossible to lay the smoke curtain which had been arranged. Furthermore, General Roberts doubted whether there would be time to contact the Camerons. Accordingly, no change in the time was made and Naval Force Commander ordered Commander McClintock to send all L.C.A. and L.C.M. to the same beaches on which they had landed their troops but decided that fire was too heavy to send in L.C.P. and L.C.T. Landing craft were to ferry troops out to the L.C.T., which were to remain one mile out to sea, returning to beaches to load again. The evacuation was to be confined to personnel, it being clearly impossible to remove the tanks. Destroyers and L.C.F. (L) were to give fire support while the R.A.F. was to bomb the two headlands.

29. **Evacuation of Green Beach (Pourville).**

At 0930 L.C.A. 521 went into Green beach but was unable to make contact with anyone on shore and was forced by heavy fire to withdraw. At 1000 L.C.A. 315 arrived inshore. Nothing could be seen but the beach party taking cover under a wall, where they were trapped by heavy fire from the western headland. One man tried to cross the beach to reach the craft but was instantly killed. The L.C.A. then retired.

At 1045 L.C.A. 198, 185, 186, 187, 188, 176, 197 from the *Prince Leopold's* flotilla supported by L.C.S. (M) 21 proceeded inshore to carry out the withdrawal. They should have gone into Red beach at Dieppe but owing to the smoke arrived instead at Pourville; L.C.A. 186 realising her error left at once for Red beach after picking up some men who were in the water. The *Albrighton* and *Bleasdale* covered this movement by bombarding the flanks and firing smoke shell. Soon after L.C.A. 170 and 215 arrived at Green beach.

Enemy fire was very heavy especially from the hill to the east of Pourville. Lt.-Cdr. Prior, (senior officer, Green beach), tried to communicate with M.G.B. 317 to arrange for a bombardment of the hill, but was unsuccessful, mainly because the beach signal party had not been landed. Troops moving down the beach towards the landing craft lost heavily from enemy fire and many swam or waded out to the approaching crafty. This caused delay as the men had to be picked up one by one. Arriving further in there was a rush to board the craft and many casualties occurred during the re-embarkation; the ramps became jammed with dead and wounded and some of the craft were overloaded and shipped a lot of water.

L.C.A. 215 was sunk during the withdrawal. The landing craft withdrew and transferred the troops to destroyers. Of the craft not disabled some returned to Green beach and embarked more troops while others endeavoured to go to Red beach according to the original plan, but it does not appear that any of the latter craft succeeded in beaching. At 1100 L.C.A. 262, 317, 251 and 214 from the Invicta's flotilla proceeded in to Green beach. The enemy's fire had increased in intensity. L.C.A. 317 was badly hit and was abandoned on the beach. L.C.A. 251 was overloaded and sank under fire 200 yards out. L.C.A. 214 too left the beach greatly overloaded; she was towed by an L.C.M. to a destroyer (probably *Albrighton*) and sank alongside. L.C.A. 262 also sank alongside the *Bleasdale* after transferring her troops.

At 1115 L.C.A. 250 and 315 having picked up some Marines who were swimming off Red beach proceeded to Green beach and took off survivors from the beach and from wrecked landing craft. Soon after 1130 the Brocklesby's bombardment[113] of positions overlooking Green beach gave some relief from enemy fire, and L.C.A. 250 and 315 were able to make two more trips into it. The *Locust* assisted by bombarding enemy positions round Green beach at this time and S.G.B. 9 also bombarded later. According to the *Locust* there was no enemy fire out to sea to the west of Dieppe.

At about 1130 Lt.-Col. Merritt commanding the South Saskatchewan Regiment, formed a rear-guard of 100 men and held the perimeter of the beach. Lt.-Cdr. Prior and the assistant beachmaster, who had both been wounded, were tireless in their efforts to evacuate all the troops, and in a last endeavour to rescue the rear-guard, Lt.-Cdr. Prior asked Lt.-Col. Merritt to set fire to the houses on the foreshore so as to withdraw under cover of the smoke, unfortunately owing to the failure of the incendiary grenades this could not be done and the gallant rear-guard had to be abandoned. The troops held on until their ammunition was exhausted and then surrendered. Lt.-Cdr. Prior was also taken prisoner.

At 1215 L.C.A. 250 and 315 made their final trip into the beach, where there was no one alive, and withdrew under heavy fire. There seems little doubt that had it been possible effectively to shell the dominating hill to the eastward of the beach the rear-guard could have been evacuated, but as the enemy's fire was never silenced,[114] the task could not be performed.

30. **Evacuation of Red and White Beaches (Dieppe).**
While this was going on at Green beach, similar strenuous efforts against heavy opposition were being made at Red and White beaches.

At 1020 the Naval Force Commander had ordered destroyers to form a line of bearing 070° to 250° from the *Calpe* and follow landing craft in towards the shore laying a smoke screen. The wind blowing on shore from the west made the smoke screen effective, its efficiency being increased by a curtain of smoke laid by aircraft between the east and west headlands from 1100 to 1200. The smoke prevented the enemy from firing effectively on landing craft until they were close inshore, but it also hid the beaches from the destroyers, interfering seriously with their covering fire and preventing the force commanders from seeing what was happening ashore.

The destroyers, the *Locust* and the L.C.F. remained at from 4 to 6 cables from the shore and gave what support they could. L.C.F. (L) 6 claimed to have shot down two Junkers 88 during two dive bombing attacks before the destroyers closed. Some of the landing craft made several journeys between the beaches and the L.C.T. under heavy fire and often dangerously overloaded. At 1040 the Flotilla officer of the *Prince Charles* went into Red beach with eight L.C.A. of these six were destroyed including the Flotilla officer's craft, but one, and probably two, embarked troops.

The Flotilla officer of the *Princess Astrid* led four craft in to White beach under very heavy fire. On touching down the boats were swamped by the weight of numbers trying to embark and one craft, hit by a heavy shell, capsized but each of the others took off about 70 men. L.C.A. 314, heavily laden, had been badly holed on the beach so the troops were transferred under fire to an L.C.T., which immediately received several direct hits and sank. L.C.A. 314 was sinking so her Commanding Officer put her alongside another L.C.T. and abandoned her. At 1100 the Flotilla officer of the *Glengyle* proceeded in to White beach with three craft of his flotilla and two or three from the *Prince*

Charles. The beach was in enemy hands with a small pocket of Canadians forming a strong point round a stranded L.C.T. These troops were removed but many were killed after embarkation.[115] The enemy fire was very heavy and they were fired on by some of our own tanks which had been captured. At least three craft were lost after leaving the beach; the troops that survived were put on board the *Calpe*.

From the report of the senior officer of "A" L.C.T., the tank landing craft which was sunk appears to have been L.C.T. 124 which in spite of orders to remain one mile off shore, had approached to within half a mile. L.C.T. 163 off White beach took troops from L.C.A. which were withdrawing and L.C.T. 166 remained off Red beach embarking troops who were ferried out. Later the senior officer of the L.C.T. in M.L. 343 proceeded to a point off the harbour entrance and came under very heavy fire. The M.L. put up a smoke screen to cover L.C.T. 166, which eventually withdrew safely in company with the M.L. and L.C.F. (L) 5 and 6. Commander McClintock, the Boat Pool officer, gave his assistant, Lt.-Cdr. Dathan, orders to supervise the withdrawal of landing craft from the eastern part of the beaches, while he himself dealt with the western half. He was off the breakwater in an M.L. leading in the landing craft when enemy aircraft attacked him with bombs and cannon forcing him to retire seawards followed by some of the landing craft. He then met a landing craft from Blue beach, which the Commanding Officer stated was held by the enemy. He accordingly came to the conclusion that it was impossible to carry out evacuation from Blue, White or Red beaches, and ordered the landing craft with him to form up on a course for home, while he himself proceeded in search of the *Calpe*.[116] Lt.-Cdr. Dathan meanwhile in M.L. 214 led his landing craft in towards the beach and at about 1145 when the last landing craft had gone in, closed the *Calpe*. As there were no special orders for him he withdrew to 3 miles off shore and collected landing craft as they came off from the beaches eventually sailing in company with them and the *Calpe* in the last group to leave.

Commander Lambert, the Principal Beachmaster, subsequently gave a graphic account[117] of these attempts as seen from the shore:

"I observed about eight L.C.A. making for White beach and was proceeding along the beach to meet them when they were heavily attacked by bombs from German aircraft while still some way off. In the meanwhile, about half a dozen other L.C.A. were seen heading for Red beach. These duly made the land through heavy fire and deployed perfectly just below the strong point. Lieutenant Bibby took charge of the loading but all except one were struck by mortars or shells as they were backing away and the troops had to be brought on shore again through a heavy fire. The only surviving officer of the boats which had been sunk was Lieutenant H.R. Hobday, R.N.V.R., of H.M.S. *Princess Beatrix*. It was subsequently reported to me that it was this officer who led these boats in and it was hard luck that his boat should have been hit on its way off after a fine attempt to rescue troops in almost hopeless circumstances.

After this incident, which left us busy for some time, it was noticed that the horizon was clear of shipping, and the Brigadier (W.W. Southam) was informed that it was unlikely that any more would be sent. He was rallying his men to further efforts but they were too exhausted for much exertion. Casualties were getting heavy, and although we kept up small arms fire as individuals, we could not reduce the increasing fire directed at us from the cliff tops. I then set out to return to Beach H.Q. about a furlong to the eastward to talk things over with the P.M.L.O., but a heavy barrage was put down and it was necessary to lie very flat until it ceased. When it suddenly stopped Germans could be seen approaching the promenade and our troops had begun to surrender. I returned to the strong point, being met by Lieutenant Bibby who told me that the soldiers had had enough and had run out of ammunition. We decided to try to escape by swimming out to a sunken L.C.T. with its bows afloat and lie up in it until dark. The Germans had no compunction about firing at us all the way out, but we got on board. However, the rising tide engulfed the bows and, as we were too exhausted to swim, the current took us close in to the breakwater where we were picked up by the enemy."

Meanwhile some of the landing craft from the *Prince Leopold's* flotilla, which had taken troops off Green beach went in towards Red and White beaches. Some of these were ordered to withdraw by destroyers before they reached shore, others picked up men swimming in the water but more of them appear to have touched down.

L.C.A. 186 made a final attempt. On arriving off White beach she found that all was quiet. At Red beach she found two L.C.T. on fire and three disabled L.C.A. The beach was clear of smoke and under heavy fire; it was covered with dead. Only two live men were seen but the craft could not, owing to heavy fire, approach sufficiently to take them off, though she picked up 30 men swimming in the sea including the Flotilla officer of the *Prince Charles* whose craft, as already recounted, had been sunk. L.C.A. 186 was the last craft to leave Red beach.

31. **Decision to abandon operation.**
By about 1130 the Naval Force Commander realized that the position ashore was deteriorating and that enemy fire was continually

increasing. At that time the *Brocklesby* was ordered to close the shore and give supporting fire. She advanced to within 500 yards of the beaches firing at gun positions on the cliffs and at houses on the front. Her action gave some relief to Green beach (see Section 36) but does not appear to have had much effect on the enemy guns, which were firing on the main beaches. The *Brocklesby* came under very heavy fire and was repeatedly hit by shells of 3-in. calibre and below and even by small arms fire; both engines were put out of action and the ship grounded by the stern. Repairs, however, were completed in three minutes and still firing at the enemy the *Brocklesby* got clear and sought protection behind the smoke.

At 1215, according to the *Brocklesby's* report the enemy were firing with small arms from the Casino and large houses to the east of the Casino. Three L.C.T. were high and dry and our troops were sheltering behind these whilst others lying on the beach were still firing. The number of troops was estimated at between 100 and 150 and one man signalled asking for boats to be sent.

At 1233, the *Fernie* attempted to give Red beach extra smoke cover but was hit and her director put out of action. Her Captain then received a request for assistance from Chasseur 13, hit and stopped off Red beach, but did not consider himself justified in approaching further. He endeavoured to pass on the request but without success. The Chasseur, however, succeeded in extricating herself, and reached home.

Meanwhile Commander McClintock, unable to find the *Calpe*, had made a signal at 1220 saying that no further evacuation was possible. The Military Force Commander, however, asked for further efforts to be made to bring off troops, so the Naval Force Commander replied "If no further evacuation possible, withdraw." The signal was reported to Commander McClintock without the word "if" and he accordingly withdrew with all landing craft in sight at about 1230 without apparently having been into the beach at all.

By this time over 400 men had been evacuated from Red and White beaches under conditions of the greatest difficulty, the crews of the landing craft showing complete contempt for danger. At 1240 the Naval Force Commander in the *Calpe* closed the beaches for a final personal inspection. Stationing L.C.A. 185 and 188, one on each bow, the *Calpe* steered for the eastern end of Red beach, opening fire with her 4-in. guns. At nine cables from the shore she came under heavy fire and as no troops could be seen on the beach, retired behind the smoke screen. It appeared impossible to bring off any more troops, but before finally abandoning the attempt Captain Hughes Hallett closed the *Locust* which was bombarding the eastern cliff, intending to consult

Commander Ryder as to whether the shallow draught *Locust*, should go in once more. At this time, however, the Military Force Commander received a signal saying that the remainder of the troops ashore were surrendering and the operation was brought to an end.

32. Loss of H.M.S. *Berkeley*.

It was shortly after the withdrawal from the French coast started, that the Force incurred its only warship loss. When the signal to withdraw was made, the destroyers were ordered to close the *Calpe* and make smoke. A number of enemy aircraft was engaged but owing to the smoke it was impossible to assess the results of A.A. fire. A general withdrawal began and destroyers were ordered to concentrate 4 miles 330° from Dieppe. Air attack at the time was almost continuous. The *Berkeley* was bombarding houses at the back of White beach when she received the signal to withdraw. On arriving at the rendezvous, her Captain intended to turn round astern of the main body in order to make smoke cover. At this juncture, at 1318 she was attacked by three Dorniers which were at once engaged by our fighters. One of the enemy, however, came on and dropped four bombs, which some of the accounts, not however that of the *Berkeley's* Captain, say were jettisoned. Two bombs hit the ship on the starboard side just forward of the bridge. The ship's back was broken, the main bulkhead at the after end of the forward mess-deck was shattered, and the forepart of the ship was flooded.

S.G.B. 8 immediately went alongside and took off the greater part of the ship's company. Lieutenant Yorke still thought that there was a chance of saving his ship and decided to remain on board with a towing party. As, however, all communications on board had broken down and the ship appeared to be sinking, the Captain reluctantly gave the order to abandon ship, which was carried out at 1321 when the S.G.B. cast off. The *Albrighton* was ordered to sink the *Berkeley* by torpedo which she did at 1338. The Captain of the *Berkeley* specially mentions the gallantry of Colonel Hillsinger of U.S.A.A.C. who had a foot blown off by the bomb but made his way to the S.G.B., where, though in great pain, he continued to act as aircraft lookout while lying on the deck.

33. Remarks on the Evacuation.

While accounts of the evacuation of Green beach are clear, the same cannot be said of the evacuation of Red and White beaches. Only a few reports from Commanding Officers of landing craft, who took part in the withdrawal from the main beaches, are available and in most cases no times are given. Under the circumstances it was no doubt difficult to keep any accurate records, but the lack of them makes it difficult to follow the sequence of events. It seems evident that several craft which might have gone into the beaches were ordered away by destroyers, and Commander McClintock[118] states that a number of craft were withdrawn before the end. It is true that except for the 100 to 150 men seen by the *Brocklesby* at 1215 reports tend to show that no troops, in a position to be evacuated were left ashore on Red and White beaches. The *Calpe* saw no one when she was close to the beach shortly before 1300. L.C.A. 186, the last craft to leave the beaches, saw only two men on Red beach, and none on White beach. It is nowhere stated at what time this craft finally left the beaches but presumably it was well after 1200. When dealing with reports that no men were left on the beaches, however, it must be borne in mind that the troops were sheltering under the sea wall at some distance from the water's edge and it might well have been impossible to discern them through the smoke from off shore. The men would not have been ordered down to the fire-swept beaches until it was known from the Naval beach parties that landing craft were about to touch down.

The original report[119] states that well over 1000 men were evacuated from Red and White beaches but this is almost certainly wrong. The Canadian History estimates the number taken off at about 368 and this is probably the maximum figure. So far as can be substantiated from the reports of the boat officers, only 18 or 19 craft, about half the number available,[120] endeavoured to touch down on the main beaches. Of these 10 or 11 were destroyed and 6 to 8 brought off troops; one craft never beached but returned safely with a number of men who were swimming off the beach. According to the reports of Commander Lambert, the principal beachmaster, and of the beachmaster at White beach,[121] both of whom were taken prisoner, only one L.C.A. got safely away from each beach. It is evident however that the beach officers were unaware of the evacuation carried out by the boats of the *Princess Astrid* and they may have counted as destroyed one or two craft which in fact returned safely. The L.C.A. were designed to carry 35 men. One craft is known to have taken off 80 and three took off 70, but craft carrying a number of wounded on stretchers must have taken considerably fewer. In addition, perhaps 50 men were rescued from the sea. Under these circumstances it is impossible to be certain about the exact number evacuated but it was probably well under 400.[122]

The Naval Force Commander commented that it was remarkable that "it proved possible to plan, promulgate, and carry out an entirely different scheme for withdrawal than that which had been contemplated in the original operation orders".[123] This involved (a) cancelling the existing operation orders, which contained a detailed plan for the withdrawal, (b) ordering the simplest possible alternative, and (c) achieving this without the use of plain language radio signals, since by this time it was apparent that these were being intercepted by the Germans.

In these circumstances, all L.C.A. were sent into the same beaches as those on which they had originally landed to take off as many troops as possible as best they could and ferry them to L.C.T. awaiting them about a mile from the shore. There is no doubt that the landing craft carried out their most difficult task with the greatest gallantry and determination and there is also little doubt that though destroyers and other craft gave them what support they could, this support was not effective. On the other hand, the smoke screen was extremely efficient and in fact without it, it is possible to think that no evacuation could have been carried out.

34. **The Return to England.**

Meanwhile the main body of landing craft and coastal craft had formed up in accordance with orders and was now slowly heading north. Destroyers took up their positions and the *Fernie* was ordered to take guide. While this was happening, the *Calpe* was attacked by enemy fighters and her bridge was shot up causing several casualties including Air Commodore Cole, the representative afloat of the R.A.F. Commander. The *Calpe* proceeded to eastward to pick up a British pilot who was reported in the sea. She thus left the protection given by the concentrated A.A. fire of all the ships, and as a result sustained two dive bombing attacks and suffered casualties and damage from near misses. Subsequently the *Calpe* re-joined the convoy which proceeded through the western swept channel on its way home.

The passage home was marked by a number of enemy air attacks, which all proved ineffective against the efficient umbrella provided by the R.A.F. About 20 miles from Newhaven the convoy was joined by the *Mackay* (Capt. D. 16) and *Blencathra* which escorted the landing and coastal craft in to Newhaven, while the destroyers and the *Locust*, with over 500 wounded on board went on to Portsmouth where they arrived shortly after midnight.

Part V

The Air Battle[124]

35. Air Forces.
In the preceding pages, little reference has been made to the part played by the R.A.F. mainly because in the nature of things, our aircraft though very active were not often seen from the ground. It should be clearly understood, however, that the Air Battle was not a separate phase but went on continuously from the first landings until dark, reaching its greatest intensity during the main withdrawal from the beaches.

The Air Battle was directed by the Air Force Force Commander, Air Vice-Marshal T. Leigh-Mallory from H.Q. of 11 Group of Fighter Command at Uxbridge,[125] and the immediate operations of fighters were directed by the fighter controller in the *Calpe*. The Air Forces detailed to take part in the operation were 56 squadrons of day fighters (50 to provide cover and six for close support), two squadrons of Hurricane bombers, two squadrons of day bombers, four squadrons of Army Co-operation forces, and three squadrons of "Smoke forces," in all 67 squadrons. In addition Coastal Command provided search patrols during the passage of the expedition throughout the dark hours. Bostons carried out bombing attacks on the east headland battery at 0510, after which a smoke screen was laid over both headlands. The two batteries behind the town were also bombed by Bostons but owing to the haze and the bad light these attacks on the batteries were considered in the words of C.C.O. "quite ineffective,"[126] "Intruder" aircraft engaged batteries, the attack by cannon-firing fighters on "Hess" battery being particularly helpful as has already been mentioned (Sections 22 and 23). Cannon-fighters supported the landing of the troops on Red and White beaches at Dieppe, and further smoke screens were laid as requested by the Naval and Military Force Commanders. Subsequent bombing attacks were made on the east headland when it was seen that the Blue beach landing at Puits was held up. Unfortunately, the bombs like the destroyers' shells had little effect on the enemy's defences. Nor can it be said that the bombing was very intensive, for the total of bombs dropped amounted only to some 220 bombs of 500 lbs. and about 90 of 250 lbs., a total of 60 tons. When it was seen that the situation on White beach was deteriorating, attacks were made at about 0930 on the west headland by "Hurribombers" and cannon-fighters.

36. Enemy Air Opposition.

At the commencement of the operation there was practically no enemy air opposition, the Luftwaffe having evidently been taken by surprise, but as time passed enemy sorties of 20 to 30 fighters appeared, and subsequently the strength of the sorties increased to between 50 and 100 aircraft. Fighter bombers also arrived and some abortive attacks were carried out on our ships, but it was not until about 1000 that heavy bombers appeared escorted by fighters. The heavies were energetically attacked by our fighters and sustained severe losses. The bombers made no attempt to attack our troops ashore and confined their attentions to the ships, but except for the sinking of the *Berkeley*, had practically no success.

At 1030 an attack was made by 24 Fortresses, escorted by Spitfires, on the fighter airfield at Abbeville-Drucat, which rendered it unserviceable for two hours and probably severely hampered the enemy fighters at the crucial moment of the withdrawal. During the withdrawal Bostons made bombing attacks on the two headlands, and a heavy smoke curtain was laid from the air. From 1200, heavy battles between formations of fighters went on over the ships and beaches, the enemy losing heavily. During the voyage home, fighter cover was maintained over the convoy and all attempts of enemy aircraft to attack the ships was foiled.[127] In the air we lost eight Bombers and smoke layers, 10 Army Co-operation and Reconnaissance aircraft, and 88 fighters,[128] while our casualties in killed and missing were 113 with 40 wounded. It is estimated that the enemy made 125 sorties with bombers and 600 with fighters. Our total sorties were stated to have been about 3,000.

At the time it was thought that the enemy's air losses were considerably greater than ours and that over a quarter of the German Air Force in Western Europe had been put out of action.[129] German records show, however, that in fact we only destroyed 23 fighters and 25 bombers, while 8 fighters and 16 bombers were damaged.[130]

These bare figures, however, do not tell the whole story. According to reliable German documents, there were in the Luftflotte 3 area (France, Belgium and Holland) 299 fighters and 175 bombers, but of these only 206 fighters and 107 bombers were fully serviceable at the time. Thus about 15% of the serviceable fighters and over 38% per cent of the serviceable bombers were either destroyed or substantially damaged.

Since the Spring of 1941, when the bulk of the German Air Force was moved to the eastern front, the small force remaining in the west had operated under severe pressure. The bomber units in particular were showing signs of extreme fatigue, resulting in a serious decline in efficiency of both aircraft and crews. Coming just after substantial losses suffered in the raids on Birmingham at the end of July, the casualties at Dieppe were a heavy blow, particularly as nearly all of the crews were lost, including two Squadron Commanders.

These losses should be viewed, too, in the light of the contemporary position of the German Air Force as a whole. Both in the Mediterranean and on the eastern front it was extremely hard pressed and the bomber force especially was stretched to the limit of its capabilities. In these circumstances it can fairly be claimed that Dieppe was an important contribution to the run down of the forces in the west, which in turn led to a severe restriction of offensive operations against the United Kingdom and British shipping.

Above: Troops about to disembark from their Assault Landing Craft during the training for the Dieppe Raid. A total of sixty LCAs such as that seen here were involved in Operation *Jubilee*. (Library and Archives Canada; 011052415)

Below: Pictured between June 1942, troops undertake their final training exercise prior to the launching of Operation *Jubilee*. (Library and Archives Canada; 011052414)

Above: Personnel landing craft draw away from ML230 to start their run-in to the beaches during the raid on Dieppe. At the time of *Jubilee*, ML230 was commanded by Lieutenant H.M. Nees RNVR. (Department of National Defence/Library and Archives Canada; PA-113247)

Below: Landing craft run in to the beaches at Dieppe under the cover of a smoke screen. (Department of National Defence/Library and Archives Canada; PA-11324

Above: Taken by Captain A.D.C. Smith, Intelligence Corps, this image shows a landing craft carrying personnel of No.4 Commando running in to land at Vasterival near Varengeville-sur-Mer. This short stretch of the French coast, on the right flank of the main assault at Dieppe, was Orange Beach One on 19 August 1942. (Historic Military Press)

Above: Douglas Boston Mk.IIIs, believed to be of 88 Squadron, lined up at Attlebridge, Norfolk, in preparation for their involvement in the Dieppe Raid. (Historic Military Press)

Above: A Douglas Boston Mk.III of 88 Squadron, flying from Ford, Sussex, heads inland over France after the bombing the German gun batteries defending Dieppe. (Historic Military Press)

Below: Bombs fall away from USAAF Boeing B-17 Flying Fortresses during an attack on the Luftwaffe airfield at Abbeville/Drucat on 19 August 1942. The bombing was undertaken in support of Operation *Jubilee*. In the foreground can be seen bombs that were released by the prior aircraft, while on the ground bombs are exploding. (NARA)

Above: The grim aftermath of *Jubilee*. The tank on the left is Mk.III T68561R named *Blossum*, which was part of 9 Troop, 'B' Squadron. It was transported aboard LCT No.121. Commanded by Lieutenant M.J.A. Lambert, it was disabled when the right track was broken by chert build-up. The tank in the foreground is Mk.III T68701R named *Bloody*, which was part of 10 Troop, 'B' Squadron, 4th Canadian Army Tank Regiment (The Calgary Regiment). It was transported aboard LCT No.124. Commanded by Sergeant R.B. Lee, it was disabled when the right track was destroyed by shellfire on the tank's return to the beach. (Historic Military Press)

Above: Abandoned Churchill tanks on the beach at Dieppe in the immediate aftermath of the attack on 19 August 1942. In all, twenty-nine Churchill tanks, comprising of assorted Mark I, II and III examples, were disembarked at Dieppe. Of these, twenty-seven would eventually get ashore – two 'drowned in deep water'. Fifteen would make it to the esplanade. Most were either hit by German fire, drowned or stranded as soon as they hit the beach. (Historic Military Press)

Above: One of the knocked-out Churchill tanks at Dieppe. One of the biggest problems encountered by the tank crews was the beach itself. At Dieppe this was composed of chert stone. As the tanks tried to cross the beach, these hard stones became jammed in the drive wheels, throwing the tracks. (Historic Military Press)

Below: British and Canadian prisoners pictured under escort in Dieppe's Rue de Sygogne as they are being marched inland away from the beaches. (Historic Military Press)

Above: Some of the German prisoners brought back from Dieppe pictured blindfolded and under guard at 'a South Coast harbour', 19 August 1942. (Historic Military Press)

Below: An American soldier receives a light for his cigarette from a compatriot at Newhaven on his return from Dieppe. This is possibly one of the Rangers who participated in the attack on the Hess Battery at Varengeville-sur-Mer with No.4 Commando.

Above: Another of the stranded Churchill tanks pictured after the attack. This tank, named *Cougar*, a Churchill Mk.III with the serial number T68173, went ashore from Tank Landing Craft 2 (No.127). It was one of five tanks fitted with the 'Beach Track Laying Device'. (Historic Military Press)

Below: German officers inspect landing craft, tanks, armoured cars and other equipment that littered the beach at Dieppe after the attack on 19 August 1942. (Historic Military Press)

Part VI

The Aftermath

37. Conclusion.
The Dieppe Raid occupies a place of its own in the operations of the war. It was the only raid in which the landing of tanks was attempted or in which more than a couple of hours was allowed for military operations. Though it can hardly be claimed that the immediate results were commensurate with the casualties incurred it is certain that it had important ulterior results that render it a notable landmark in the history of the war. For example, it convinced the Germans that an invasion could be defeated on the beaches; hence reliance of Hitler's "western wall" and the tactics which led to the military disaster that overtook them after the Normandy landings.

In its general aspect it shed an illuminating ray on the urgent need for meeting the long-standing requirements of Combined Operations.[131] In particular the question of close fire support received immediate and thorough investigation and steps were taken to build a number of special types of support craft. A further sequel was the introduction of the landing craft gun and landing craft rocket to support assaults. Other naval lessons, forming an important aggregate, were the necessity for ample smoke protection, for a higher standard of aircraft recognition, for careful timing of the assaults, for ample briefing with due regard to security considerations and for an accurate and comprehensive system of control and communications. In this connection it was noted that R/T messages in plain language were speedily intercepted and exploited by the enemy.[132] Another important lesson, which was finally accepted by the Admiralty, was the necessity for "the formation of permanent naval assault forces" possessing a "coherence comparable to that of any other first line formations".[133] Up to the date of the raid scattered units had been collected together as required for a particular operation and the important elements of a permanent command and continuity of training had been wanting. Measures were taken to remedy this deficiency and in due course Force "J" came into being. This led to the issue of Force "J" fighting instructions, which standardised the technique of assault forces and permitted an immense shortening of future operation orders.[134]

But the principal lesson of the Dieppe Raid was that a direct attack on a defended port had little chance of success and that landing forces must be put ashore on beaches at some distance from the port. This policy was followed in all the Mediterranean assaults and also in the Normandy Landing. The necessity for prolonged maintenance over beaches caused the possibility of the construction of a temporary harbour to be investigated, with the result that the "Mulberry" was evolved, in time for the latter great operation.

Part VII

Apendices

A	List of H.M. Ships on Operation "Jubilee"	55
B	Organization of H.M. Ships on Operation "Jubilee"	62
C	Military and Air Forces on Operation "Jubilee"	65
D	Casualties	67
E	Types of Landing Craft	71
F	Analysis of Bombing Attacks in Support of Operation "Jubilee"	72
G	Summary of the Lessons learnt	74
H	Extracts from German Reports on Dieppe Raid	77
I	Naval Operational Order No.I	126
J	List of Ships, Groups and Senior Officers	132
K	Operation "Jubilee" – Instructions to L.S.I.	137
L	Operation "Jubilee" – Instructions to Destroyers	141
M	Orders for Naval A.A. Fire	146
N	Operation "Jubilee" – Orders for Coastal Craft	148
O	Table of Movements of Coastal Craft After the Assault	153
P	Operation "Jubilee" – Instructions to Cutting Out Force	156
Q	Orders for Withdrawal of Troops and Return Passage	163
R	Orders for Naval Beach Parties	168
S	Detailed Military Plan	172
T	Information – Enemy	178
U	Assault and Occupation	182
V	Schedule of Timings	185
W	Detailed Air Plan	200
X	Officers in Command	221
Y	Report by Naval Force Commander	231
Z	Report by Military Force Commander	242
AA	Report by the Air Force Commander	250
BB	Order of Battle of the Royal Air Force	265
CC	Analysis of Bombing Attacks	268
DD	An Estimate of Enemy Aircraft Seen over Dieppe During the Action	270
EE	Reactions of the German Air Force	271
FF	Medical Arrangements for Casualty Evacuation	276
GG	Medical Evacuation at a Dockyard	282
HH	Security Arrangements	284
II	Security Lapses and Action Taken	291
JJ	German State of Readiness	293
KK	Enemy Defences and Weapons	294
LL	Enemy Defences Summarised	298

Appendix A

LIST OF H.M. SHIPS ON OPERATION JUBILEE

Naval Force Commander: Captain J. Hughes Hallett, R.N. (in H.M.S. *Calpe*). Chief of Staff: (Acting) Captain J.D. Luce, D.S.O., R.N.

Ship. *Commanding Officer.*
Destroyers
H.M.S. *Calpe*
(Headquarters Ship)   Lt.-Cdr. J.H. Wallace, R.N.

H.M.S. *Fernie*
(2nd Headquarters ship)   Lt. W.B. Willett, R.N.

H.M.S. *Brocklesby*   Lt.-Cdr. E.N. Pumphrey, D.S.O., D.S.C., R.N.
H.M.S. *Garth*   Lt.-Cdr. J.P. Scatchard, R.N.
H.M.S. *Albrighton*   Lt.-Cdr. R.J. Hanson, R.N.
H.M.S. *Berkeley*   Lt. J.J.S. Yorke, R.N.
H.M.S. *Bleasdale*   Lt. P.B. North-Lewis, R.N.
O.R.P. *Slazak* (Polish)   Cdr. R. Tyminiski.

Sloop and Gunboat
H.M.S. *Alresford*   Cdr. R.E.C. Dunbar, R.N. (Ret.).
H.M.S. *Locust*   Lt.-Cdr. W.J. Stride, M.B.E., R.N. (Ret.).

Minesweeper Flotillas
9th Minesweeper Flotilla   Cdr. H.T. Rust, D.S.O., R.N.
13th Minesweeper Flotilla   Cdr. L.J.S. Ede, D.S.O., R.N.

Landing Ship, Infantry (Large)
H.M.S. *Glengyle*   Captain D.S. McGrath, R.N. (Ret.).

APPENDICES

Landing Ships, Infantry (Medium)
H.M.S. *Queen Emma*   Captain G.L.D. Gibbs, D.S.O., R.N. (Ret.).
H.M.S. *Princess Beatrix*   Cdr. T.B. Brunton, R.N. (Ret.).

Landing Ships, Infantry (Small)
H.M.S. *Prince Charles*   Cdr. S.H. Dennis, D.S.C., R.N. (Ret.).
H.M.S. *Prince Albert*   Lt.-Cdr. H.B. Peate, R.N.R.
H.M.S. *Prince Leopold*   Lt.-Cdr. W.S. Byles, R.D., R.N.R.
H.M.S. *Princess Astrid*   Lt.-Cdr. C.E. Hall, R.N.R. (Ret.).

Landing Ships, Infantry (Handhoisting)
H.M.S. *Invicta*   Cdr. A.I. Robertson, R.D., R.N.R.
H.M.S. *Duke of Wellington*   Lt.-Cdr. J.F.H. Coombes, R.D., R.N.R.

Senior Officer, Landings
"Yellow" Beach   Cdr. D.B. Wyburd, R.N.
"Orange" Beach   Lt.-Cdr. H.H.H. Mulleneux, R.N.
"Green" Beach   Lt.-Cdr. R.M. Prior, D.S.C., R.N.
"Blue" Beach   Lt.-Cdr. H.W. Goulding, D.S.O., R.N.R.
"White" Beach   Lt.-Cdr. C.W. McMullen, R.N.
"Red" and "White" Beaches
and Principal Beach Master   Cdr. G.T. Lambert, R.N.
Officer Commanding
Cutting-Out Party   Cdr. R.E.D. Ryder, V.C., R.N.
"White" Beach Beachmaster   Lt. P. Ross, R.N.V.R.[135]
"Red" Beach Beachmaster   Lt. D.T. Bibby, R.N.V.R.[136]

Landing Craft
Commanding Officer
First Flotilla. Group 5. ("Yellow" Beach):   L.C.P. No.
Lt. D.R. Stevens, R.N.V.R. (Flotilla Officer)   1
Sub-Lt. H.A. Hancock, R.N.V.R.   80
Sub-Lt. B.K. McCosh, R.N.V.R.   81
Sub-Lt. A.M. Button, R.N.V.R.   85
Sub-Lt. R.E.D. Fenning, R.N.V.R.   86
Sub-Lt. N.W. Dunn, R.N.V.R.   87
Lt. G.W. Holt, R.N.V.R.   95
Sub-Lt. A.L. Oates, R.N.V.R.   118
Sub-Lt. J. Rutherford, R.N.V.R.   128
Sub-Lt. M.V. Nicholl, R.N.V.R.   145
Sub-Lt. K. Child, R.N.V.R.   157

Second Flotilla. Group 6. ("Green" Beach):

Lt. G. Byerley, R.N.V.R. (Flotilla Officer)	19
Sub-Lt. Franklin, R.N.V.R.	88
Sub-Lt. M. Easton, R.N.V.R.	94
Sub-Lt. D.H. Botly, R.C.N.V.R.	119
Sub-Lt. R.M. Smith, R.C.N.V.R.	124
Sub-Lt. D.L. Marchant, R.N.V.R.	125
Sub-Lt. J.E. O'Rourke, R.C.N.V.R.	129
Sub-Lt. D. Masson, R.N.V.R.	147
Sub-Lt. J.D. Nisbet, R.N.V.R.	156

Fourth Flotilla. Group 7. (Floating Reserve):

Lt.-Cdr. W.L.N. Wallace, R.N.V.R. (Flotilla Officer)	186
Lt. J. Hawkes, R.N.V.R.	195
Lt. F. Lock, R.N.V.R.	187
Lt. R.A. Durham, R.N.V.R.	212
Sub-Lt. S.G.P. Walker, R.N.V.R.	175
Sub-Lt. W.E. Ibell, R.N.V.R.	170
Sub-Lt. D.B. Corcoran, R.N.V.R.	188
Sub-Lt. C.T. Kitching, R.N.V.R.	192
Sub-Lt. R.C.A. Barnes, R.N.V.R.	174
Sub-Lt. C.H. Lindfoot, R.N.V.R.	173
Sub-Lt. G.W. Lindfoot, R.N.V.R.	199
Sub-Lt. G.M. Doaman, R.N.V.R.	172
Sub-Lt. N. Sparks, R.N.V.R.	53
Sub-Lt. J.H. Vellacott, R.N.V.R.	28

Fifth Flotilla. Group 7. (Floating Reserve):

Lt.-Cdr. N.C. Roulston, R.N.V.R. (Flotilla Officer)	163
Lt. R.F.H. Morgan, R.N.V.R.	164
Lt. A. Wilson, R.N.V.R.	165
Lt. E.R.C. Hunt, R.N.V.R.	166
Lt. C. Newman, R.N.V.R.	167
Lt. C. Tymms, R.N.V.R.	209
Lt. K.D. Cox, R.N.V.R.	210
Sub-Lt. J. Vaughan, R.N.V.R.	208
Sub-Lt. T. Williams, R.N.V.R.	155
Lt. R.F. McRae, R.C.N.V.R.	45
Sub-Lt. G.E. Evans, R.N.V.R.	31
Sub-Lt. D.B. Rogers, R.C.N.V.R.	163

APPENDICES

Sixth Flotilla. Group 6. ("Green" Beach):
Lt. J. Murray, R.N.V.R. (Flotilla Officer)	127
Lt. P. Moss, R.N.V.R.	130
Lt. D.R. Tride, R.N.V.R.	131
Sub-Lt. L.C. Breeze, R.N.V.R.	132
Sub-Lt. J. Whiting, R.N.V.R.	134
Lt. C.W.R. Cross, R.N.V.R.	135
Sub-Lt. A.D. Waters, R.N.V.R.	136
Sub-Lt. T.L. Rankin, R.N.V.R.	153
Sub-Lt. J. Murts, R.N.V.R.	158

Seventh Flotilla. Group 6. ("Green" Beach):
Lt.-Cdr. H. Garrard, R.N.V.R. (Flotilla Officer)	101
Sub-Lt. H.A. Carter, R.N.V.R.	83
Sub-Lt. B.T. Heath, R.N.V.R.	84
Lt. J. Mattinson, R.N.V.R.	99
Lt. C. Lawrie, R.N.V.R.	102
Lt. J. Cassidy, R.N.V.R.	104
Lt. E.N. Russel, R.N.V.R.	110
Sub-Lt. R.G. Holmes, R.N.V.R.	113
Lt. M.L. Bateson, R.N.V.R.	159
Lt. G. O'Keefe Wilson, R.N.V.R.	160

Twenty-Fourth Flotilla. Group 5. ("Yellow" Beach):
Lt.-Cdr. C.L. Corke (Flotilla Officer), R.N.V.R.	42
Sub-Lt. A.D.H. Kelly, R.N.V.R.	3
Sub-Lt. B. Purden, R.N.V.R.	4
Sub-Lt. Plummer, R.N.V.R.	13
Lt. H.T. Buckee, R.N.V.R.	15
Sub-Lt. R. Hough, R.N.V.R.	23
Sub-Lt. G.E. Green, R.N.V.R.	34
Sub-Lt. P.J. Record, R.N.V.R.	40
Sub-Lt. D.H. Spring, R.N.V.R.	41
Lt. G. Brown, R.N.V.R.	43
Sub-Lt. B. Faragher, R.N.V.R.	44
Sub-Lt. M.S. Pilkington, R.N.V.R.	115
Midshipman A.B. Potter, R.N.V.R.	7, 8 (Navigational)

2nd L.C.T. Flotilla.
Lt.-Cdr. H.P. Brownell, R.A.N.V.R (Flotilla Officer and of 1st L.C.F. Flotilla)	L.C.T.

APPENDICES

Lt. C. Brookes Hill, R.N.V.R.	121
Lt. G.H. Reynolds, R.N.V.R.	145
Lt. L.A. Gwinner, R.N.V.R.	124
Lt. T.A. Robertson, R.N.V.R.	125
Lt. A. Cheney, R.N.V.R.	126
Skpr. B.D. McPherson, R.N.R.	127
Sub-Lt. W.H. Cooke, R.N.V.R.	159
Skpr. T.A. Cooke, D.S.C., R.N.R.	163
Skpr. C.L. Barber, R.N.R.	165
Sub-Lt. S. Alanson, R.N.V.R.	166

1st L.C.F. Flotilla	*L.C.F. (L)*
Lt. E.L. Graham, R.N.V.R.	2
Lt. N.R. Woodeson, R.N.V.R.	4
Lt. H.C. Trickiey. R.N.V.R.	6
Lt. T.M. Foggtt, R.A.N.V.R.	1
Lt. E. Arundale, R.N.V.R.	3
Lt. C. Grantham, R.N.V.R.	5

4th L.C.T. Flotilla

Lt.-Cdr. C. Masterman, R.A.N.V.R. (Flotilla Officer)	*L.C.T. No.*
Lt. F.F. Appleton, R.A.N.V.R.	305
Lt. P. Drew, R.N.V.R.	304
Lt. P. Bull, R.N.V.R.	303
Sub-Lt. S. Carr-Smith, R.N.V.R.	302
Lt. D.J.B. Morris, R.A.N.V.R.	306
Lt. L. Bailey, R.N.V.R.	308
Lt. R.M. Thacker, R.N.V.R.	376
Lt. K.B. Porteous, R.N.V.R.	361
Lt. F.F. Welcome, R.N.V.R.	309
Sub-Lt. R. Dewhurst, R.N.V.R.	310
Skpr. E.J. Brown, R.N.R.	360
Skpr. C.D. Powdrall, R.N.R.	307
Lt. R.E. Green, R.N.V.R.	318
Skpr. A.C. Tavandale, R.N.R.	325

Escorting Craft Commanding Officer	*M.G.B. No.*
Sub-Lt. L.H. Ennis, R.N.V.R.	50
Sub-Lt. G. Clarke, R.N.V.R.	51
Lt. W.B.G. Leith, R.N.V.R.	52
Sub-Lt. C.C.P. Broadhurst, R.N.V.R.	57

Lt. A.R.H. Nye, R.N.V.R.	312
Lt. J.L. Lloyd, R.N.V.R.	315
Lt.-Cdr. T.M. Cartwright, R.N.V.R.	316
Lt. J.H. Coste, R.N.V.R.	317
Lt. N.W. Hughes, R.N.V.R.	320
Lt. B.L. Bourne, R.N.V.R.	321
Lt. G.C. Fanner, R.N.V.R.	323
Lt. R.D. Russell-Roberts, R.N.V.R.	326

	S.G.B. No.
Lt. G.H. Hummel, R.N.R.	5
Lt. H.C.T. Bradford, D.S.C., R.N.V.R.	6
Lt. I.R. Griffiths, R.N.	8
Lt. P.M. Scott, R.N.V.R.	9

	M.L. No.
Sub-Lt. G.F. Bayne, R.N.C.V.R.	114
Lt. E.K. Jones, R.N.V.R.	120
Lt.-Cdr. R.N. Wood, R.N.V.R.	123
Lt. C.J. Jerram, R.N.V.R.	171
Lt. G.N. Johnstone, R.N.V.R.	187
Lt. B.H. Lloyd, R.N.V.R.	189
Lt. R.W. Ball, R.N.V.R.	190
Lt. H. Leslie, R.N.V.R.	191
Lt. J.F. Humphreys, R.N.V.R.	193
Lt.-Cdr. W. Whitfield, R.N.R.	194
Lt. J.S.E. Page, R.N.V.R.	208
Lt. I.D. Lyle, R.N.V.R.	214
Lt. H.M. Nees, R.N.V.R.	230
Lt. D.H. Titcombe, R.N.V.R.	246
Lt. J.B.C. Lumsden, R.N.V.R.	291
Lt.-Cdr. G. Shaw-Brundell, R.N.V.R.	292
Lt.-Cdr. F. Hellings, R.N.V.R.	309
Lt. G.A. Wright, R.N.V.R.	343
Lt. L.E. Barker, R.N.V.R.	344
Lt. A.D. Fear, R.N.V.R.	346

	Chasseurs
Lt. W.H.P. Loftie, R.N.	14
Lt. de Vaiseau, Y.J. Boja, F.N.F.C.	43
Officier des Equipages J. Parc, F.N.F.C.	42

Lt. E.G. Egerton, R.N. 13
Lt. J.E. Syms, R.N. 41
Enseigne de Vaiseau Chanlieau, F.N.F.C. 10
Officier des Equipages M. Ibarlucia, F.N.F.C. 5

Landing Craft from the L.S.I. Flotillas consisted of: 60 L.C.A. (Assault); 8 L.C.S. (Support); 7 L.C.M. (Mechanised).

Appendix B

ORGANISATION OF H.M. SHIPS ON OPERATION JUBILEE

Lists are taken from B.R. 1887 and Report of N.F.C.; these do not give the names of flotilla officers in every case. The number of assault craft attached to each ship is taken from Plan 3. The total number of L.C.M. on Plan 3 (Diagram VI of B.R.) does not correspond with the text in B.R.

Destroyers
Calpe   H.Q. ship 1st Destroyer Division, Captain J. Hughes-Hallett, R.N. Naval Force Commander.
Fernie   "Stand-by" H.Q. ship.
Garth   S.O., 2nd Destroyer Division.
Albrighton
Berkeley
Bleasdale
Slazak   S.O., 3rd Destroyer Division.
Brocklesby

Group 1 ("Orange" beach)
Prince Albert   6 L.C.A., 1 L.C.S., Flotilla Officer, Lt. P. McKinnon, R.N.V.R.
M.G.B. 312
S.G.B. 9
S.O. Landings   Lt.-Cdr. H.H. Mulleneux, R.N.

Group 2 ("Green" beach)
Princess Beatrix 10 L.C.A., 2 L.C.S., 2 L.C.M. Flotilla Officer Lt. J.H.F.
Invicta   Thomson, R.N.V.R. Flotilla Officer
M.G.B. 317
S.G.B. 6
S.O. Landings   Lt.-Cdr., R.M. Prior, R.N.

APPENDICES

Group 3 ("Blue" beach)
Queen Emma   12 L.C.A., 2 L.C.S., 1 L.C.M. Flotilla Officer, Lt. N.E.B. Ramsay, R.N.V.R.
Princess Astrid   Flotilla Officer, Lt. J. Howitt, R.N.V.R.
M.G.B. 316
S.G.B. 8
S.O. Landings   Lt.-Cdr. H.W. Goulding, R.N.R.

Group 4 ("Red" and "White" beaches)
Glengyle   10 L.C.A., 1 L.C.S., 2 L.C.M. Flotilla Officer, Lt. P. Cork, R.N.V.R.
Prince Charles   8 L.C.A., 1 L.C.S. Flotilla Officer, Lt. Phillips, R.N.V.R.
Prince Leopold   8 L.C.A., 1 L.C.S. Flotilla Officer, Lt. R. Chancellor, R.N.V.R.
M.G.B. 326
M.L. 291
Locust
S.O. Landings
"Red" and "White" Beaches   Cdr. G.T. Lambert, R.N.
S.O. Landings "White" beach   Lt.-Cdr. A.W. McMullen, R.N.
Duke of Wellington
("Blue" Beach) 6 L.C.A.,   Flotilla Officer, Lt. S. Breach, R.N.V.R.

Group 5 ("Yellow" beach)
1st L.C.P. Flotilla
24th L.C.P. Flotilla
S.G.B. 5
M.L. 346
L.C.F. (L) 1
S.O. Landings   Cdr. B.D. Wyburd, R.N.

Group 6 ("Green" beach)
2nd L.C.P. Flotilla
6th L.C.P. Flotilla
7th L.C.P. Flotilla
M.L. 190
M.L. 194
S.O. Group and Boat Pool Officer   Cdr. H.V.P. McClintock, R.N.

Group 7 (Floating Reserve)
4th L.C.P. Flotilla
5th L.C.P. Flotilla

M.L. 214
M.L. 230
S.O. Group   Lt.-Cdr. J.H. Dathan, R.N.

Group 8
L.C.T. 145, 127, 159, 126, 121, 163
L.C.F. (L) 2, 6   (Numbers of L.C.F. (L) not certain)
M.L. 343
S.O. Group   Lt.-Cdr. Earl Beatty, R.N.

Group 9
L.C.T. 124, 125, 165, 166
M.L. 191
S.O. Group   Lt. H. Leslie, R.N.V.R.

Group 10
L.C.T. 305, 304, 303, 302, 313, 314
M.L. 193
S.O. Group   Lt.-Cdr. G.H. Stevens, R.N.

Group 11
L.C.T. 306, 308, 376, 361
M.L. 189, 187
L.C.F. (L) 3, 5
S.O. Group   Lt. N.B. Lloyd, R.N.V.R.

Group 12
L.C.T. 309, 307, 310, 360
M.L. 344
L.C.F. (L) 4   (Number not certain)
S.O. Group   Lt. L.E. Barker, R.N.V.R.

Group 13
Chasseurs 14, 43, 42, 13, 41, 10, 5
Alresford
S.O. Group   Lt. M. Buist, R.N.

Not attached to groups
M.G.B. 315, 321, 320, 323, 50, 51.
M.L. 246, 123, 114, 120, 292, 309, 171, 208.
Carried in landing ships, 60 L.C.A., 7 L.C.M., 8 L.C.S.

Note: The total number of landing craft lowered and sent in from the landing ships are in B.R. but the number from each ship and the flotilla identity numbers are not given.

Appendix C

MILITARY AND AIR FORCES ON OPERATION JUBILEE

2nd Canadian Division: Major-General J.H. Roberts, M.C.

Regiment	Commanding Officer
4th Canadian Infantry Brigade	Brigadier W.W. Southam, E.D.
6th Canadian Infantry Brigade	Brigadier Sherwood Lett, M.C., E.D.
Royal Hamilton Light Infantry	Lt.-Col. R.R. Labatt.
Essex Scottish	Lt.-Col. F.K. Jesperson.
Queen's Own Cameronians	Lt.-Col. G.W. Gostling.
Royal Regiment of Canada	Lt.-Col. D.E. Catto.
South Saskatchewan Regiment	Lt.-Col. C.C.I. Merritt.
Les Fusiliers Mont-Royal	Lt.-Col. D. Menard.
Calgary Regiment (14th Canadian Tank Battalion)	Lt.-Col. J.G. Andrews.
2nd Canadian Light Field Ambulance, R.C.A.M.C.	Lt.-Col. K.A. Hunter.

Commandos
No. 3 Commando	Lt.-Col. J.F. Durnford-Slater, D.S.O.
No. 4 Commando	Lt.-Col. The Lord Lovat, M.C.
Royal Marine Commando	Lt.-Col. J.P.P. Phillips, R.M.

R.A.F.
Air Vice-Marshal T. Leigh-Mallory, C.B., D.S.O., R.A.F.

Fighter Squadrons   611, 131, 129, 111, 43, 3, 32, 174, 124, 616, 64, 122, 81, 154, 165, 65, 242, 56, 51, 266, 610, 253, 232, 602, 130, 66, 118, 501, 87, 245, 175, 19, 41, 222, R.A.F. 402, 412, 416, 401, 411, 403, R.C.A.F. 485, R.N.Z.A.F.

APPENDICES

	350, Belgium.
	340, French.
	306, 317, 302, 303, 308, Polish.
	71, 121, 133, *Eagle*.
	331, 332, Norwegian.
	310, 312, Czechoslavakian.
	307, 308, 309, U.S.A.A.C.
Bomber Squadrons	88, 107, R.A.F.
Army Co-operation Squadrons	26, 239, 414, R.A.F. 400, R.C.A.F.
Smoke Forces	13, 614, 226.

Appendix D

CASUALTIES

Note. The figures which follow differ from those given in B.R. 1887 pp. 35, 36, which were compiled shortly after the raid.
The figures adopted in the following statement have been obtained from the following sources:

Royal Navy and Royal Marines from the Naval Force Commander's Report and the Admiralty, N.C.W. (casualties); Commandos from Amphibious Warfare H.Q.; R.A.F. from Air Ministry, Historical Branch. These were all checked in June 1958. Canadian losses from official History of Canadian Army, Vol. I. p. 389.

I. Allied Losses

Naval (exclusive of Royal Marine Commando, but including R.M. serving in L.C.F.):

(a) Personnel:	Officers	O.R.	Total
Killed and died of wounds[137]	25	123	148
Prisoners of War	16	96	112
Wounded,[138] returned to U.K.	18	245	263
	<u>59</u>	<u>464</u>	<u>523</u>

(b) Material:
1 destroyer (H.M.S. *Berkeley*), 5 L.C.T., 8 L.C.P. (L), 1 L.C.M., 1 L.C.S. (M), 1 L.C.F., 17 L.C.A.

Military

(a) Personnel:[139]	Officers	O.R.	Total
Killed and died of wounds[140]	66	914	980
Prisoners of War	126	1884	2010
Wounded,[141] returned of U.K.	45	590	635
	<u>237</u>	<u>3388</u>	<u>3625</u>

APPENDICES

(b) Material:
29 tanks[142], 10 cars and carriers, 3 motor cycles, mortars, small arms, ammunition etc.

Air

(a) Personnel:	Officers	O.R.	Total
Killed or died of wounds	20	33	53
Prisoners of War	9	13	22
Wounded, returned to U.K.	7	20	27
	36	66	102

(b) Material:
88 fighters, 10 army co-operation and reconnaissance, 8 bombers and smoke laying aircraft, 3 high speed launches.

In addition to the foregoing the Combined Operations Headquarters Staff suffered 10 casualties of which 2 were fatal.

The Germans claimed a total of 2217 prisoners (German report, para. 70) and said they had buried about 600 of our dead.

The proportion of casualties to the troops engaged of the 2nd Canadian Division, Nos. 3, 4, 6 and 10 Commandos, the R.M. Commando and the U.S. Rangers was as follows:

| Engaged | 6088 | 59.5% of these 980, |
| Casualties | 3625 | 16% were fatal. |

The following table shows the proportion of casualties to the number engaged by Services. Column 3 shows casualties from all causes (killed, wounded, missing, prisoners of war) on the conclusion of the raid i.e. the loss to the war effort at that time until they had been made good: Column 4 gives fatal casualties (killed, died of wounds, died in captivity, permanently missing, presumed killed) as finally determined on the conclusion of the war.

(1) Service	(2) Number engaged	(3) Casualties from all causes		(4) Fatal casualties	
Naval	7750	523	6.7%	148	1.9%
Royal Marine Commando	370	76	20%	29	7.8%

Commandos	705	169	24%	37	5.2%
Canadian Forces	4963	3367	67.8%	907	18.2%
U.S. Rangers	50	13	26%	7	13%
R.A.F.	1179	102	8.6%	49	4.1%
C.O.H.Q. Staff	22	10	45%	2	9%
Grand Total	15039	4260	28.3%	1179	7.8%

II Enemy Losses

(*a*) Personnel.
Two sets of figures of losses are given in the German report (paras. 38 and 70) which are not reconcilable, but the probable losses were:

Navy.
Killed and missing, 78. Wounded, 35.

Army.
Killed, 115. Missing, 14. Wounded, 187.

Air Force.
Killed and missing, 104. Wounded, 58.

This makes a total of 591 enemy casualties for the three services; not far from the estimate of 500 in B.R., p. 35. Our prisoners consisted of 25 naval ratings from the armed trawler UJ 1404, eight soldiers, and four air force personnel. (B.R., p. 35)

(*b*) Material:

Naval.
Two armed trawlers sunk.
One small tanker sunk.
Two armed trawlers probably damaged.

Air Force.
48 aircraft destroyed.
24 damaged.

Military.

Military damage is difficult to assess. A number of fortified houses, the Casino and tobacco factory all facing Red and White beaches were set on fire by shell fire or bombs, and gutted. A certain amount of damage was done to other fortifications.
Four 5.9-in. guns of "Hess" battery were destroyed, and other guns are thought to have received direct hits.

Appendix E

TYPES OF LANDING CRAFT

L.C.T. — Landing craft, tank. Craft of about 250 tons, with length of 160 ft. and upward. Armament, two 2-pdr. pom-poms. No armour. Crew 2 officers and 10 ratings. Carries three tanks.

L.C.F. (L) — Landing craft, flak, (large). Craft of about 400 tons. Length about 160 ft. Converted L.C.T. The armament of L.C.F (L) 1 was two twin 4-in. H.A./L.A. and three Oerlikons. L.C.F. (L) 2 to 6 were armed with eight 2-pdr. pom-poms and 4 Oerlikons.[143]

L.C.S. (L) — Landing craft, support, (large). Craft about 46 ft. long. Armament, one 2-pdr., two .5-in. M.G., two Lewis guns. One 4-in. smoke mortar. These craft are armoured against .5-in. fire. Crew 1 officer, 11 ratings.

L.C.M. (1) — Landing craft (Mechanised) (*i.e.* for carrying mechanised transport). Craft about 40 ft. long. No armament. Partially armoured. Used for carrying Bren carriers or jeeps; will take one medium tank. Crew six ratings, one officer to three craft.

L.C.A. — Landing craft (assault). Craft about 38 ft. long. Armament one Bren gun. Partially armoured against small arms fire. Carries 35 men, crew 4 ratings. One officer to three craft.

L.C.P. (L) — Landing craft (personnel). Craft about 36 ft. long. Armament one M.G. No armour. Carries 25 men. Crew 1 officer and 3 ratings.

Appendix F

ANALYSIS OF BOMBING ATTACKS IN SUPPORT OF OPERATION JUBILEE

Target	Squadron	No. of Aircraft	Bombs dropped	Result
"Rommel"	No. 2 Group	14	55 x 500 48 x 40	Not observed but believed "target area and to E"
	174	10	12 x 250 6 x 250	Bursts in target area Houses s. of "Rommel"
	175	18 10	16 x 250 20 x 250	Six bursts in target area Direct hits on emplacements
"Bismarck"	No. 2 Group	12	48 x 500	Target straddled and entire area covered with smoke
	Army Co-op Smoke Laying	14	156 smoke bombs	Objective reached
	174	12	18 x 500	No target seen on landfall.
	6 x 250			Targets selected were 2 miles east of Dieppe (houses and woods)
"Hitler"	No. 2 Group	13	39 x 500 92 x 40	South and east of target overshot
	174	12	18 x 500	Many bursts in target area

APPENDICES

Target	Squadron	Sorties	Bombs	Results
	605	1	4 x 250 10 x 40	Results not observed
"Goering"	No. 2 Group	1	3 x 500 8 x 40	South and east of target. Unobserved
	418	3	30 x 40	Target located and bombed
"Hindenburg"	No. 2 Group	12	36 x 500 92 x 40	Most bombs in target area
Road Dieppe/ Rouen	No. 2 Group	6	—	Bombed railway at Ouville
"Red, White Beaches"	Army Co-op. Smoke Laying	4	36 smoke bombs bombs	Effective screen
		2	—	—
		2	—	Successful. Mole w. headland
		4	—	Successful screen. East and w. headland
		3	—	Did not attack target
		3	—	Task successfully completed
"Green Beach"	Army Co-op. Smoke Laying	6	60 smoke bombs 72 smoke bombs	Smoke screen good Task completed
W. Headland	175	—	24 x 250	Bursts on houses and church used as flak post

Appendix G

SUMMARY OF THE LESSONS LEARNED[144]

1. **Naval**
(a) The need for overwhelming fire support, including close support during the initial stages of the attack.
(b) The necessity for the formation of permanent naval assault forces with coherence comparable to that of any other first line fighting formations. Army formations intended for amphibious assaults must without question be trained in close co-operation with such naval assault forces.
(c) The necessity for fire support in any operation where it has been possible to rely on the element of surprise. This fire support must be provided by heavy and medium Naval bombardment, by air action, by special vessels or craft working close inshore, and by using the fire power of the assaulting troops while still sea-borne. Special close-support craft, which should be gunboats or some form of mobile fort, do not exist and must be designed and constructed.
Support by the Royal Air Force is effective within the limits imposed by time and space.
(d) Tanks should not be landed until the anti-tank defences have been destroyed or cleared.[145] L.C.T. carrying tanks must not linger on the beaches beyond the time required to disembark their loads.
(e) A far higher standard of aircraft recognition is essential both in the Royal Navy and the Army. This should be achieved by means of lectures, photographs and silhouettes. If possible, personnel of the Royal Observer Corps should be carried in ships.
(f) Beach signal parties should not land complete with the first wave, but only when the beach has been secured.
(g) The importance and necessity of using smoke cannot be over-emphasized and larger quantities of smoke must be carried in any operation of the size of the assault on Dieppe.

2. General

(a) The necessity for planning a combined operation at a combined Headquarters where the Force Commanders and their staff can work and live together.

(b) The necessity to plan a raid so as to be independent of weather conditions in the greatest possible degree. A plan based on the assumption that the weather conditions will be uniform is very likely to fail; therefore, a plan which can be carried out even when they are indifferent or bad is essential.

(c) The necessity for flexibility in the military plan and its execution. To achieve this, the assault must be on the widest possible front limited only by the possibilities of control and the amount of naval and air support available.

(d) The allocation to the assault of the minimum force required for success and the retention of the maximum force as a reserve to exploit success where it is achieved.

(e) The necessity for as accurate and comprehensive a system of control and communications as it is possible to establish.

(f) The dissemination of knowledge to officers and other ranks, each of whom should know the intention of his superior, the outline of the operation and the details of the task of his unit and those on the flanks.

(g) The value of special training particularly in amphibious night operations. Such training must include rehearsals and the testing of inter-communication arrangements.

(h) Assaults must be carefully timed. Whether to assault in darkness, at dawn or dusk or in daylight, must depend on the nature of the raid, and on certain conditions, such as tide and distance, which will vary in every case.

(j) Great and continuous attention must be paid to security problems and greater use made of subordinate officers who should be put partly in the picture, so that they can control the men under them. Only important extracts from Operation Orders should be taken ashore. These should be kept in manuscript form and have their official headings removed.

(k) Briefing of the troops should take place as late as possible.
If airborne troops are used, arrangements must be made to increase the number of models available so as to cut down the time needed for briefing.
Airborne troops provide means of achieving surprise and should be used as often as possible subject to the limitations of the weather. It should be regarded, however, as exceptional for a plan to depend for success entirely on their use.

APPENDICES

(*l*) Unless means for the provision of overwhelming close support are available assaults should be planned to develop round the flanks of a strongly defended locality rather than frontally against it.

(*m*) Some form of light or self-propelled artillery must be provided once an assault has got across the landing place and is making progress ahead.

Appendix H

EXTRACTS FROM GERMAN REPORTS ON DIEPPE RAID

This report is derived from the translation of an Italian copy which came into Allied hands. Some matters of no Naval interest have been omitted. Times, which were German, have been altered one hour to correspond with British time, and paragraphs have been numbered to facilitate reference. Comments are in italics.

Of particular interest is the fact of the incorrect appreciation that a small British Channel convoy was a large troop convoy. (Sections 11 and 39.) As shown in Section 39 the Germans derived a considerable amount of information from numerous documents, which they captured including the operation orders of the 2nd Canadian Division and the Orders of the Naval Force Commander. Sections 40 to 46 and 54 to 57 have been omitted as the matter in them consists merely of an abstract of our operation orders.

Extracts from Report of German C.-in-C., West, Commanding D Group of Armies

I – Anticipatory Events.

1. From middle of June, the results of photographic and visual reconnaissance of Air Squadron 3 and information from Agents collected by Headquarters revealed the concentration of numerous small landing craft on the South Coast of England.

An air photographic reconnaissance carried out, in spite of weather conditions, just at the end of July, confirmed the concentration of Naval forces which were later increased in comparison with the large numbers already observed in June.

It was *not* possible, up to 15th August, to obtain other details regarding a British landing operation except the information furnished by Agents which could not be checked. All the same, from middle of June onwards Headquarters considered the situation was such that an operation by the enemy on a large scale would certainly take place at some time at some part of the coast. For this reason, the submarine bases and defence sectors were reinforced to full establishment both with personnel and supplies (also the shore-fronts), and the defence organisation was continually exercised to make certain that all the local reserve sections, air and army, should be ready to come quickly into action.

Special importance was given by H.Q. to the fact that its motorised reserves of the Army Group should be stationed near enough to the coast to be able to come into action in mass on the first day of a landing.

On 15th August, occurred a sudden change in British wireless traffic which made it more difficult for our Interception service. Numerous flights over the Channel coast pointed to increased reconnaissance action and the crews of the machines brought down were mostly American.

No other change in the enemy situation could be discovered, however, up to 0350 hours on 19th August, even by the daily recco of the 3rd Air Squadron.

1a. Weather conditions, tides and force of the wind were carefully observed each day and communicated to the troops.

On 18th August, the weather forecast for the Channel area for the coming night was as follows.

Light winds chiefly from the South, increasing later to a minimum of two to four. Few clouds, visibility about 4 to 10 kilometres, morning mist in the coast with decreasing visibility. Later on an increased haze may be expected from the West with a ceiling of low cloud:

Moon sets	2320 hours, 18th August.
Night period	From 2115 of 18th to 0510 of 19th August.
Visibility	Increasing from 0510 hours.
High water at Dieppe	0403 hours on 19th August.

These conditions make an enemy landing appear possible to the 4th Group of M.T.B.s (4 units) stationed at Boulogne to be ready to move at a half hours' notice from midnight onwards.

(*Note* – No orders were given for the employment of this force on the 19th, as the enemy attack took place at dawn, and it was considered useless to use it against destroyers.)

No other Naval forces were available in the Channel Area as the 5th Flotilla M.T.B.s were minelaying in Lyme Bay during the night 18/19th.

APPENDICES

On 18th August, at 2000 hours, one of our convoys left Boulogne for Dieppe, steaming 6 knots. It consisted of five small coasting motor schooners, escorted by three submarines.[146]

On 19th august, between 0330 and 0400 hours, this convoy was off the coast opposite Dieppe.

II – **First Contact with the Enemy.**
(*Naval engagement off the Dieppe sector, 302nd Infantry Division.*)

19.8.42

2. At 0445 hours the following signal from Naval H.Q. West was received:

"At 0350 hours attack on our convoy by surface-forces, 4 kilometres off Dieppe. Particulars not yet known. It is the opinion of the Naval Command that it has been one of the usual attacks on convoys."

At 0500 hours, 15th Army Command signalled to Army H.Q.:

"According to information from 81st Army Corps, one of our convoys has been attacked by fast British ships at 0400 hours, at about 20 kilometres off the port of Dieppe. Troops have intensified their lookout. Navy and Air authorities have been advised."

(*Note* – It became known later that this convoy was caught up in the first wave of British landing craft and had partially upset the enemy's plan of times and operations, and at least had had a delaying effect.)

The noise of the engagement between our units and the enemy gave the alarm to the coastal sector.[147]

III – **The Enemy's Attempt to Land Near and Around Dieppe (302nd Infantry Division)**
Initial Situation of Air Arm

3. *Reconnaissance* – Air reconnaissance had been organised (with special intensity in certain sectors) from May, 1942, by agreement between Army H.Q. and Air Squadron 3.

Taking part in this were:

9th Air Corps, 123rd Recco Group and Atlantic Air Command.

Zone of Reconnaissance: From the North Sea as well as the Channel as far as the Atlantic.

Sectors in which reconnaissance was carried out with special intensity: Mouth of the Thames, English South Coast ports, British Channel, Bay of Biscay.

APPENDICES

Evening Reconnaissance: Area between the Scheldt and the mouth of the Thames, English South Coast and the zone round Britain as far as the mouth of the Gironde.

Night Reconnaissance: Zone of the Channel of Cape Griz Nez, Gulf of the Seine, and the area of sea round Normandy.

To augment the reconnaissance all the fighting planes available had been employed up to the limit of their range.

Fighter Groups

Two Fighter Commands with six groups of fighters, two fighter-bomber squadrons and complementary formations were continuously employed by air-defence work.

Fighting Detachments

9th Air Corps (six fighting groups and some complementary groups).
Atlantic Air Command (three fighting groups, one complementary group).

(*Note* – The 3rd Air Squadron, especially the fighting portion, was, on 19th August, about 35 to 40 per cent. of its normal strength.)

Readiness for immediate action, and similarly for regrouping of all squadrons of complementary groups fit for flight, was assured by 3rd Air Squadron.

All measures for the defence of aerodromes, etc., had already been taken.

Air Situation. Up to the beginning of the fighting on 19th August, the enemy's air activity by day and night did not show any characteristics pointing to an imminent attempt to land.

Wireless Situation. There was also little variation from normal detected by the watch on wireless traffic and drill in England.

Initial Naval Situation

4. Three harbour lookout ships were stationed off Dieppe. Up to the moment of receiving news of the Naval fighting off Dieppe, our D/F service had not signalled the presence of any enemy Naval forces. Single objectives detected after 0300 hours by the Treport apparatus in the area between 10 miles North and North-West of Dieppe, were intercepted only for brief periods, and were considered in view of the noise of the motors causing their detection to be *aerial* objectives.

The Landing
0530 *hours*

5. 15th Army Command (AOK 15) signals to H.Q.:
"Information received from 81st Army Corps that at 0505 hours bombs

were dropped on Dieppe and enemy attempted landing in the areas Berneval-Dieppe-Pourville and Quiberville."

At the same time the General staff at Army H.Q. has been advised of the situation, as well as the Liaison Officers of the Navy and Air Force (The Duty Officer at Army H.Q., has passed the information received from AOK 15 to Navy West and to 3rd Air Squadron).

First Appreciation of the Situation by Army H.Q.
6. It cannot yet be decided whether the operation is of a local nature and of what it consists. As however, the attempted landing has taken place at various points (for the first time) on a front of 20 to 25 kilometres and in daylight, the invasion may have larger proportions. And there is also the possibility of an attack in other sectors. The situation is not yet by any means clear.

0600 *hours*
Army H.Q. gives orders that, as a preventative measure, the 10th Armoured Division, the S.S. Division "Adolf Hitler" and the 7th Air Division shall be warned as follows:

"Information about enemy attempted landing still not clear. The alarm will probably be given."

0625 *hours*
Army H.Q., gives an order to the 10th Armoured Division "Alarm No. 2".

0628 *hours*
Army H.Q. orders the S.S. Division A.H. "Alarm No. 2".

0632 *hours*
The Commanding Officer, Navy West, signals that according to information received from the Seine-Somme Command, the enemy was attempting to land at 0525 hours near Berneval. Naval battery is in action against enemy ships.
At the same time, AOK 15 signals:

"Chief of Staff of 81st Army Corps states that the enemy has landed near Berneval. Counter attack begun with about three companies, details not yet known, bombardment of Dieppe continues. An attempt to land near Pourville has been repulsed. The situation round Quiberville is not yet clear."

0640 *hours*
Officer Commanding Navy West signals that according to what he has

heard from Admiral Francia's[148] Command, communication with the Officer commanding Dieppe Port is interrupted. Dieppe Naval Semaphore Station signals.

"The enemy continues to land at Dieppe. Destroyers making smoke along the coast. Up till now 12 tanks have been landed of which one is on fire."

Second Appreciation of the Situation by Army H.Q.
7. The operation is of large proportions and evidently aims at the occupation of Dieppe as a bridge-head.

0700 *hours*
The Chief of Headquarters Staff calls the Chief of General Staff, Artillery General Jodl, and informs him of the enemy's position, and of the measures adopted by us (counter attack by the local reserves, alarm passed to the reserves of the Army Group, 10th Armoured Division and S.S. "Adolf Hitler" Division) and asks the Officer Commanding Submarines that the submarines may be employed against the flank of the enemy formation.

0700 *hours*
First operational signal, first priority, secret, to Army H.Q.:
"At 0525 hours enemy attempted to land at and around Dieppe. Fighting proceeding. Detailed signal will follow."

0715 *hours*
Chief of Staff, Army H.Q. speaks with the General of the 81st Army Corps, who judges the enemy operation to be a local action up to now.

0725 *hours*
The officers commanding the Armies in Netherlands and the Air Forces are informed of the situation at Dieppe. *The utmost vigilance is necessary.* At the same time the Military Commander in France is informed who passes it to the Military Commander in Belgium and in Northern France.

0730 *hours*
Commanding Officer, Navy West, sends the following signal received from Naval C.-in-C., France (received at 0720 hours) to Army H.Q.:
"Dieppe Naval Semaphore Station signals: A.A. firing against troops landing near the Casino (the Casino on the beach at Dieppe had been partially blown up for security reasons) and against attacking fighter-

planes. A troop transport has been sunk in front of the Casino. German fighters over Dieppe. A second transport on fire. The British are trying to land from assault vessels."

0745 *hours*
Commanding Officer, Navy West, signals:
"Our convoy has been dispersed to the North of Dieppe during the enemy landings. An enemy unit destroyed by ramming. Several hits on M.T.B.s and a destroyer; brought down, two planes. A small part of the convoy off St. Valery-en-Caux. The divisions stationed in the respective defence sectors of the Channel have been advised by the Naval Group."

0750 *hours*
Army H.Q. to 3rd Air Squadron after conversation with the 81st Army Corps:
"Commanding Officer 81st Army Corps requests air support against everything under-weigh afloat, and asks for no intervention in land fighting. This intervention will be required later."

0815 *hours*
Naval Commander, Seine-Somme, signals through the N.O.I.C. channel coast:
"British continue to land round Dieppe, 17 to 20 tanks are on the beach firing at the town. Destroyers making smoke. One troop-transport sunk to the east of Dieppe. Guns on board enemy destroyers also attacking." (Time missing in signal.)
Immediately afterwards the same Command completes the signal:
"0635 hours the British landed detachments. Destroyers made smoke screens. About 20 tanks on the beach. Four destroyers patrolling in front of the port. English destroyers watching the landing from 3 miles out."

0823 *hours*
8. 3rd Air Squadron signals (through the Air Liaison Officer) that the 9th Air Group has been engaged since 0800 in continuous air attacks against enemy Naval targets.
Contradictory information about the appearance of enemy cruisers off St. Valery-en-Caux (afterwards found incorrect).

0840 *hours*
9. Third appreciation of the situation by Army H.Q.:

The enemy situation is becoming clearer. Enemy attempts to land continue, but the local reserves of 302nd Infantry Division are already counter attacking. While the heights on the two sides of Dieppe are entirely in our hands, it is not yet possible to say anything about the situation inside the town. It seems that more to the West, near Pourville, the landing may still be going on. In any case there are still movements of vessels to and from the beach going on in that sector. Around Quiberville the situation is not clear and it has not yet been established whether Quiberville itself has been attacked or not. Near St. Aubin an attempt to land by the enemy is still possible.

Based on this estimate of the situation, in which an idea of the size of the enemy's landing force has been recognised, amounting to two regiments at least and perhaps a whole division, and as it is not yet possible to foresee the ultimate development of the operation, Army H.Q. decides to employ the 10th Armoured Division.

0844 *hours*
Orders from Army H.Q. to 10th Armoured Division (information of AOK 15 and 81st Army Corps):
"The 10th Armoured Division is placed under the orders of General Kuntzen (Commanding 81st Army Corps) for the immediate clearing-up of the situation round Dieppe. The advanced portion of the Division will move up at 1000 hrs. and the main body at 1100."

(This order was received over the telephone by AOK 15 at 0847 hours; by 10th Armoured Division at 0851 hours; and by 81st Army Corps at 0845 hours).

0900 *hours*
10. Second signal to Army Headquarters:
"Enemy attempts to land continue. Our Army forces have commenced to counter attack with local reserves. Situation at Dieppe not yet clear. Heights at the sides of Dieppe entirely in our hands. Landings continue near Pourville. Position at Quiberville not clear. It seems that at St. Aubin a further attempt to land is being prepared."

0903 *hours*
Chief of Staff of 81st Army Corps signals as follows about the position at Dieppe:
"Situation at Berneval seems clearer. Battery[149] is again firing with four guns. Enemy is in flight, apparently to the foot of the cliffs (low tide) in North-East direction. The intervention of the fighting planes is

APPENDICES

requested here. Position at Puits to the north-east of Dieppe is also clearer. The 302nd Division signals that the enemy has lost 500 men between dead and prisoners. The heights on both sides of Dieppe are in our hands, as well as the heights to the East of Pourville. The enemy is on the height to the West. Battery 813[150] near St. Marguerite had fallen into enemy hands, but has been retaken. It is again firing with two guns."

0947 *hours*
11. Commanding Officer, Navy West, refuses the employment of submarines for reconnaissance in the Channel requested by Army H.Q., as submarines lend themselves very little for reconnaissance and their employment to the east of Cherbourg is not possible owing to the risk of mines and enemy superiority. Their employment at the Western exit of the Channel and in the Bay of Biscay is not considered necessary at present.

1010 *hours*
Third Air Squadron signals (through Air Liaison Officer) the following results of Recco (Reconnaissance plane returned to base at 0910 hours):
(a) At Dieppe two large groups of fires in the roadstead, five to six destroyers making artificial smoke, 50 to 80 landing craft identified.
(b) Forty kilometres to the North-West of Dieppe six large transports, presumably carrying tanks and fully loaded.
(c)[151] Sixty kilometres North-West of Dieppe, three merchant ships of medium tonnage and 1 M.T.B.
(d)[152] In the zone of Selsey Bill (England) 26 large transports of 6,000 tons each, crowded with troops escorted by three destroyers.
(e) To the South-East of Eastbourne ships of small tonnage steering east, apparently a security force.
(f) Nothing observed in other areas.
(g) The number of British fighter planes over Dieppe is very large, bitter fighting with the smaller number of our fighters.
Clauses (b), (c) and (d) gave rise to thought. The immediate question from H.Q. as to what course the 26 large transports were steering could not be answered (at least not immediately).[153] From these signals H.Q. had to judge the position from a new point of view.

Fourth Appreciation of the Situation by H.Q.
12. The ships mentioned in clauses (b) and (c) belong to "the reserves afloat" of British landing plans. If this is linked up operationally with

the fleet of transports further behind mentioned under (d), the enemy operation may represent the beginning of the attempt to form "the second front".

It is, therefore, possible that the enemy is carrying out the attack on Dieppe to draw off the attention of the defending forces and to bring to Dieppe the motorised reserves of Army H.Q. so that a major operation can be carried out in another locality – H.Q. thinks possibly Brittany.

The essential thing, therefore, is that the enemy around Dieppe shall be routed and destroyed in the shortest possible time with all the means available. The position is now cleared to the point that it is certain that the reserves employed there will be more than sufficient for this object.

If the enemy is unable to establish a bridge-head at Dieppe, neither his "reserves afloat" nor the fleet carrying his "operative reserves" can be used.

He may then hold the 26[154] transports ready for another step in a main operation – probably against Normandy.

From these considerations, after a brief interval, H.Q. decides to give the alarm to the whole sector of AKO 7 (Normandy and Brittany).

1020 *hours*
Advice received of an enemy wireless signal just intercepted:
"At Dieppe four tanks destroyed, position serious."

1030 *hours*
13. Order from Army H.Q. to AOK 7:

(For information to: 81st Army Corps, Army Motorised Reserves including 7th Air Division, Herman Goering Brigade, and the Reserves of the Army Group constituted by the 337 Division).

"Air reconnaissance has sighted in the latitude of Isle of Wight, 26 transports crowded with troops.[155] Orders for the 7th Army and for the Reserves of Army Groups – 7th Division, 6th Armoured Division, 337 Infantry Division, Herman Goering Division – Alarm II -." von Rundstedt. General Field Marshal. (The S.S. Division "Das Reich" was not put into the state of Alarm II but was immediately informed of the measures taken by Army H.Q. as were also Navy Command West and the 3rd Air Squadron).

1050 *hours*
3rd Air Squadron reports (through Air Liaison Officer) from the 123rd Recco Group:

APPENDICES

From conversations with an air commander, a convoy (26 ships of 6,000 tons each) is loaded with troops; at 0830 hours, it was proceeding North-westerly from Selsey Bill, direction Portsmouth. Later information will be given about 1200 hours by reconnaissance plans.

This action gives rise to New Considerations by Army Headquarters
Probably the enemy Command had already understood that the Dieppe action had failed. It did not seem advisable therefore to take the valuable tonnage into the area threatened by the fighting air forces of the Germans. All the same the fact that the enemy convoy was proceeding to the strongly protected port of Portsmouth might not mean that the enemy had abandoned his intentions.

1100 *hours*
14. Ic/LW of Army Headquarters signals from 3 (F) Squadron 122. – 0830 to 0835:
"Sighted in the Fécamp-Dieppe area at 3-6 kilometres from the coast seven large warships, heavy and light cruisers 10-15 escorts ships, 1 light cruiser, another Naval unit, steering towards the English coast."

This return movement may also be connected with that mentioned above. All goes to show that the enemy, recognising the failure of the Dieppe operation, breaks off the action. This may mean the destruction of his troops already landed.

Army headquarters had doubts about the size and types of warships reported above (large destroyers, it has been proved by experience, may easily be mistaken for cruisers).

1120 *hours*
Army headquarters decides to communicate with the General Commanding Communications in the West (and had sent a liaison officer to the officer of the Operations Division of Army Headquarters) that in view of the favourable development of the situation there need not even be taken into consideration the necessity of suspending the civil railway traffic and the cancelling of permits.

All precautions are to be taken, however, that the railways may be taken over by the Germans at any moment.

The Maritime Commander of the Channel Coast signals through Navy Command, West
15. (Received at 1120 hours):
"There are no more ships off Dieppe. The destroyers have left. Landing craft are in flames on the beach. Several tanks are still moving

here and there on the beach and come under the gunfire of the army positions. It appears that the beach is blocked."

At the same time Army Headquarters is informed of the following British wireless messages:

At 0645 hours:
"All well."

At 0944 hours:
"Many tanks destroyed. The situation is serious. The enemy has great possibilities."

At 0958 hours:
"An unknown British commanding officer requests smoke screen for re-embarking."

1135 *hours*
16. Signal from 3rd Air Squadron to Army Headquarters:
"Up to 1130 hours, 288 fighter planes were employed, among these 18 fighter-bombers. Successes: 24 planes brought down certain, 4 probables. One destroyer damaged, 3 of our planes lost. Fifty-four battle planes employed so far; no information yet about results obtained."

1149 *hours*
81st Army Corps signals its opinion about the situation at the moment:
"The position to the east of Dieppe is cleared. There is no danger around Penly and Berneval. At Dieppe about a dozen tanks have been destroyed. Repelling action along the beaches proceeds well. West of Dieppe the enemy still resists near Pourville, a counter attack with two battalions is proceeding well.

They have penetrated into the western part of Pourville. Apparently, no more reinforcements from the sea are arriving. General impression: 'giving up!'".

1210 *hours*
17. Signal from Ic Army Headquarters with wireless interception shows that the enemy is retiring but it seems that counter orders have been given for a second operation at the same time.

This confirms the opinion of 81st Army Corps and of headquarters with regard to the 26 transports sighted,[156] the enemy still had the intention of landing other troops if the Dieppe action had succeeded and thus to begin operations against the important key point Le Havre, or at any rate a second action against Normandy and Brittany. This brings us to the 5th Appreciation of the situation by Army Headquarters.

The Enemy gives up. He is completely beaten to the east of Dieppe and is being repelled to the west of Dieppe at Pourville and in the woods and on the cliffs to the west of it, and it is now only a question of time. Everything possible is now being destroyed and with this object every weapon is being employed. Army Headquarters then gives the following orders:

1215 *hours*
To
(1) AOK 15 (first priority).
(2) 81st Army Corps.
(3) Navy Command West.
(4) 3rd Air Squadron.
The enemy landed at Dieppe is giving in.

It is necessary that as much as possible of the enemy forces shall be destroyed. With this object strong detachments of the 10th Armoured Division, tanks and artillery should immediately go forward. Every weapon available must now contribute to the total destruction of the enemy. All fronts on which the enemy had landed must now be cleaned up in the shortest possible time.
(*Signed*) von Rundstedt,
Field Marshal,
C.-in-C., West.

18. The Military Chief of Staff then called up the General Chief of Staff Jodl and instructs him in the opinion of Army Headquarters on the general situation.

Immediately afterwards Ic Army Headquarters gives instructions regarding the procedure of the Propaganda Arm and also for the collection of prisoners of war in a camp already prepared by the military commander, France. All prisoners will be handled by AOK 15. Interpreters and interrogating officers provided for special cases are already available for AOK 15.

1230 *hours*
Army H.Q.'s appreciation of the position is confirmed by a signal from 3rd Air Squadron (123rd Recco Group) that the enemy Naval traffic between Eastbourne and Dieppe in a southerly direction had now ceased.

1233 *hours*

81st Army Corps signals:

"The enemy force landed to the east of Dieppe has been destroyed. At Dieppe itself the situation has been cleared up. Small centres of resistance still remain. Estimate of prisoners taken is about 1,000. The heights to the west of Dieppe as far as Pourville have remained all the time in our hands. Battalion I/571 has commenced an attack on Pourville into which it has partially penetrated. To the west of Pourville in the cliff and wooded area, there is still an enemy bridge-head about 1 kilometre deep and 6 kilometres wide. Reserves of 302nd Division have been made available to support Battalion I/571 attacking the Pourville-Varengeville sector from Ofranville. A battalion at St. Marguerite has been sent forward to prevent the enemy in the bridge-head getting away from it.

At sea the enemy is making a dense smoke screen, apparently to facilitate the return of the troops who were landed.

All forces are employed in attacking and destroying the enemy.

General Kuntzen was personally at Dieppe and is now at the south of Pourville. He intends to make use of the 10th Armoured Division."

1400, 1415 *hours*

19. The following signals reached Army H.Q.:

(a) From AOK 15. The number of tanks destroyed at Dieppe appears to be 18.

(b) From 3rd Air Squadron. Enemy asking by wireless for air (fighter) support as, on account of strong defences, he cannot drop his bombs on the coastal fortifications, and requires Mustangs for the protection of his ships which are being attacked from the air. Thirty-four planes brought down against nine of ours. Direct hit with 500-kilo bomb on 1,500-ton ship, and well-placed release among enemy vessels.

1425 *hours*

Army H.Q. orders AOK 15 to report within an hour:

(a) An estimate of the force employed by the enemy;

(b) The successes obtained by the defence forces so far, especially the booty, material destroyed, number of prisoners, etc., with a summary of the operations.

1445 *hours*

81st Army Corps, reports:

"Dieppe and Pourville in our hands. Some of the forces landed still in Varengeville wood. During the last hour three destroyers, two torpedo boats and various landing craft have been sunk by our gunfire. Operation may be considered finished; prisoners calculated at about 1100. 10th Armoured Division arrived. Advance force should now be at Dieppe. 302nd Infantry Division had made its own arrangements in collaboration with the Artillery and Air Forces."

20. With this the enemy's operation against Dieppe has been broken-up in little more than nine hours. The extent of the enemy's defeat was already evident at 1100, but form 1600 onwards detailed reports arriving made it appear always greater. He must have had very serious losses not only ashore but also at sea, it being possible only to *estimate* the latter.

Our losses appear moderate, and very much lower in comparison than the enemy's.

1610 *hours*
Signal received at H.Q. through AOK 15 confirming the above opinion and which is at once elaborated for report to Army Headquarters West.

From this and other signals it is considered that at least two regiments and additional forces of the British Army carried out the attack besides the "Commandos". Tanks were landed only at Dieppe where they were all destroyed. The number of landing-vessels put into the sea from transports is estimated at 300 to 400; these came shorewards in waves of 40 to 60 at a time. In the first hours of the morning appeared numerous forces of enemy fighter planes, about 16 squadrons, some accompanied by fighter-bombers, for the protection of ships in the convoy. These forces were continually being renewed. At 1000 hours an attack took place by a numerous formation of fighters (about 15 squadrons) together with 12 bi-motor battle-planes in the Abbeville zone, bombs being released from a height of 4,000 metres.

The British protecting fighters, continually renewed, remained in the skies over Dieppe until towards 1400 hours, and were reinforced by other planes about 1300 hours. Afterwards there was a gradual reduction of British air activity.

1640 *hours*
21. Orders from Army H.Q. that the Senior Tank Officer was to go to Dieppe immediately to examine the enemy tanks destroyed there.

At about the same moment the Military Chief of Staff signals General Jodl:
"No armed British remaining on terra-firma,"
and informs him of the successful end of the action.

APPENDICES

1650 *hours*

The Admiral Commanding in France signals that the net defence of the port of Dieppe is intact, although there has naturally been some damage to it by gunfire and air bombardment.

1700 *hours*

81st Army Corps signals:

"At Dieppe and on both sides of the town, all is again in order. Twenty-eight enemy tanks have been destroyed round Dieppe. The number of prisoners has increased to 60 officers and 1,500 men. The principal weight of the struggle has been borne by the 571st Infantry Regiment which has also made the greatest number of prisoners.

At the same time the Air Liaison Officer at H.Q. receives a signal from the 3rd Air Squadron:

"57 enemy fighter planes brought down so far."

1715 *hours*

22. Third signal to Headquarters West (for information Army H.Q./Operations Section):

"Army reports that no armed enemy remain on terra firma. 302nd Division have sunk in the concluding period three enemy destroyers, and two torpedo boats which had ventured too close in, as well as various landing-vessels.

One thousand five hundred prisoners taken, amongst whom 60 Canadian officers, 28 tanks destroyed, including some American. Details will follow. Enemy has suffered heavy bloody losses. Prisoners being interrogated. They include Canadians, British, American and Free French.

The operation appears as follows:

A landing group of 300 to 400 units protected by 13 to 15 cruisers and destroyers and various groups of fighter-planes. Behind these a reserve of 6 transports and 3 merchant ships. An operative reserve of 26 transports between terra firma and England. As far as can be ascertained so far, about 3 regiments and 30 tanks were landed.

Our losses not yet known but they are limited.

Battery 813[157] near Pourville has held on to its fort in hand-to-hand fighting, but blew up its guns; the battery has had heavy and bloody losses. The port of Dieppe has not been damaged, the net-defence of the harbour is intact; off the entrance a fighter-bomber has sunk a "Hunt" class destroyer. Material, etc., at Berneval is intact. The personnel defended the fortress in collaboration with Army Coastal Battery 2/770 in violent hand-to-hand fighting."

(*Signed*) Rundstedt.

With this the shore fighting was terminated.

1845 *hours*
23. The following from Military Headquarters was communicated to AOK 15, 81st Army Corps, 302nd Infantry Division, as well as to Naval Command West, 3rd Air Squadron and Admiral Commanding, France:

"British, American and Canadian troops on 19th August, attempted a landing on a large scale in the sector of 81st Army Corps at Dieppe. This has been beaten off by the brave 302nd Division in collaboration with the Air Arm, local reserves, artillery reserves, part of the 10th Armoured Division and Coastal artillery stationed in the sector.

The enemy has suffered heavy and bloody losses. He has many landing craft, some cruisers, destroyers, torpedo boats and many aircraft.

1,500 prisoners have been taken.

I extend to all Commanding Officers and troops who have taken part in the action my praise and my thanks. Today I have been able to report "The troops have fought well."

My thanks are also extended to the air squadrons who with their continuous action have helped the Division and incessantly attacked the enemy at sea, and I thank also all those of the Navy who before the landing fought an action afloat and those who were employed ashore."

(*Signed*) C.-in-C., West.

von Rundstedt, Field Marshal.

IV – **Following-up by the Air Arm**

24. Attack by the Air Arm on the enemy fleeing by sea continues off Dieppe and nearly up to the centre of the Channel the sea had been cleared of enemy ships by about 1615 hours; this fact was immediately signalled. The 3rd Air Squadron then again joined up with the air forces employed at Dieppe, making themselves available to the respective commands.

9th Air Corps and the Atlantic Air Command received orders to attack Portsmouth with a moderate-sized force, disregarding the weather conditions. Fifty planes were employed and the attack which was to be of a destructive nature was continued into the night of 19

August. Numerous bombs were concentrated on the town of Portsmouth and on the quays and harbour. The following results were obtained against Naval objectives, torpedo motor boats, and vessels returning from Dieppe:

Sunk – two transports totalling 5,000 to 6,000 tons.

In addition, four bombs of medium calibre dropped in the middle of 10 landing craft returning to base in close formation.

The defensive fire was very heavy, so that it was impossible to ascertain whether other targets were hit; but in any case, this is very probable.

V – Sixth (and Last) Appreciation of the Position by Army H.Q.

1915 *hours*

25. The enemy has been defeated and wiped out at Dieppe. No immediate renewal of his attempt to land is therefore likely, but there is always the possibility of small intrusive attacks and reconnaissance's as well as of air attacks.

Further the general situation is not yet sufficiently cleared up to the point of being able to cancel "the Alert" to the 7th Army (Normandy-Brittany). It is always possible that a second operation on a large scale may be attempted, as all attention is concentrated on Dieppe. It is not yet known whether the fleet of transports[158] has again unloaded at Portsmouth.

VI – Last Enemy Signals

2140 *hours*

26. AOK 15 signals that Interception Station Etretat has intercepted the following British wireless messages:
(1) "Help, we are sinking."
(2) (From the Portsmouth-Southampton area). "Return immediately to places of departure."

VII – Army H.Q.s Remarks on the Enemy – Landing at Dieppe

What were the Objects of the Enemy?
(1) The landing operation at Dieppe organised on a large scale and which after some months' preparation has been carried out with almost too *much* precision and detailed arrangement, on account of the forces employed – one Canadian Division reinforced by "Commandos" and special troops – cannot be described as merely a Raid.

For an action of that kind, too many men and too much material were employed. For a Raid, one would not sacrifice at least 29 or 30 tanks.

(2) It is considered that the enemy with such a large force thought that he could win in a short time the bridge-head of Dieppe after having eliminated the defending artillery, and then be able to use the harbour installations for disembarking the reserve and operative forces which were afloat.

With the reserves afloat there were 28 tanks, certainly of the same type as those landed. Now the employment of altogether 58 similar tanks cannot be connected with a brief sabotage operation. Although operational orders have also fallen into our hands, it is not possible to deduce whether it was a question of an operation of local character, or – in case of success – if it would form the initial stage of "Invasion". The British directive for the landing operations elaborated also the evacuation and re-embarkation, but it is not a proof of the enemy intentions if in the orders both these latter were treated with great clearness and in detail.

(3) Thus Commandos 3 and 4 had orders that, having carried out their mission and re-embarked, they were to await instructions whether to return to England or to remain with the reserve forces (only in case the enterprise failed and retirement was ordered were they to return immediately to England).

(4) Further there were indications in the orders that the troops were not to destroy the gasometer in Dieppe at any rate until the pioneers had come into action and this left open the possibility of other orders being given at an opportune moment.

If Dieppe had fallen it may be considered certain that such new orders would have been given.

(5) The behaviour and employment of the British Air Force was strange. It is incomprehensible why, at the beginning of the landing, the bridge-head of Dieppe and other points of disembarkation were not subjected to continuous air-bombardment, to prevent or at least to delay the action of the local reserves.

One explanation may be that the British wished to keep the employment of large air forces as a *second phase*, that is for the beginning of the "Invasion", after having gained Dieppe. As the enemy knew exactly where the 10th Armoured Division was stationed and that it would certainly come into action, it may be that this contributed to his decision to hold back his fighting Air Force.

He will not do that a second time!

APPENDICES

VIII – **Conclusions**

20th August, 1942

27. Chief of Staff, Army H.Q., visits the 302nd Infantry Division at Dieppe to gather personal impressions of the battle, and to examine on the spot the different phases of the action carried on by Battery 813.[159]

As the enemy's position is such as to make it improbable that another landing will be attempted (*see* VI, "Last enemy signals") the order is given to terminate Alarm II for all interested Commands as well as for the 10th Armoured Division of 81st Army Corps.

In the course of the day the first information about our losses which, even if they are not to be considered exact until hospital returns, etc., are confirmed, show that those of the Army have been moderate.

With regard to Naval Command, West, information is received that one of the three harbour patrol vessels which were off Dieppe when the action began and retired into harbour was sunk there without its crew, probably by a hit received during the battle.

28. Third Air Squadron reports, through Ic Army H.Q., that the number of enemy planes brought down has increased to 112.
Teleprinter signal from 3rd Air Squadron confirms previous signal:

Completely sunk	5 merchant ships, totalling 13,000 tons.
	1 destroyer.
	1 coastguard vessel.
	1 motor-torpedo boat (probable).
Damaged	4 cruisers.
	4 destroyers.
	5 merchant ships, totalling 15,500 tons.
	3 motor-torpedo boats.
	1 rescue vessel.
	1 landing craft.
	1 tug.
Probably damaged	4 merchant ships, totalling 12,000 tons.
	1 motor-torpedo boat.

About 1700 hours the Chief of Staff, Army H.Q., returns to H.Q. and reports his impressions. The following is sent to General Jodl by teleprinter, most urgent (first priority).

29. (1) Personal impression of action:
Heavy and bloody British losses.

Although many have already been interred, there are still British dead everywhere, especially in front of our heavy gun-positions. In front of one machine-gun post which flanked the narrow strip of beach between the sea and the cliffs, there are piles of dead (more than 100 only in this spot); much booty in equipment and infantry weapons, light and heavy. The British fought well.

Prisoners make a good impression, young, fresh, intelligent. The aspect of one part of the beach to the west of Dieppe recalls that of Dunkirk. Three large burnt-out transports, high and dry at low tide, with many landing vessels and about 20 tanks which were all knocked out during the landing operations. At other places, still more landing vessels, tanks and funnels and masts sticking out of the water. At Dieppe, damage has been serious at some points, moderate at others. The behaviour of the civil population during the battle has been correct. No cases of sabotage or interference with military measures. Shops re-opened as early as midday on the day of the attack. In the sectors where the most violent combats developed, the civil population is still terrorised.

Our rapid intervention and the powerful aspect of the Armoured Division made a great impression on the populace.
Further details will follow.
Military Chief of Staff,
Army H.Q.
(*Signed*) Zeitzeler,
Major General.

30. (2) Personal Impressions of Battery 813 ("*Hess*")
Battery 813 is situated on a height, about 1 kilometre from the coast, which at this point is very precipitous. All round there are arrangements for defending against close attack, which, however, were only lightly manned, as not enough men were available. The battery was employed against Naval objectives. Fighter planes attacked it, swooping down and igniting the cartridges of nearly all the guns with small incendiary bombs. The personnel had to extinguish these fires. At the same time the enemy attacked from both sides with about 150 men. The battery-crew fought gallantly; the attack lasted nearly two hours, until at last the battery had to surrender. The guns still intact continued firing to the end at 200 metres range. The battery, whose fighting personnel was 112 men, had the following losses: 30 dead, 21 wounded who were got away, amongst them the Commander of the battery seriously wounded, and up to now apparently 10 missing, the greater part of whom were presumably brought to safety by our troops. It seems that two men of

the battery were taken prisoner, but it is doubtful whether they were taken on board the enemy's ships. A telephone operator defended his blockhouse until the arrival of reinforcements, and is now in hospital, seriously wounded. The guns have been damaged by explosive charges.

(3) Enemy losses: 2,095 prisoners, among them 617 wounded; 500 to 600 dead; an unspecified number wiped out.

Military Chief of Staff, Army H.Q.
(*Signed*) Zeitzeler,
Major General.

21*st August*, 1942

31. The following teleprinter message from the Fuhrer to the Supreme Command has been received at Army H.Q.:

"To C.-in-C., West, Field Marshal General von Rundstedt. Thanks to the accurate preparations conscientiously carried out by officers and men, a great British attempt to land has been repulsed.

I request you, Field Marshal General, to express my approval and my thanks to all units of the three Armed Forces who have taken part in the action. I know I can safely rely in the future also on the Command and on the troops of the armed forces in the West."

(*Signed*) Adolf Hitler.

32. **Fundamental Remarks from Army H.Q.**, No. 8, 23rd August, 1942. (First reports on the enemy's large-scale attempt to land at Dieppe. Further reports will follow when collected and confirmed.)

(1) *Time for Landing Operation*

The landing took place as day was breaking, just when it might be considered unsuitable for such an operation.

Lessons deduced. H.Q. has repeatedly pointed out in its orders and fundamental remarks (*see* Fundamental Remarks No. 1, paragraph 3), that:

"The Commanding Officer responsible must always calculate that everything, even the most unlikely, if possible."

The enemy may even come at noon in full daylight and also at low tide. He possesses means for landing, and also material much more modern than anything hitherto considered.

(2) *Smoke Screens*

At the time of landing the enemy made great use of artificial smoke. Ships and landing craft were rapidly hidden in it. The smoke was produced either by ships or by aircraft. At some points the approach to the shore and the actual landing was possible only thanks to the smoke;

APPENDICES

as the latter was coming towards the shore, the firing of the defence's guns was made less effective.
Lessons deduced.
(a) Exercises of every kind carried out at night and with smoke should accelerate training.
(b) Army H.Q. has been asked to put chemists on research work to find means of making smoke.

(3) *Counter-attacks*
33. The rapid counter-attacks of our reserves were very successful and decisive. It is necessary, however, for reserves to have with them some guns.
   Lessons deduced. Re-examine again everywhere whether the reserves are in a state of readiness to be employed immediately. They must also, in the case of large units, have some artillery. It is wrong to employ *all* the divisional artillery in the front line.

(4) *Coastal Batteries*
There are still many coastal batteries in absolutely wrong positions and which could not oppose a close infantry attack well led. The reason lies in the fact that these were established in 1940-41 when conditions were quite different to the present (then more of an offensive nature firing against distant naval targets. Now it is coastal defence against landing operations and supporting the principal fighting forces).
   Lessons deduced. The winter programme for the work of fortification must eliminate this trouble. We shall have to find and will fins a solution so that these batteries will be able to protect themselves.

(5) *Consumption of Ammunition*
34. One group of troops not used to fighting, wasted a great deal of ammunition. H.Q. had indicated this fact already in its Order No. 20. Of course, a young soldier sometimes loses his nerve. One battery for example fired 1,300 rounds in the fighting up to midday. There was also a want of ammunition for the machine guns. One machine gun company had fired away all its ammunition during the forenoon.
   Lessons deduced. Continue to educate the troops "Ammunition tactics", to prevent excessive barrage fire. Take care, however, that there is sufficient ammunition since a landing operation presents many suitable targets.

(6) *Conservation of Ammunition*
British fighter planes ignited the cartridges of one battery with tracer

bullets, obliging the personnel to employ themselves in extinguishing the fire, after which the enemy attacked the battery with infantry.

Lessons deduced. Re-examine all the arrangements of ammunition, especially of cartridges, to see that they are in safe places.

(7) *The Landing of Tanks*

35. There were landed from 4, or at a maximum from 5 motor boats, 29 tanks in a sector of 1,000 metres. Twenty-four of these were put out of action by our artillery and remained stranded among the pebbles on the high levels of the beach. Only five arrived on the roadway beside the sea.

The pebbles on the beach proved a very good obstacle against the tanks which easily got stuck in them. This has been a valuable help in preventing them getting to the road. The tanks were not able to get into the town quickly but had to wander to and fro along the beach, becoming easy targets for the guns of the defence.

Lessons deduced. (a) Make still better use of the deep pools and pebbles which are natural obstacles against tanks. In districts of the town near the shore, obstruct all the streets at right angles to the beach with numerous large walls. In streets which must be left open hold mobile obstructions in readiness.

(b) H.Q. will carry out trials to see how tanks may be placed on the high levels of the beach.

36. *Lessons deduced.* Nearly all the tanks have been hit by our projectiles of every calibre including those of 75 mm. but only two have been perforated by medium calibre projectiles. Serious effects on the bullets, which apparently are of non-ductile material, and which therefore break easily. Do not fire at too great range. 37-mm. projectiles had little effect.

Note. Para. 8 omitted as being without interest.

(9) *Cliffs*

The enemy climbed the cliffs by the help of various means, even places considered impracticable. The valleys having been mined he approached from the sides of them.

Lessons deduced. No point is "inviable" every possibility must be reckoned with.

(10) *Maps*

The enemy was in possession of good charts which showed nearly all our arrangement of defences and minefields up to June, 1942.

Lessons deduced. It is necessary to make still more use of camouflage

which is one of the most effective weapons of our forces. Intensify still more our measures against espionage. In this regard further orders will be issued.
(*Signed*) von Rundstedt,
General Field Marshal.

37. British Operational Orders for the Dieppe landing comprising 121 pages (operation "Jubilee") were photostated after rapid and partial translation, and distributed to all the military authorities, divisions, and to the other Services under the title:

Fundamental Observations of Army H.Q., No. 9
(British Operational Orders for Dieppe Landing)

I have had these translated and photostat copies made. According to the German conception these are not orders but a collection of notes of procedure with an exercise on the chart.

In any case it contains many points of great value to us; first about the enemy himself; secondly, details of his methods of landing and fighting.

All Commands must therefore take the greatest care to benefit by these experiences for our coastal defences and for the training and education of out troops. It would be a mistake to think that the enemy will organise his next operation in the same manner. He will learn lessons from the errors and lack of success this time, and will act differently next time. All the same, some details of his orders are instructive for us.
Army H.Q.,
(*Signed*) von Rundstedt,
General Field Marshal.

Losses

38. Our total losses in the three Services including those of the Navy, personnel ashore and Air reconnaissance troops amount to:

Army   115 dead.
             187 wounded.
             14 missing (of these, according to British broadcasts, four at most in enemy hands).

Navy   78 dead and missing (the missing are from the E-Boat sunk).[160]
            35 wounded.

Air Force 104 dead and missing (the latter brought down).
        58 wounded.

(*Signed*) Zeitzeler,
Major General.
Chief of Staff.

German Army Headquarters Report on the Enemy Situation

39. **Summary of report on enemy situation during the operations at Dieppe, 19th August, 1942**

A. Compiled from the following sources:
(*a*) Numerous documents captured including operational orders nearly intact, of the Second Canadian Division, and the orders of the Naval Commanding Officer.
(*b*) Interrogations of prisoners.
(*c*) Results of wireless interceptions of all three Services.

B. *Scheme of Operations.*
Forces taking part:

Army   2nd Canadian Division with 1 Armoured Group, 3rd and 4th British Commando.

Navy   8 destroyers.
         16 gunboats.
         1 river boat.
         26 light units (motor boats and chasers).
         8 transports carrying 65 landing vessels, rescue vessels and material.
         100 large motor boats for landing.
         2 minesweeping flotillas.
         1 Commando of Royal Marines (about 100 men).

A convoy of 26 transport ships seen off Portsmouth by our Recco planes; these were laden with troops and were probably held ready as a reserve in case the landing operation had succeeded.

Air Force. Appears to be two fighter groups with a total of about 30 squadrons for action in various waves. Some squadrons of twin-engined bombers.

Note. Sections 40 to 46 have been omitted as they consist of an abstract of British orders.

Effective execution of the Operation
47. The concentration of troops and the embarkation took place according to the plan arranged. At 0348 hours the invading forces met at about 4 miles to the North of Dieppe a small German convoy which was dispersed by units of the British escort. In consequence of this there was a delay of about a quarter of an hour and the alarm was given to the German coastal defence. Doubts arose among the landing troops as to the preservation of secrecy (some prisoners spoke of a betrayal).

At the sides of Dieppe only the landing of the 1st waves succeeded everywhere. Owing to the weak support of gunfire and to the heavy fire of the German defences many landing craft were sunk and the bodies of troops on the beaches suffered heavy losses. In only one point the preparation of a corridor for tanks was made and the main body remained blocking the higher levels of the beach. Thirty tanks could not be landed and remained afloat.

The landing of the Commandos on the wings was more successful No. 4 Commando was able to signal at 0745 hours that it had already fulfilled its task (putting out of action battery 813) and to be re-embarked. No. 3 Commando arrived with its party in the middle of the attack but was immediately repulsed and forced to re-embark during which it suffered heavy losses.

The retreat and the re-embarkation resulted in a complete chaos. Not even one tank could be re-shipped. Numerous landing craft were sunk by the powerful attacks of the German Air Force, by the gunfire of the coastal batteries, and by parties of German troops. More than 2,000 men surrendered with heavy losses.

48. In case new enemy attempts are made to land, the coastal defence must presumably reckon with the following changes in the fighting arrangements that he will make:
(*a*) Intensification of measures to preserve secrecy.
(*b*) In the first landing waves the mass of men and material landed will not be considered so important as choosing an unexpected locality and the fighting value of the troops who will first touch land. This is proved by the fact that the action of No. 4 Commando of 200 men succeeded, while the action at Dieppe in which 10 times as many men supported by tanks, was a complete failure.
(*c*) When the surprise factor fails owing to meeting enemy units the

principal precaution for the success of the operation is wanting; therefore, it is better to return to the base of departure. Daylight landings are very difficult unless there is an enormous superiority of air force and gunfight support with Naval batteries. Landings by night offer greater probability of success.

(d) It is only advisable to land tanks on difficult ground when the pioneers disembarked by night together with the 1st Assault troops, have created the possibility of movement for the tanks themselves.

(e) To support a re-embarkation which is to be carried out under enemy pressure, very powerful fighter and bomber air forces must be available.

49. British Losses

(1) *Prisoners*   2,195 including 1 Brigade General, 15 Staff Officers, 112 other officers.

(2) *Deaths*   About 600 buried ashore.
Losses at sea not known but very considerable according to statements by prisoners.

(3) *Air*   127

(4) *Ships sunk*   5 transports, 3 destroyers, 6 escort units and numerous landing craft.
Damaged   An unspecified number of all classes.

50. Booty

(a) *Vehicles*   29 Churchill tanks, including   4 of Mark I,
7 of Mark II,
18 of Mark III,
6 Armoured cars with machine guns (Dingo)
1 Petrol carrier.

(b) *Weapons*   1,300 rifles.
170 machine guns.
60 machine pistols.
70 light mortars.
16 heavy mortars.
700 bayonets.

(c) *Ammunition* 1,210 rounds for tank guns.
2,180 rounds for light mortars.
356 rounds for heavy mortars.

1,230 rounds for anti-tank rifles.
400 rifle bombs.
150,000 rounds for machine guns.
75,000 rounds for rifles.
4,220 rounds for machine pistols.
2,000 hand grenades.
250 kilogrammes of explosives of various kinds.
50 metres of explosive tubing.

(d) Equipment   1 Assault ladder in six parts
6 lifebelts.

German Report on Operations by 81st Army Corps during British Attack on Dieppe, 19th August, 1942

Initial Situation

51. The defensive arrangements in the Division's sector extended for a length of 70 kilometres, including high cliffs with numerous ravines at right angles to the sea. For this reason, the defence was not continuous but concentrated at points of special importance, *i.e.*, near ports where a landing was possible and probable. It was laid out for the defence of each single valley with the smallest possible force. With such an arrangement of defence it was not possible to prevent the well-equipped British Commandos obtaining temporary successes at certain points along the coast as at Berneval and Varengeville. To have any possibility of repelling an attack from the sea or from the shore there would have to be much more strength than is now possible at the most important points in the vicinity of the ports; and it is further necessary to have numerous reserves in hand both to help the blockhouses and immediately to counter-attack the enemy forces landed in the intermediate zone.

It is specially important to hold back some strong reserves, because it may be considered certain that the enemy in a large scale operation, will employ airborne troops and parachutists to eliminate the coastal defence while he is attacking from sea and land.

52. In the Dieppe Sector there were employed:
1 Infantry regiment (Infan. Reg. 571) with 2 battalions of infantry;
1 Pioneer battalion with 2 companies of pioneers;
8 Anti landing guns and three 47-mm. guns served by infantry;
The 3rd Group, 302nd Artillery Regiment with 2 batteries of light field-howitzers and 2 range-finding batteries.
The coastal battery of heavy field-howitzers of Post 265.

For Flak:
1 heavy battery (of 75 mm.).
1 platoon (50 mm.).
1 platoon (37 mm.).
2 platoons (20 mm.).
About 200 men of various Naval detachments.
60 men of the police.
1 experimental company of 60 men.

53. *Army Reserves* were:
Infantry Regiment 676 at Doudeville.
1st Battalion of Infantry Regiment 676 around Hericourt.
3rd Battalion of Infantry Regiment 676 around Yvetot.
3rd Battalion of Infantry regiment 570 around Baqueville.
81st Armoured Company at Yvetot.

The last named was stationed so as to be able to come into action immediately both in the sector of the 302nd Infantry Division and the 332nd Infantry Division.

This grouping of the reserves was proved efficient on the 19th August, 1942.

The 332nd Artillery Regiment was use for coastal defence at Fecamp and from there was transferred to the zone of the Army Reserves.

Note. Sections 54 to 57 have been omitted as being an abstract of British orders.

58. It is not known whether other forces would land if the attack succeeded. It is possible that the convoy of 26 ships[161] which had left Portsmouth at midday and then reversed its course was intended to form the second wave in case the operation was successful. This supposition is supported by the fact that many prisoners spoke of help which should have arrived after 1600 hour and of alternatives.

The enemy was provided with the very best maps, which were of great help to him in carrying out the operation. By means of perfect photographic reliefs, the German positions had been reproduced to the very smallest detail. There were even shown the anti-tank walls barring passage to the sea-promenade. All possible points of access to the coast were clearly shown. But from the maps it did not appear that the local French-English espionage had worked well. The regimental tactical Headquarters were not known. The Divisional H.Q.s were believed to be at Arques la Bataille where they had been many months earlier. The 110th Infantry Division was supposed to be in the line instead of the 302nd Division.

APPENDICES

Progress of the Operations

59. The British Forces proceeding towards the French coast met, at 0400 hours, a German convoy about 20 kilometres off Dieppe. A violent action took place between the two formations, which, though short, gave the alarm to all the coastal defences. While enquiries were still being made as to whether they were our own or enemy ships off Dieppe, heavy air-attack with the dropping of bombs and firing on Dieppe itself and the sides of the town was taking place. While this air attack was going on, evidently with the object of neutralizing the coast defences, groups of landing-craft in waves of 40 to 50 emerged from the clouds of artificial smoke made by the aircraft, and under cover of the British Naval gunfire, proceeded towards the shore. Natural fog, as well as the artificial smoke and the dim light of dawn, prevented out artillery from scattering the landing craft already very close in, so that the fire of the guns and heavy weapons had to be concentrated on them when they were practically on the beach. On the beach itself there was so much fog and smoke as to make observation very difficult.

60. To the East of Dieppe the enemy had landed at the opening of the valley near Berneval, presumably in the strength of a Commando of 250 men, with orders to take and to destroy the battery in position there. They had succeeded in scaling the sides of the cliffs with the help of ladders, ropes and other gear, and attack the battery. The latter was situated in a blockhouse, and consisted of a machine-gun squad under the command of an Officer of the Berneval sector. The battery was able to repel, partly with direct gunfire at close range and partly with machine-gun fire, the fierce enemy attacks. A position near the battery with a personnel of 100 men was also attacked, but all the attacks were repelled, mostly by counter attacks.

61. The 302nd Infantry Division had, on hearing of the attack on Berneval, ordered a counter-attack to be made by the 302nd Anti-tank Group under Major von Blucher, together with the Cyclist Squadron stationed at St. Nicholas and the 3rd Pioneer Company stationed at Arques la Bataille. Major von Blucher also assumed the command of the 3rd Company of the 572nd Infantry Regiment which came out from St. Martin. The Berneval battery repelled the enemy attack. Major von Blucher succeeded in wiping out the enemy forces at Berneval and captured 2 officers and 80 men.

62. A similar action to that described above was taking place to the west of Dieppe against the battery near Varengeville by a special Commando

of 300 men. Protected by smoke this Commando landed on the coast on both sides of Varengeville whilst another Group attempted to land opposite the Quiberville blockhouse where a platoon of the 3rd Company of the 571st Infantry Regiment was stationed. The attempt was frustrated by the concentrated fire of the Company.[162] On the other hand some Commandos were able to get ashore at various points in the area around Varengeville where small wooded cliffs run down to the sea and where it was possible to clamber up.

This enemy force, about 300 men, attacked the battery from two sides with hand grenades, machine guns, and revolvers and mortars, while air bombardment neutralised the defence of the battery with continuous diving raids. Tracer bullets ignited the cartridges which were stored in the battery. The battery defended itself bravely right up to the end as is proved by the 28 dead and 29 wounded, including the Commanding Officer who directed the fire and did his best to hold out. When at last the battery passed into British hands practically all the guns had been rendered unserviceable by the ignition of the ammunition.

It was probably 0800 hours when the British Commandos re-embarked taking with them 4 prisoners and there were many dead and wounded of their own.

Evidently both the actions at Berneval and Varengeville were carried out with the object of wiping out the two heavy coastal batteries in order to facilitate later landings and subsequent re-embarkations at Dieppe.

The two coastal batteries were outside the main sector of Dieppe and through lack of personnel were not able to be defended sufficiently by infantry. The critical position of 813 was known, and its inclusion in the Dieppe defences proper should have been made earlier.

The Principal Attack against Dieppe

63. This took place on a wide front with three principal centres at Puits, Dieppe itself and Pourville.

The attack at Puits was broken up by the concentrated fire of the heavy artillery with serious losses to the enemy. No British troops were able to force a passage through the defences. The enemy was literally wiped out by flanking fire in front of the barriers, on the high walls running along the beach and on the beach itself. Beside numerous prisoners taken there were 150 dead at this point alone.

The battalion which was landed immediately to the west of Dieppe Harbour, up to the Rue Duquesne, was dispersed and destroyed together with the tanks which had been landed. The gunboat *Locust*, which had come up to the entrance of the harbour at 0600, found herself under the fire of the anti-landing guns and was hit several times; she tried to back out under a smoke screen and was probably sunk, as during an interval of good visibility the stern of a large sinking ship with 200 or 300 men on board was clearly seen.

The two battalions which with tanks had landed on the two sides of the Casino, suffered the same fate. They were dispersed during the landing operation on the beach and on the promenade, and with the exception of some patrols did not succeed in entering the town. All the tanks landed there were destroyed.

64. The 6th Battalion, however, succeeded in entering the western part of Pourville with the aid of darkness and smoke screens and overcame the weak garrison (1 platoon of infantry and men of the Todt Organisation). The battalion then tried to reach the objectives assigned to them. Two companies setting out from Pourville westwards overcame all the positions along the coastal road in the Valley of the Scie and got as far as the anti-tank positions where they put the gun out of use. Practically all the personnel serving the gun were killed. A part of the British were able to get over the Scie and arrive at the northern side of the Quatre Vents Farm. Here they were destroyed.

The two companies did not succeed in breaking through the line of the principal defences of Dieppe. The line began only at the anti-tank positions whilst Pourville had an advanced post only weakly defended.

The other two companies presumably reached their first objective occupying the south side of Pourville and the machine gun positions on the heights towards the west forming with it a bridgehead.

65. The 7th Battalion which had orders to land behind the 6th Battalion and to advance along the west bank of the Scie as far as the Airport of St. Aubin arrived in the zone of Hautot by going through the woods on the heights to the west of the river; they then came under the flanking fire from Quatre Vents Farm and met the Cyclist Platoon pushed forward by the 571st Infantry Regiment and other patrols from the same regiment. The intentions of this Canadian Battalion are not clear; they had met only slight resistance as there were only few German troops in the locality but they found it impossible to carry out orders to advance in the direction of the Airport of St Aubin. Probably they were held up by an order from the British Command as the frontal attack against Dieppe and Puits had not succeeded.

From the British orders it appears that the troops landed ought to have reached their fixed objectives before 1130 hours and that the retirement and re-embarkation ought to have started at that time. This operation had to be finished by 1430 hours. Numerous other vessels approached the beach at Dieppe up to midday. On account of the smoke it was not possible to see whether these vessels landed other troops or if they were taking on board those who had previously landed.

Measures Adopted by Army Command

66. When shortly after 0500 hours the width of the attacking front was known and it was seen that there were no attacks at Le Tréport, at the mouth of the Somme, and in the sector of the 332nd Infantry Division the latter had, as already mentioned, sent from Arques la Bataille to Berneval the Cyclist Squadron and 3rd Pioneer Company under the orders of Major von Blucher to help the Berneval Battery.

At 0610 hours the 571st Infantry Regiment stationed at Dieppe ordered its first battalion at Ouville to be prepared to attack in the Pourville direction.

The G.O.C. 81st Corps who at 0540 hours gave the Alarm II to all divisions and reserves put the third Battalion of the 570th Infantry Regiment at the disposal of the 302nd Infantry Division and ordered it forward to Offranville, while the remainder of the reserves were given orders to advance to Bacqueville (14 kilometres southwards of Dieppe). The 1st Battalion of the 571st Infantry Regiment was ready at 0900 hours in the Hautot area for the attack against Pourville. At 1030 hours the battalion began the attack against Pourville, cleared the enemy from the heights to the west and took about 200 prisoners.

The position at Dieppe itself was cleared up by 1100 with the employment of five companies of the 571st Infantry Regiment, with some of the 302nd Pioneer Company. The counter attack by this force caused the surrender of the British troops landed who were completely demoralised. About 100 prisoners were taken.

What was the cause of the Failure of the British Operation?

67. It was an absolutely mistaken estimate of the extent of the German defence which decided the enemy to take the bull by the horns and to land the main forces of his troops and tanks frontally at Dieppe, even though as appears from his charts he had a clear knowledge of the organisation of the coastal defences, the cement fortifications, the anti-tank walls, the machine gun positions, and the anti-landing guns. It is also hard to understand why no tank support was given to the patrols landed at Pourville. Probably the attack by tanks coming from Pourville against the heights west of Dieppe and the Quatres Vents Farm would have been successful even if getting through the anti-tank walls and over the Scie would have been a formidable obstacle.

Against all expectations neither airborne troops nor parachutists were employed by the British. If Puits had been attacked from the East by airborne troops and at the same time from the sea, the position of the defence in the area would have been very critical especially at first.

The enemy certainly thought that his air attack would have a demoralising effect on the coastal defences and hoped therefore, to be able to overcome the German lines fairly easily with his battalions. Probably the precision and the efficiency of the British air attacks was considerably influenced by the smoke cover over Dieppe.

68. The enemy landed both light and heavy mortars but in all his orders only one light battery and one light A.S. Squadron is mentioned which was to be landed near Puits. As the landing, therefore, failed these guns were not employed. Probably some light assault artillery would have been of greater service initially than tanks.

69. Since the large Naval vessels were not able to see the results of their gunfire on account of the artificial smoke there was a want of any artillery support for the enemy forces.

The British under-estimate of our defences is as surprising in view of their air reconnaissance as is the brief lapse of time in which they believed they could carry out the whole operation.

Their operational orders extending over 100 pages gave the fullest details of the task of each unit and detachment. Their detail gave rise in itself to the germ of failure in case unforeseen difficulties presented themselves.

70. The British attack against Dieppe completely failed with very great losses to the enemy thanks to the valiant defences of all our Armed Forces. The enemy left 95 officers and 2,122 men prisoners in our hands. Up to the 24th August, his dead are estimated at 475. More corpses are continually being washed up by the sea. A large percentage of losses which cannot be estimated was caused afloat by our gunfire, our air bombing, and the sinking of landing vessels, lighters and destroyers. The enemy losses must amount to 60 or 70 per cent. of the landing force.

German Losses
302nd Infantry Division:
5 Officers, 14 non-commissioned officers, 68 men dead.
1 non-commissioned officer, 9 men missing.
5 officers, 27 non-commissioned officers, 124 men wounded.

Total Losses: (Army, Air Force, Todt Organisation):

6 officers, 144 non-commissioned officers and men dead.
15 non-commissioned officers and men missing.
5 officers, 270 non-commissioned officers and men wounded.

Booty

28 tanks.	60 machine pistols.
7 motor lorries.	42 anti-tank rifles.
1 petrol waggon.	70 light mortars.
1,300 rifles.	60 heavy mortars.
170 machine guns.	

In addition, a quantity of ammunition, hand grenades, explosives and equipment.

German Report of 15th Army on British Attack on Dieppe on 19th August, 1942
(Headquarters, 27th August, 1942)

Enemy landings
71. The fact that the British were able to land a considerable number of men is explained by their use of so many landing craft (about 300 to 400) which were protected while proceeding to the beaches by both air force and naval gunnery and especially by artificial smoke and natural cloud prevailing. The latter caused our own gunfire to be obscured at the critical moment of the landing operations, that is when the landing craft were still afloat within range of the guns of the defences. The attack has again proved that the prompt recognition of an attempt to land and the immediate opening of fire by the defences are of enormous and decisive importance in breaking up and destroying the Naval objectives while these are still at some distance from the coast.

Also, in future the employment of smoke by the enemy must be taken into consideration.

The success of the Defences
72. From the large number of prisoners taken it may be thought that the fighting qualities of the British and Canadian troops are not too high, this is not the case. The enemy troops, nearly all Canadian soldiers, who took part in the battle fought well and bravely. The principle reasons for the large number of prisoners and the heavy losses are:-
(1) The lack of artillery support. The Naval guns were obscured by

the smoke. As soon as his tanks had been eliminated the enemy had no more heavy weapons at his disposal.

(2) The British had under-estimated the forces of the defence and at all the landing points, but especially at Puits and at Dieppe, were in a desperate position from the very start.

(3) The effect of the German defensive weapons was greater than the offensive weapons employed by the enemy.

(4) The craft which had been relied on for the re-embarkation were nearly all hit and sunk.

Reserves in the Sector

73. The opinion of the 81st Command is confirmed with regard to the employment of reserves in the sector. These reserves which can rapidly be got hold of should come into action without any hesitation, even if the position is not clear, so as to suffocate at birth any initial success of the enemy.

Mobile Artillery

The request that part of the Army's reserves of guns should be quickly placed on motor lorries is justified.

Reserves of Army Corps

The proposal to reduce these reserves and to assign them to the divisions is not favoured.

The Corps reserves arrived too late on the 19th August, not because there were too far from the coast but because their movement orders were given only at 0630 hours. The Corps reserves were at the disposal of the 81st Corps from the beginning so that the hands of their Commanding Officer were not tied in any way with regard to their employment.

Anti-tank Defence

74. It appears necessary to strengthen the passive anti-tank defences covering a greater area. It is also absolutely necessary to strengthen the active anti-tank defence.

These first trials against British tanks have shown that the Anglo-American tanks are certainly vulnerable.

According to telephone communications from the 10th Armoured Division the tanks were perforated at short range by our anti-tank rifles and by anti-tank 37mm. guns with armour-piercing shells, Model 40, and were also blown up with ordinary 37mm. shells for anti-tank guns (it appears that on 19th August, these had been fired at too long range as well as badly aimed). It is a question of giving the personnel serving the anti-tank guns more confidence in their weapons and of training the gunlayers with regard to efficient ranges. With this object it seems that the training of the personnel in war conditions, should be intensified.

Anti-Landing Guns

A larger organisation for anti-landing batteries had been repeatedly requested.

In view of the absolute necessity for reinforcements the urgency of the increase is again pointed out.

Military Coastal Artillery

The indispensable inclusion of Army guns in the sector of the harbour works is again emphasised to those commands where it has not hitherto been possible for want of personnel.

Collaboration with the Air Arm

75. To accelerate collaboration with the Air Arm an Air Liaison Officer should be sent to the Corps H.Q. with a wireless unit.

Liaison of the Corps with only one officer of the Air Arm does not seem workable; the one Command, which in the Army's point of view, could be taken into consideration is the Air Force. This, however, is not possible, the distance being too great.

Minefields

The arrangement of many false minefields (those at sea being charted) is a valuable factor.

Otherwise there are no improvements to propose.

It is possible that experience from other sectors can be obtained.

The creation of more telephone call boxes would be advisable, but perhaps this is a question of wire being available.

Wireless

76. The provision of wireless apparatus is not sufficient. It is absolutely necessary to have a third wireless apparatus in the batteries.

Civilian Traffic

The orders to stop all civilian traffic in the battle area must be given by the division itself on receiving the Alarm II signal.

Booty

Ascertaining the real situation with regard to booty has been impeded and delayed by various Commands intervening (even the High

Consumption of Ammunition

77. The consumption of ammunition has been much too high. The importance of munition tactics should be continually inculcated to the troops.

The ammunition which is available ought not to be *destroyed* too quickly.[163]

The stowage of ammunition should be re-examined (especially that of cartridges with regard to safety from incendiary projectiles). The stowage should be in small quantities at safe distances, under cement, if possible.

H.Q. has given the necessary orders.

Medical Services

78. The medical authorities in the sector of the 81st Command are being examined.

Fuel Supplies

The problem of fuel supplies for gasogene vehicles will be taken up by H.Q.

German Weapons

79. There have been no difficulties or special breakdowns in our arms and apparatus. The introduction of some sort of electric lighting for blockhouses is urgently necessary.

British Weapons

There do not appear to be any new or unusual British weapons.
Their abandoned equipment with explosives of every type is worth pointing out.

Behaviour of the Troops

80. The behaviour of our troops has been good. An example was given by the non-commissioned officers who have done their duty everywhere. The fighting has shown the special importance of having good non-commissioned officers with detachments stationed in small nests of resistance and in blockhouses.

The collaboration between detachments of the Army, of the Air Force, and of the Navy became more marked in the course of the fighting.

(Signed) HAASE,
Commander-in-Chief.

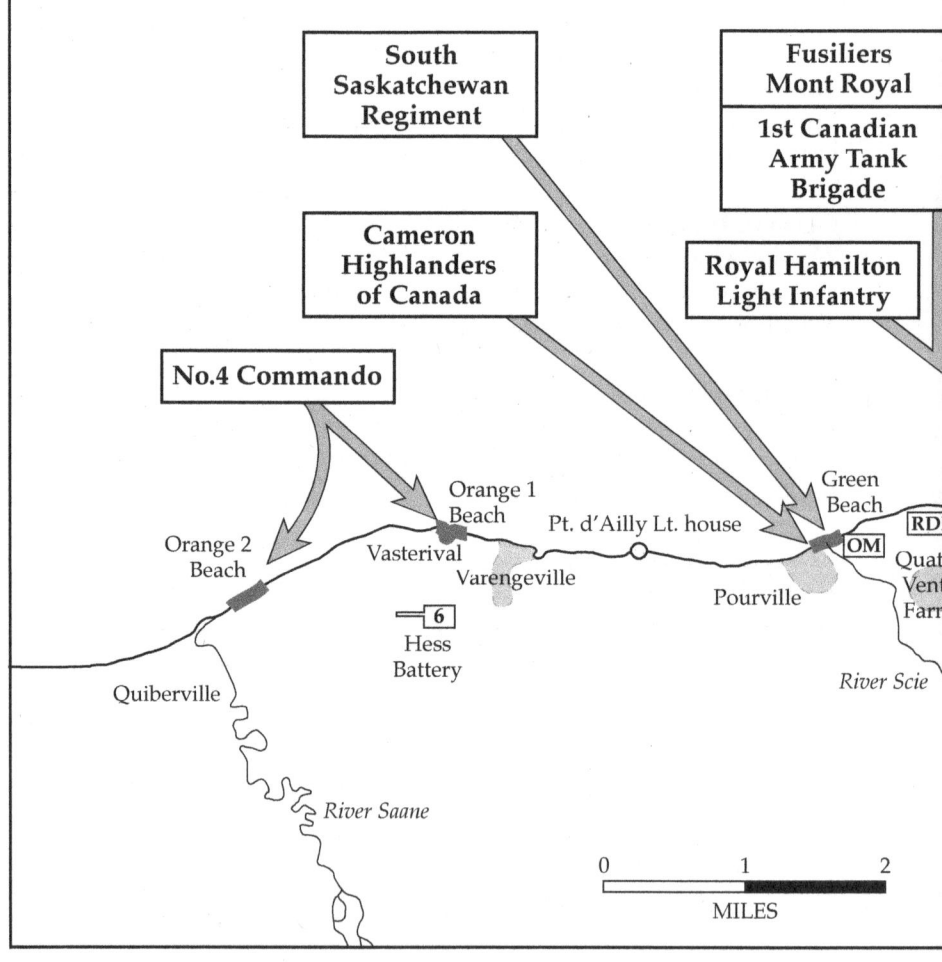

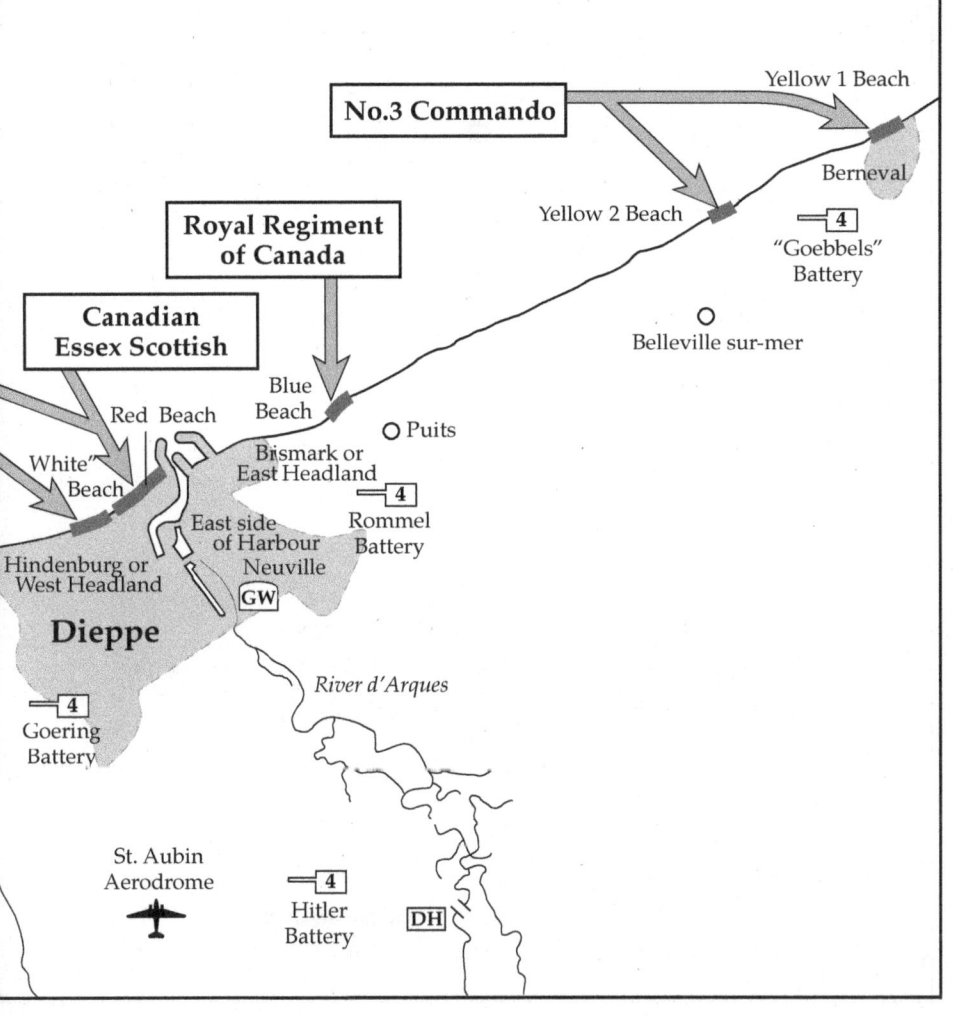

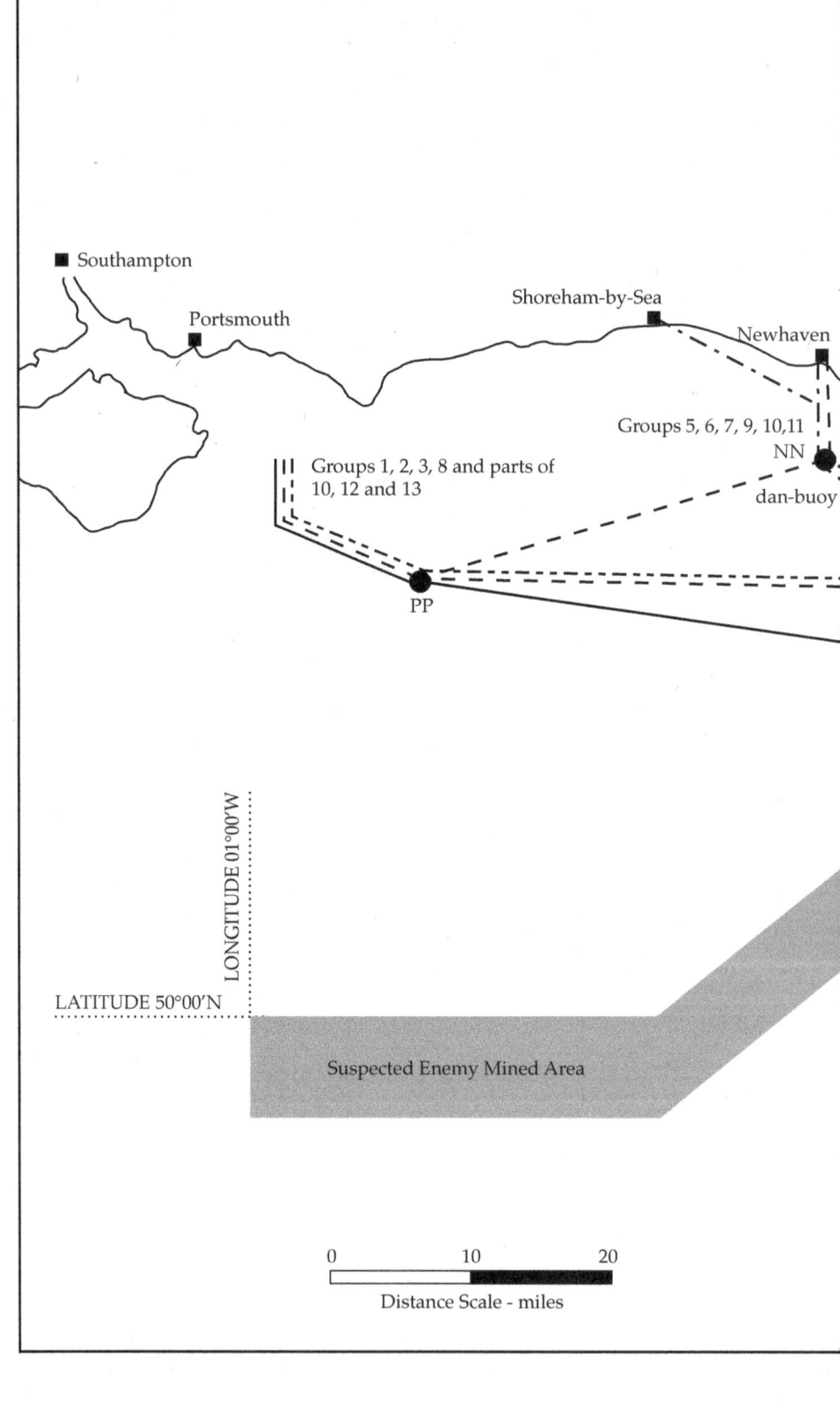

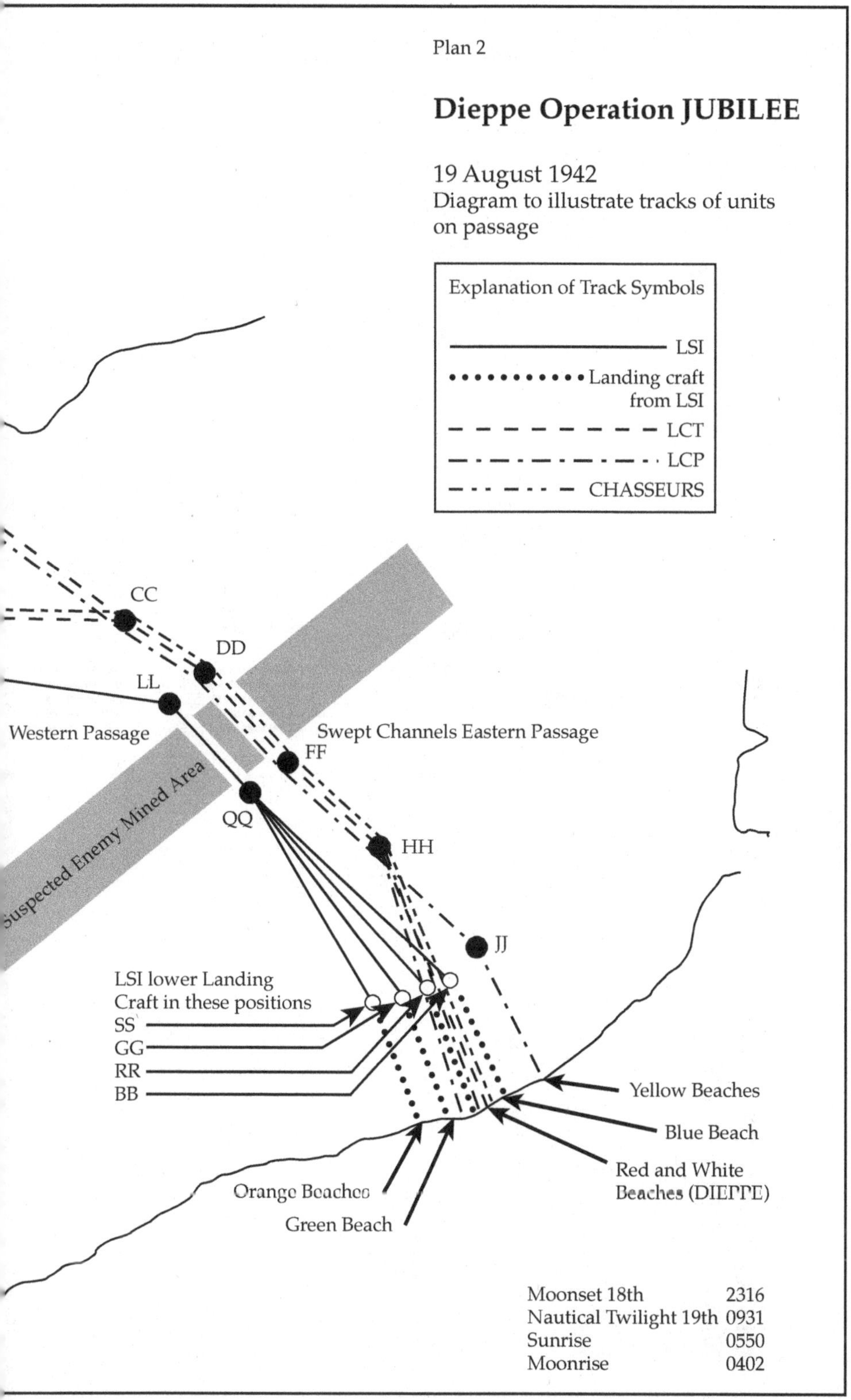

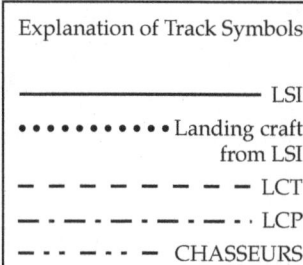

Plan 2

Dieppe Operation JUBILEE

19 August 1942
Diagram to illustrate tracks of units on passage

Explanation of Track Symbols	
──────────	LSI
••••••••••	Landing craft from LSI
─ ─ ─ ─ ─ ─	LCT
─ · ─ · ─ · ─ · ·	LCP
─ · · ─ · · ─	CHASSEURS

Western Passage
Swept Channels Eastern Passage
Suspected Enemy Mined Area

LSI lower Landing Craft in these positions
SS
GG
RR
BB

Yellow Beaches
Blue Beach
Red and White Beaches (DIEPPE)
Orange Beaches
Green Beach

Moonset 18th	2316
Nautical Twilight 19th	0931
Sunrise	0550
Moonrise	0402

Plan 3

DISPOSITION OF NAVAL FORCE DURING THE PASSAGE

DIEPPE
August 19th 1942

NAVAL SHIPS AND LANDING CRAFT	
DESTROYERS	9
MINESWEEPERS (Not shown)	15
GUNBOAT	1
CHASSEURS	7
LANDING SHIPS	9
SGBs	4
MGBs	12
MLs	16
	73
Landing Craft Tank	24
Landing Craft Flak	6
Landing Craft Support	8
Landing Craft Mechanised	7
Landing Craft Assault	60
Landing Craft Personnel	74
	179
	252

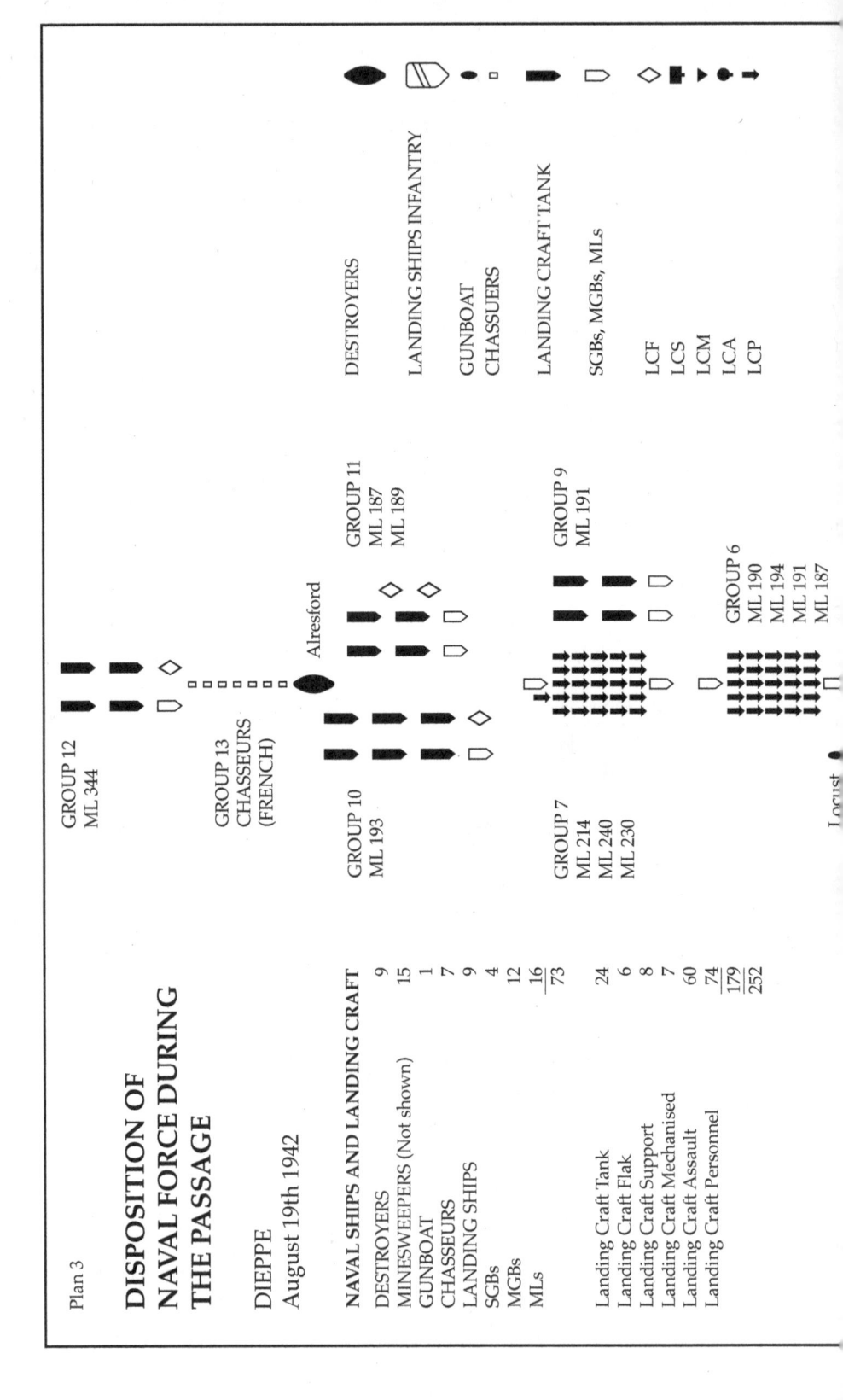

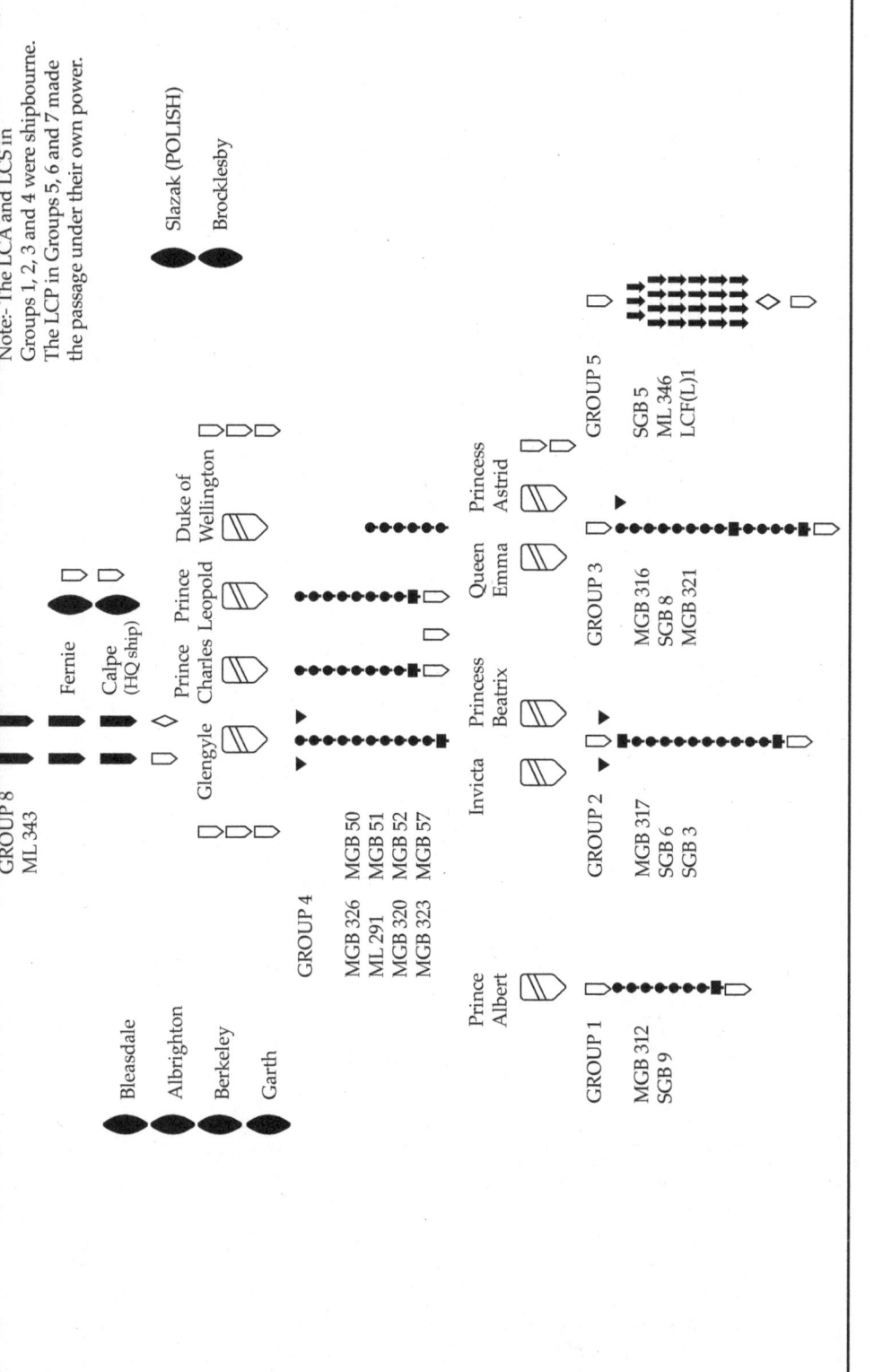

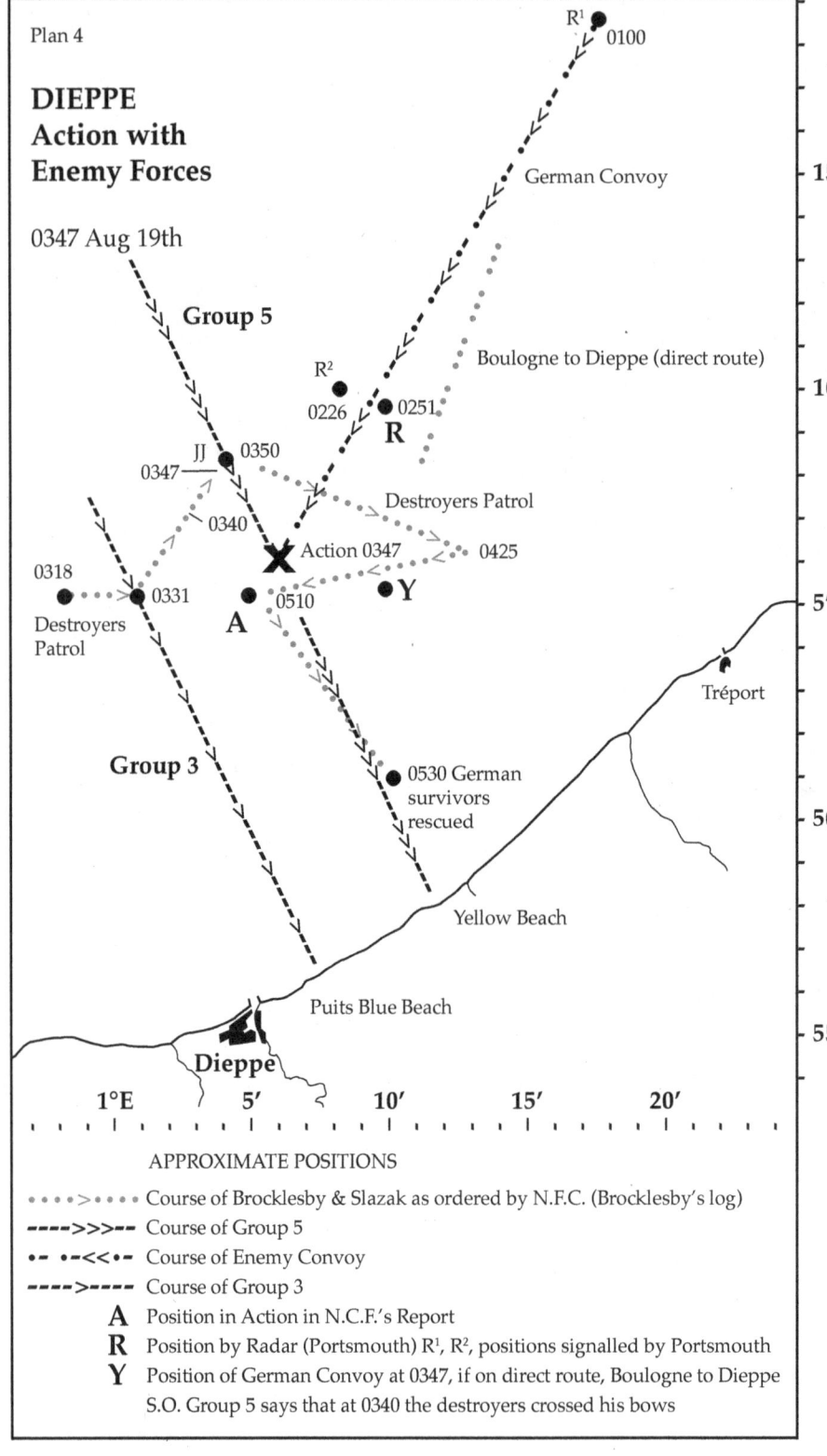

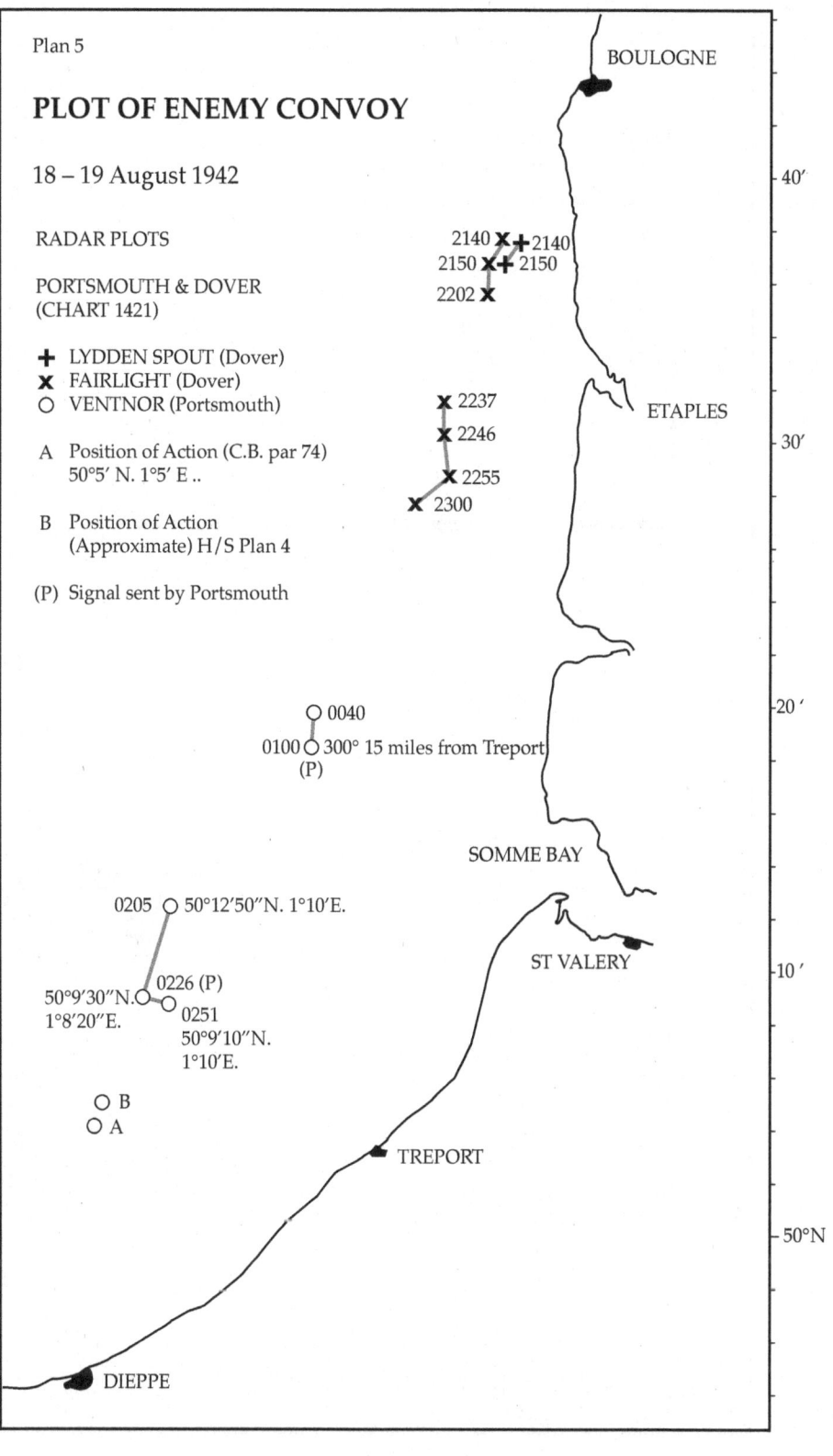

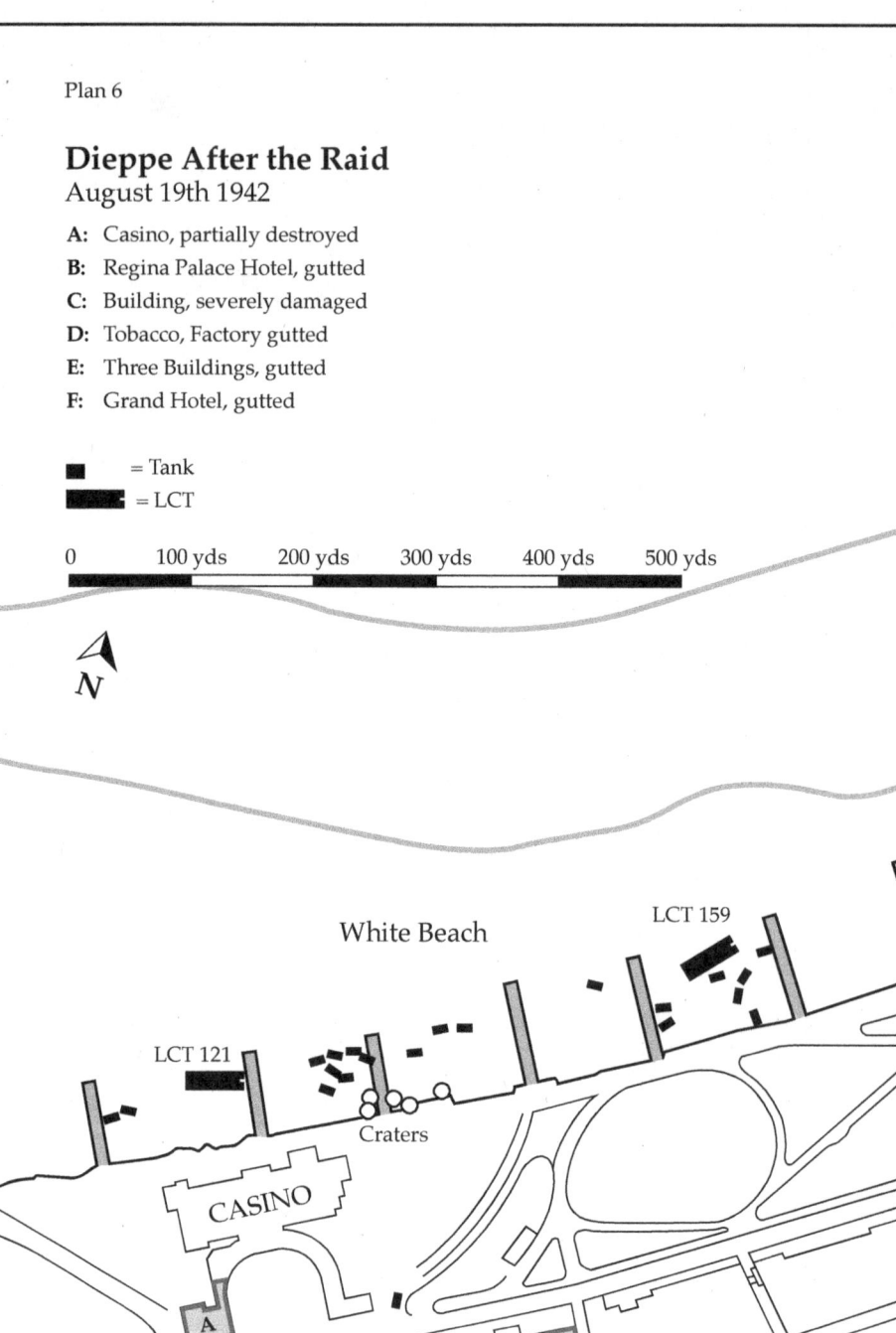

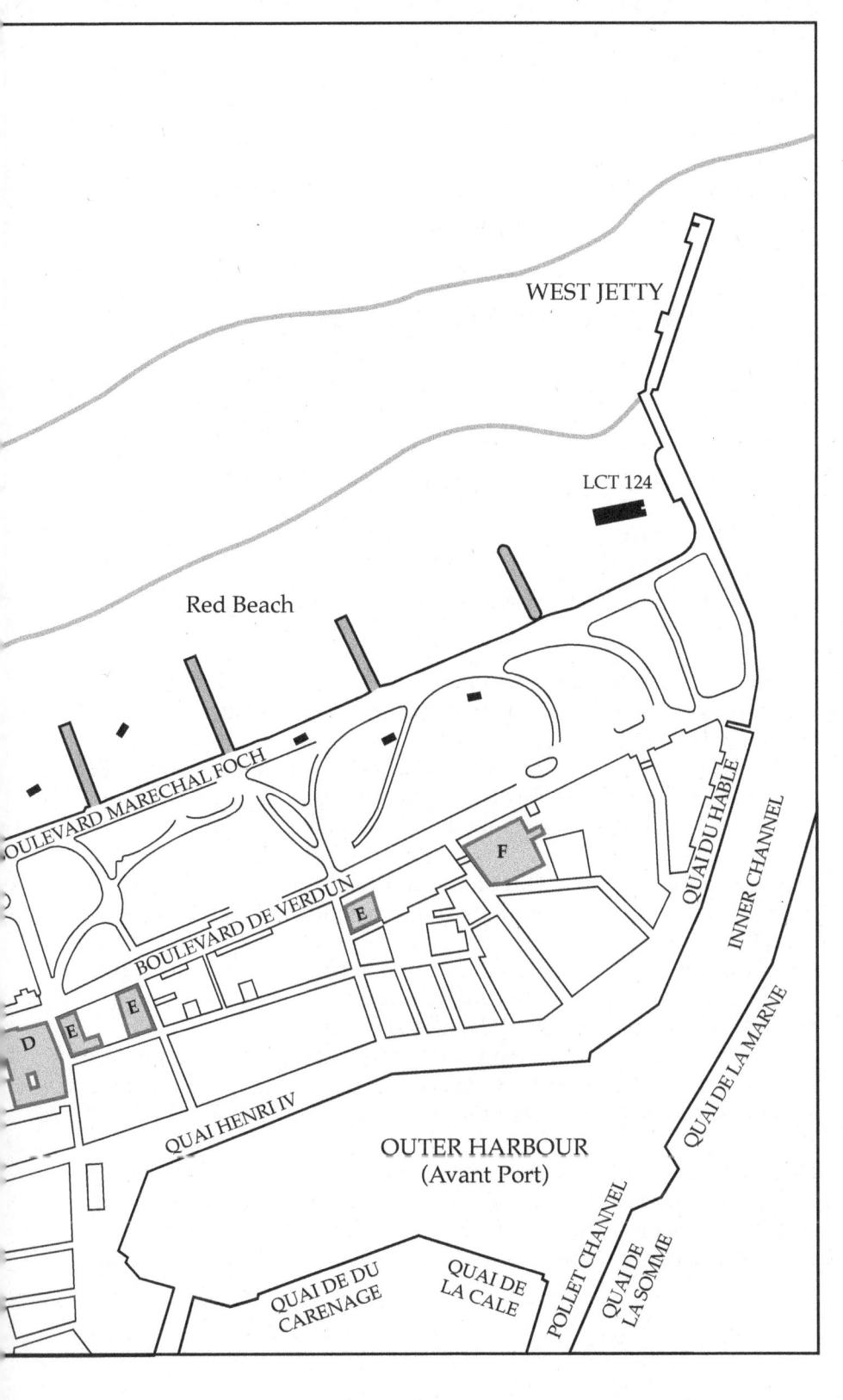

Appendix I

NAVAL OPERATION ORDER NO.1

Appendix   A: List of Ships, Groups and Senior Officers.
             B: Table, giving movements of Groups and Ships.
             C: Navigational Data.
             D: Diagram III.
All Times are British Summer Time.

Date
Operation "Jubilee" will take place on the first day when weather conditions are suitable, between the following dates inclusive:
18th August to 23rd August.
    The day previous to the assault, the day on which the force sails, will be known as D-1 day and the day previous to that, D-2 day. The day on which the operation is carried out will be D+1 day.

Executive Order to Carry Out the Operation.
Preparatory Order – If conditions indicate that the weather will be suitable during the next 48 hours, a provisional decision to carry out the operation will be made p.m. on D-2 day (the earliest date for this decision is 16th August). This will be the executive order to embark tanks during the dark hours of the night D-2/D-1.
    Executive Order – The preparatory order to carry out the operation will be made by 1030 on D-1 day. This signal will be the executive order to embark troops and carry out the operation.

Details of times of embarkation of the troops are issued to Commanding Officers. If troops have not arrived in time to allow the ship to sail at the correct time, Commanding Officers are to report to Commander-in-Chief, Portsmouth, stating the time at which the ship will be ready to sail. This signal is only to be made if there is a delay. No signal will indicate that the embarkation is going according to plan.

Sailing of Ships and Units
Ships and units are to sail to comply with Appendix B. In some cases the time of passing the gate or harbour entrance only is given, in which case ships and units are to arrange their time of sailing in conjunction with the local naval authority in order to comply. Details are given in J.N.O. 2, J.N.O. 3, J.N.O. 4 and J.N.L.C.

Flag Officer-in-Charge, Southampton, Naval Officer-in-Charge, Newhaven, and Resident Naval Officer, Shoreham, are requested to inform Commander-in-Chief, Portsmouth, if any of the groups sailing from their respective commands are delayed, stating the actual time at which they do sail. Commander-in-Chief, Portsmouth, is requested to ensure that this information is passed to the Naval Force Commander.

The Passage
The timing and routeing of the various groups referred to in *Appendix* A and B are governed both by timing of the landings, and by the necessity of passing through a German minefield (QZX 771). Two passages will be swept and cleared by fleet minesweepers. The minesweepers will sail from the Portsmouth area on D-1 day and will give the impression that they are carrying out their normal minesweeping duties in the Beachy Head area during daylight hours.

The routes and timings of all ships other than the minesweepers are given in *Appendix* B. The times given for passing the gate or leaving harbour and for touching down and lowering landing craft are exact. The times for passing other positions are approximate as all ships and groups have time in hand for the passage.
  It is important, however, that:
  Groups 1, 2 and 3 do not pass "LL" before 0115.
  Groups 5 and 8 do not pass "DD" before 0030.

The movements of the minesweepers and the details of the swept channels are given in Jubilee Naval Orders for Minesweepers 2.

During the passage across the channel there are a large number of ships manoeuvring close to each other at varying speeds. It is of the utmost importance that Commanding Officers and in particular Senior Officers of groups in company and Senior Officers of detached groups keep to their proper routes and timing by accurate navigation, not only so that the landing may be carried out according to plan, but also to avoid ships and groups meeting at night.

Commanding Officers are to work out the movements of ships and groups which are likely to be near them during the passage so that they will be prepared for possible chance contacts with friendly forces. Attention is drawn to the relative positions of groups at certain times.

Attention is drawn to the necessity of accurate station keeping. In order to prevent ships straggling with the possibility of becoming detached, senior officers of groups are to keep their groups closed up as much as possible at all times.

Approach
After passing through the minefield, a total of six destroyers will provide cover, two to the Eastward and four to the Westward of the assaulting force. They will proceed out clear from the assaulting force, rejoining as the main landing force closes the shore. Details are given in J.N.O. 3. Coastal Craft will remain with their various groups as shown in *Appendix* B. Details of their duties are given in J.N.O. 4. After lowering landing craft, the L.S.I. return to England.

Return routes are given in *Appendix* B and detailed instructions for L.S.I. in J.N.O. 2. Movements of landing craft and coastal craft during the Approach phase are given in *Appendix* B.

Assault
Details of the position and times at which landing craft touch down are given in *Appendix* B.
Details of Naval support are given in J.N.B.

Operations of Cutting Out Party
On completing her preliminary task of supporting the left flank of the landing at "Red" beach, H.M.S. *Locust* will enter the harbour when ordered. The Royal Marine Commando, followed by demolition parties, etc., will be landed from the *Locust* and from seven *Chasseurs*. The Cutting Out Force will remove as many barges as possible in the time available, destroying the remainder and any other ships which it is not possible to remove. Details are given in J.N.O. 5.

Movements of Naval Units during Occupation
Details of movements of ships and craft during the occupation are given in the following orders:

Destroyers	J.N.O. 3.
Coastal Craft	J.N.O. 4.
Landing Craft and L.C.F. (L)	J.N.L.C.

Withdrawal and Return Passage
General description of the withdrawal of the troops and the factors governing it are given in J.N.O. 6. This order also includes detailed arrangements for the re-embarkation of troops and tanks, also for the return passage, as far as it is possible to forecast events during this period.

Casualties to Landing Craft
Should any landing craft suffer defects causing a reduction in speed, the Senior Officers of Groups are not to delay their groups but are to proceed according to the timetable. Defective craft are to make their best speed independently to their respective beaches. The same principle applies if damaged by enemy action.

Action if Contact is made with the Enemy
Senior Officers of Groups in company and Senior Officers of detached groups must take drastic avoiding action if contact is made with enemy forces or to avoid contact if the enemy are known to be in the vicinity. But the proper course must be resumed as soon as it is considered safe to do so as timely arrival of groups, particularly the early ones is vital to the operation. The method to be used in signalling emergency turns is given in the orders to different types of ships and craft.

Signals on Passage and W/T Silence
Commanding Officers must bear in mind that in an operation of this complexity there is a great danger of signal congestion causing breakdown of communications. It is for this reason that the operational orders are prepared in much greater detail than would be necessary in a normal operation.

The object to be aimed at is to complete the operation with the minimum of signals. This will be achieved by Commanding officers refraining from making any signal so long as they are able to conform to the plan.

Commanding Officers, when deciding whether to make a report, must ask themselves whether that which they are proposing to report really affects the conduct of the operation. At the same time, Commanding Officers must bear in mind that both Force Commanders and Senior Officers of groups must be informed at once of any circumstances which *are* likely to affect the operation.

In a special case of ships or units carrying troops, Commanding Officers must consult with the Senior Military Officer in this matter.

W/T silence by H.M. Ships is to be preserved from the time of sailing until the landing on "Red" and "White" beaches has taken place. This rule may be relaxed as follows:
- (a) By all ships to make an enemy report if it is obvious that enemy forces are aware of the presence of our ships.
- (b) By L.S.I.s if it appears that their landing craft are going to be more than 15 minutes late touching down.
- (c) By Senior Officer of Group 5 if by delays or casualties it is the opinion of the Senior Military Officer that the success of the landing at "Yellow" beach is seriously jeopardised.

Senior Officers of other groups are to report by W/T to the Naval Force Commanders if they are going to be more than 20 minutes late or have suffered casualties. This signal is to be made after W/T silence has been relaxed.

Cancellation
If the operation is cancelled during the passage, Senior Officers of groups are in principle to return by the reverse route of the outward passage, adjusting speed so as to arrive off their ports of departure at the beginning of morning civil twilight. Detailed instructions are given in the orders for different types of ships and craft.

Recognition Signals
Current recognition signals will be used.

Command and Headquarters Ships
The Naval Force Commander is Captain J. Hughes Hallett, Royal Navy. Naval forces taking part in the operation will come directly under his orders from their time of sailing until completion of the operation. Until the time of sailing, Naval forces will be under the orders of the Commander-in-Chief of the area in which they are situated through their normal train of command.

APPENDICES

The Military Force Commander is Major-General J.H. Roberts, M.C., General Officer Commanding 2nd Canadian Division.

The Air Force Commander is Air Marshal T. Leigh-Mallory, C.B., D.S.O., who will control all Air Forces from Headquarters, No. 11 Group, Uxbridge.

The Military and Naval Force Commanders will be embarked in H.M.S. *Calpe*. Air Commodore A.T. Cole, C.B.E., M.C., D.F.C., who will represent the Air Force Commander, will also proceed in H.M.S. *Calpe*. H.M.S. *Fernie* will act as 2nd Headquarters Ship, where additional Naval and Military Staff are carried, and will remain in close proximity to H.M.S. *Calpe* throughout the operation.

Chain of Naval Command
Should the Naval Force Commander become a casualty, his duties devolve on officers in the following order:
1. Acting Captain J.D. Luce, D.S.O., Royal Navy.
2. Commander H.V.P. McClintock, Royal Navy.
3. Commander R.E.D. Ryder, V.C., Royal Navy.
4. Commander G.T. Lambert, Royal Navy.

If H.M.S. *Calpe* becomes disabled, H.M.S. *Fernie*, the 2nd H.Q. Ship, takes over, officers transferring as necessary.

Appendix J

LIST OF SHIPS, GROUPS AND SENIOR OFFICERS

(i) Ships operating in Groups

Group 1.
Prince Albert	Lt.-Cdr. H.B. Peate, R.N.R.	6.9.38	No.4 Commando.
M.G.B. 312	Lt.-Cdr. H.H.H. Mulleneux, R.N. (Senior Officer Landings, "Orange" Beach)	1.8.41	–
S.G.B.	–	–	–

Group 2.
Princess Beatrix	Cdr. T.B. Brunton, R.N. (Retd.)	–. 12.39	S. Saskatchewan Reg.
Invicta	Cdr. A.J. Robertson, R.N.R. (Retd.)	–	S. Saskatchewan Reg.
M.G.B. 317	Lt.-Cdr. R.M. Prior, D.S.C., R.N. (Senior Officer Landings, "Green" Beach)	15.7.24	–
M.G.B. 323	–	–	–

Group 3.
Queen Emma	Captain G.L.D. Gibbs, D.S.O., R.N. (Retd.)	30.6.15	Royal Reg. of Canada.
Princess Astrid	A/Lt.-Cdr. C.E. Hall, R.N.R.	17.4.42	Royal Reg. of Canada.
M.G.B. 316	A/Lt.-Cdr. H.W. Goulding, D.S.O., R.N.R. (Senior Officer Landings, "Blue" Beach)	–	–
S.G.B.	–	–	–

Group 4.
Glengyle	Captain D.S. McGrath, R.N. (Retd.)	27.8.41	Royal Hamilton Lt Inf.

APPENDICES

Prince Charles	A/Cdr. S.H. Dennis, D.S.C., R.N.	–. 2.41	Essex Scottish Reg.
Prince Leopold	Lt.-Cdr. W.S. Byles, R.D., R.N.R.	18.4.39	Essex Scottish Reg.
M.G.B. 326	Cdr. G.T. Lambert, R.N. (Senior Officer Landings, "Red" and "White" Beaches, and P.B.M.)	30.6.41	–
M.L. 291	Lt.-Cdr. A.W. McMullen (Senior Officer Landings, "White" Beach)	1.6.37	–
Locust	Cdr. R.E.D. Ryder, V.C., R.N. (Officer Commanding Cutting Out Party)	31.12.40	Royal M. Commando.
L.S.T. *Duke of Wellington*	–	–	–

Group 5.
20 L.C.P.

1st Flot	–	–	No. 3 Commando.
24th Flot	–	–	–
S.G.B. 5	Cdr. D.B. Wyburd, R.N. (Senior Officer Landings, "Yellow" Beach)	31.12.39	–
M.L. 346	–	–	–

Group 6.
25 L.C.P.

2nd Flot	–	–	Camerons of Canada.
6th Flot	–	–	Camerons of Canada.
7th Flot	–	–	Camerons of Canada.
M.L. 190	Cdr. H.V.P. McClintock, R.N. (Senior Officer of Group)	31.12.36	–
M.L. 194	–	–	–

Group 7.
25 L.C.P.

4th Flot	–	–	Fusiliers Mount Royal.
5th Flot	–	–	Fusiliers Mount Royal.

APPENDICES

M.L. 214	Lt.-Cdr. J.H. Dathan, R.N. (Senior Officer of Group)	15.7.35	–
M.L. 230	–	–	–

Group 8.
6 L.C.T.

Flight 1 145	–	–	9 tanks.
129	–	–	9 tanks.
159	–	–	9 tanks.
Flight 1A 126	–	–	9 tanks.
121	–	–	9 tanks.
163	–	–	9 tanks.
M.L. 343	Lt.-Cdr. The Earl Beatty, R.N. (Senior Officer of Group)	31.8.36	–
2 L.C.F. (L)	–	–	–

Group 9.
4 L.C.T.

Flight 2 124	–	–	12 tanks.
125	–	–	12 tanks.
166	–	–	12 tanks.
165	–	–	12 tanks.
M.L. 191	Ty. Lt. H. Leslie, R.N.V.R. (Q.O.) (Senior Officer of Group)	20.12.39	–

Group 10.
6 L.C.T.

Flight 3 305	–	–	13 tanks, stores, carriers etc.
304	–	–	13 tanks, stores, carriers etc.
303	–	–	13 tanks, stores, carriers etc.
302	–	–	13 tanks, stores, carriers etc.
313	–	–	13 tanks, stores, carriers etc.
314	–	–	13 tanks, stores, carriers etc.
M.L. 193	Lt.-Cdr. G.H. Stevens, R.N. (Senior Officer of Group)	15.2.29	–
15.2.29	–		

APPENDICES

Group 11.
4 L.C.T.

Flight 4	306	–	–	15 tanks.
	308	–	–	15 tanks.
	376	–	–	15 tanks.
	361	–	–	15 tanks.
M.L. 189		A/Lt. N.B.H. Lloyd, R.N.V.R. (Senior Officer of Group)	30.8.40	–
M.L. 187		–	–	–
L.C.F. (L) 3		–	–	–
L.C.F. (L) 5		–	–	–

Group 12.

4 L.C.T.	309	–	–	Empty.
	307	–	–	Empty.
	310	–	–	Empty.
	360	–	–	Empty.
M.L. 344		Ty. Lt. L.E. Barker, R.N.V.R. (Senior Officer of Group)	26.4.40	–

Group 13.
6 Chasseurs

A	–	–	Cutting Out Party.
B	–	–	Cutting Out Party.
C	–	–	Cutting Out Party.
D	–	–	Cutting Out Party.
E	–	–	Cutting Out Party.
H.M.S. *Alresford*	Commander R.E.C. Dunbar, R.N.	–	–

(ii) **Ships NOT attached to Groups**

Destroyers:

Calpe	Lt.-Cdr. J.H. Wallace, D.S.C., R.N.	1.10.40	Combined HQ Staff.
Fernie	Lt. W.B. Willett, R.N.	1.3.42	Shore comb HQ Staff.
Brocklesby	Lt.-Cdr. E.N. Pumphrey, D.S.O., D.S.C. R.N.	16.5.41	–
Garth	Lt.-Cdr. J.P. Scatchard, D.S.C., R.N.	1.9.41	–
Albrighton	Lt.-Cdr. R.J. Hanson, D.S.C., R.N.	1.5.42	–
Berkeley	Lt. J.J.S. Yorke, D.S.C., R.N.	1.7.35	–

APPENDICES

Bleasdale		Lt. P.B. North Lewis, D.S.C., R.N.	16.12.35	–
Slazak		Kdrpopov R. Tyminiski		–
4 M.G.B.s:				
(From	315	–	–	–
the	321	–	–	–
Nore)	320	–	–	–
	323	–	–	–
M.G.B.s:	50	–	–	–
(70 foot)	51	–	–	–
4 M.L.s:	246	–	–	–
	123	–	–	–
	114	–	–	–
	120	–	–	–
4 M.L.s:				
	292	–	–	–
	309	–	–	–
	171	–	–	–
	208	–	–	–

Appendix K

OPERATION JUBILEE INSTRUCTIONS TO L.S.I.

Sailing of L.S.I. and Deception of the Enemy
In order to comply with the times of landing troops it is necessary for L.S.I. to leave their berths at Portsmouth and Southampton before dark. Those L.S.I. so fitted will disguise themselves as they leave their berths to resemble a convoy of merchant ships sailing; they proceed at reduced speed when forming up in their respective groups inside the Gate. In this way it is hoped to deceive the enemy's evening reconnaissance which is unlikely to be photographic owing to the failing light. Disguises are to be removed at 2130.

Order of Leaving Harbour
Queen Emma is to pass the Gate at 2110 followed by remaining L.S.I. of Groups 1, 2 and 3 and coastal craft, proceeding at 15 knots.

Glengyle is to pass the Gate at 2120 followed by L.S.I. of Group 4 and coastal craft, proceeding at 15 knots.

Destroyers will follow in the order the *Calpe*, then four destroyers attached to groups 1, 2 and 3, then the remaining two.

Passage
Groups 1, 2 and 3. – *Queen Emma* is the guide of Groups 1, 2 and 3 and will be responsible for navigation of L.S.I. until dispersal at QQ. After passing PP (E.A. 5 buoy) *Princess Astrid* is to set course for LL, increasing speed as requisite to conform to the timetable. Escorting forces will take station as shown in the cruising diagram.

As Groups 1, 2 and 3 approach LL, *Calpe* will open the distance ahead of *Queen Emma* to allow the four destroyers to take action station between her and *Queen Emma*. *Calpe* will lead the destroyers round through the passage in the minefield to QQ.

At QQ, L.S.I. disperse in their various groups to their lowering positions. *Calpe* will proceed clear and wait for Group 4. The four destroyers will proceed to the South and West of the L.S.I. to provide cover. Coastal craft will proceed with their respective groups. M.G.B.s "A" and "B" will proceed with Group 3.

After lowering landing craft, L.S.I.s are to return by the routes given. Times are to be strictly adhered to, to avoid possible chance contacts between our own forces. This particularly applies to Group 3 which passes close to groups 5 and 8 between 0315 and 0345. Group 3 will also pass close to Group 13, when proceeding from KK to QQ and will probably make contact with Group 4 at QQ. M.G.B.s "A" and "B" will remain with Group 3 until QQ when they will rendezvous with M.G.B.s "C" and "D" with Group 4.

Group 4. *Glengyle* is the guide of Group 4 and is responsible for navigation of the group. After passing PP (E.A. buoy) *Glengyle* is to set course for QQ, increasing speed as necessary to conform to the timetable and then by the route given.

After lowering landing craft, Group 4 is to return by the route given being careful to avoid Group 8 which will be in close proximity after landing craft have been lowered. Group 4 should sight Group 3 at about 0500 at QQ.

If *Locust* is unable to keep up she is to follow astern at her best speed. This applies to M.L. 291 who is to attach herself to *Locust* if both are dropping astern and then join the Group and the landing craft in the vicinity of RR.

Before entering the swept channel at QQ, the two destroyers will drop astern, then come up on the port beam after passing through and finally parting company at the lowering position to provide cover for the landing craft.

The coastal craft other than those proceeding with the landing craft will escort Group 4 on the return journey. M.G.B.s "C" and "D" will break off at position QQ, rendezvous with M.G.B.s "A" and "B" and return to

APPENDICES

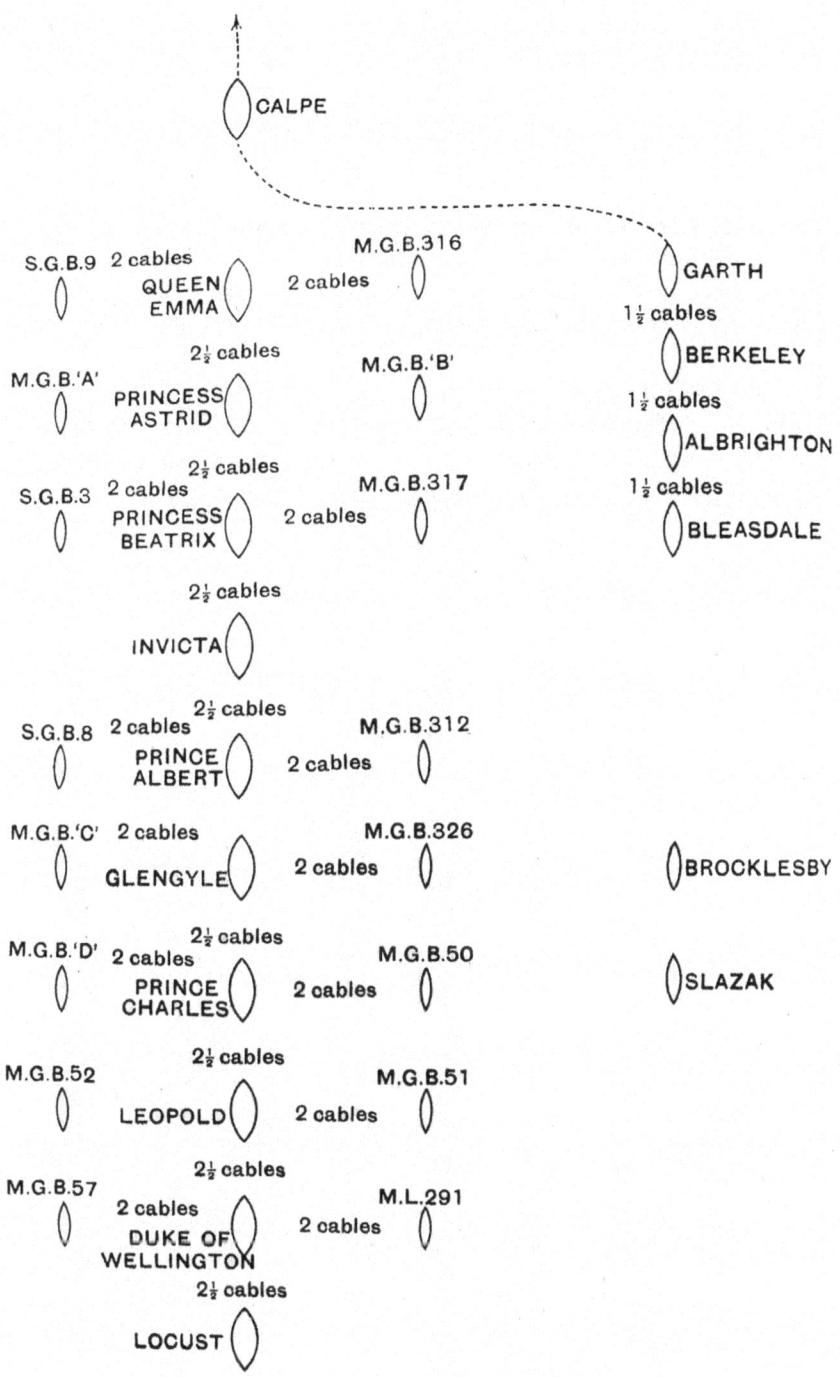

the vicinity of Dieppe, the remainder breaking off in the vicinity of NN and proceed to Newhaven.

L.S.I. *Duke of Wellington* is sailing with this Group but her L.C.A. are to proceed to "Blue" Beach.

Avoiding Action and Emergency Turns
Should it be necessary to take collective action to avoid the enemy, the Senior Officer of L.S.I. of groups in company is to manoeuvre his ships by W/T, resuming the original course as soon as possible.

Shaded Stern Lights
Dimmed shaded stern lights are to be shown by ships in company. Care is to be taken to ensure that they are not too bright, and that they are extinguished when they serve no special purpose.

Appendix L

OPERATION JUBILEE
INSTRUCTIONS TO DESTROYERS

Organisation of Destroyers
Destroyers will be organised as follows:

(a) *1st Division*:
   H.M.S. *Calpe*. Fleet No. 1 Headquarter Ship.
   H.M.S. *Fernie*. Fleet No. 2, 2nd Headquarters Ship.

(b) *2nd Division*:
H.M.S. *Garth*	Fleet No. 3
H.M.S. *Berkeley*	Fleet No. 4
H.M.S. *Albrighton*	Fleet No. 5
H.M.S. *Bleasdale*	Fleet No. 6

This division will provide cover to the west during the approach and bombarding ships during the assault and occupation.

(c) *3rd Division*:
   | H.M.S. *Brocklesby* | Fleet No. 7 |
   | O.R.P. *Slazak* | Fleet No. 8 |

Any other destroyers taking part.

This division will provide cover to the eastward during the approach and main cover during the assault and occupation.

During the return passage it is not possible to lay down any duties for divisions as destroyers will have to be detached for escort of return groups.

Destroyers will be transferred from one division to another during the operation but will retain their original fleet numbers.

This organisation is to be assumed on receipt of the executive order to carry out the operation.

H.M.S. *Calpe* will sail at 2000.

Passage
Cruising Orders for Groups accompanied by destroyers. Groups and destroyers will take up their cruising orders on passing PP (E.A. 5 buoy).

The duties of 2nd and 3rd Divisions are to provide cover against surface craft attack.

Movements of H.M.S. *Calpe* and 2nd Division from LL to Main Assault
On approaching LL, H.M.S. *Calpe* will proceed sufficiently far ahead of H.M.S. *Princess Astrid* to allow the 2nd Division to take station between H.M.S. *Calpe* and H.M.S. *Princess Astrid*. 2nd Division is to take station astern of H.M.S. *Calpe* without signal.

At position QQ Groups 1, 2 and 3 will disperse to their respective lowering positions. H.M.S. *Calpe* will proceed clear to the eastward and ease down to wait for Group 4.

2nd Division is to cover the L.S.I. of Groups 1, 2 and 3 during their passage from QQ to their respective lowering positions by keeping to the south-westward of H.M.S. *Prince Albert*.

At 0300, when L.S.I. of Groups 1, 2 and 3 are lowering landing craft, 2nd Division is to make a sweep to the south and westward to cover the approach of the landing craft as follows:

From SS proceed at about 15 knots through positions
    (*a*) 49° 58' N., 00° 41' E.
    (*b*) GG.
    (*c*) 50° 01' N., 01° 01' E.,

thence to approach "Red" and "White" beaches astern of the landing craft in company with H.N.S. *Locust*, which will be positioned on the eastern flank of the landing craft. Attention is drawn to the anticipated positions of units at 0400.

The ordering for fire support by the destroyers and H.M.S. *Locust* also their movements, are given in J.N.B. In general, 2nd Division and H.M.S. *Locust* should keep back from the landing craft until the last mile or so, so as not to disclose the presence of the landing craft by themselves being sighted, then closing up at the final stage of the approach.

H.M.S. *Calpe* with H.M.S. *Fernie* in company will follow astern of the 2nd Division.

Movements of 3rd Division from LL to Main Assault
3rd Division is to take station astern of Group 4 when passing through the swept channel. After passing QQ, the 3rd Division is to take station on the port side of Group 4.

On arrival at RR, the 3rd Division is to make a sweep as follows to the eastward to cover the passage of the landing craft to the beaches:
From RR steer to pass through positions BB and JJ at 10 knots. (Care is required on approaching BB to keep clear of units in Group 3).

At JJ, increase speed to about 15 knots and proceed through the following positions:
   (*a*) 50° 06′ N., 01° 13′ E.
   (*b*) 50° 05′ N., 01° 05′ E.

thence to be in position 1½ to 2 miles off "Red" and "White" beaches at 0530. Attention is drawn to the anticipated positions of units at 0400.

Movements of H.M.S. *Fernie* up to Main Assault
H.M.S. *Fernie* will lead Group 8, then join H.M.S. *Calpe*.

Movements of Destroyers after the Assault
H.M.S. Calpe and H.M.S. Fernie. H.M.S. *Calpe* and H.M.S. *Fernie* will remain approximately in the position given.

2nd Division. H.M. ships *Garth*, *Albrighton* and *Bleasdale* are to take over bombardment duties. The *Berkeley* is to join the 3rd Division without further orders on completion of her bombardment duties in J.N.B. She will remain as spare bombarding ship.

APPENDICES

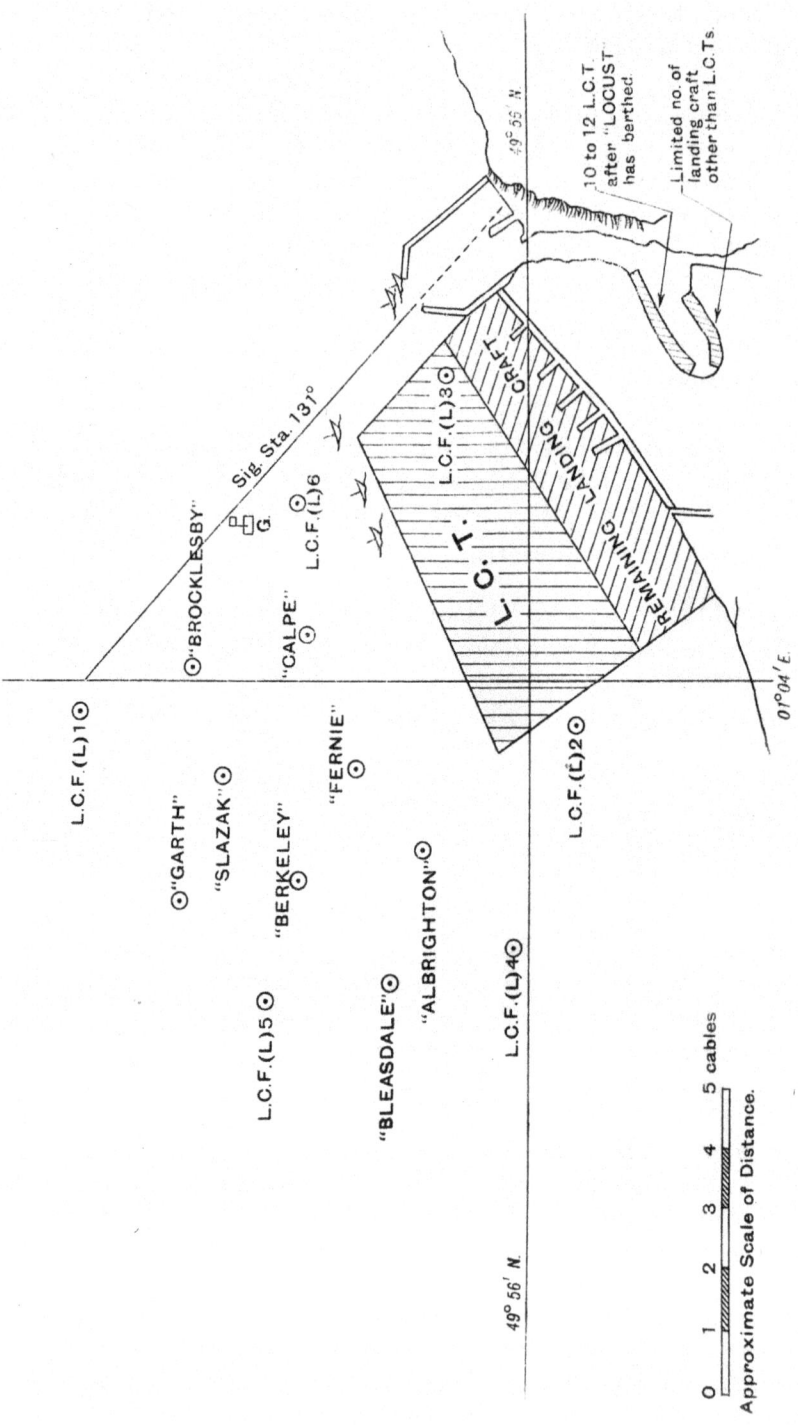

3rd Division. The 3rd Division to which will be added H.M.S. *Berkeley* will act as the main covering force against surface attack. The division is to remain in the approximate positions given when not otherwise employed.

There will be two forces of gun-boats on patrol to the eastward and westward to report approaching enemy surface forces. When proceeding to intercept enemy forces the 3rd Division is not to proceed further than about 25 miles from Dieppe.

Movements of Destroyers during Return Passage

No definite duties can be laid down for destroyers during the return passage. Some will be required to provide cover while others may be employed on close escort to return Groups.

Action if Contact is made with Enemy during the Passage

Should contact be made with enemy forces during the passage and approach, commanding officers must bear in mind that their function is to prevent the enemy from sighting the groups and other craft. They should not, therefore, pursue the enemy further than is necessary to ensure this, or become embroiled in close action which is not necessary to achieve this object.

Air recognition of Surface Craft

Destroyers are to show a recognition sign consisting of yellow, red, yellow strips which are to be displayed on the forward and aft gunshields. They should not be shown until after dark on D-1 day.

Appendix M

OPERATION JUBILEE
ORDERS FOR NAVAL A.A. FIRE

Although a high degree of protection by our own fighters may be anticipated a proportion of enemy aircraft must be expected to escape interception, and ships and craft must be prepared for attack by fighter and fighter-bomber aircraft throughout the day.

If ammunition outfits and reserves are to last throughout the day, it is essential that a high standard of fire discipline be observed. Fire must be withheld until aircraft are within effective range and should not be continued at retiring aircraft or opened against aircraft already heavily engaged unless it is making a direct attack on the ship concerned. Fire discipline of this nature must be enforced if necessary by stationing an officer or petty officer at each A.A. weapon to take charge of the gunlayer.

A.A. Gunfire. The operation is divided into two periods during which a different degree of freedom as regards the use of A.A. gunfire is permitted. These are:

Period I, 0450-0540
During this period large numbers of our own fighters will be flying low in support of the landings, and it is not expected that many enemy aircraft will be in the vicinity during this period. For these reasons great care must be taken to identify aircraft before opening fire.

Period II, 0540 Onwards
During this period, Fighter Cover will be somewhat thinner. Our own aircraft will not normally fly below 3,000 ft. or 2,000 ft. unless in pursuit of enemy fighters. Aircraft flying low or diving towards a ship are to be regarded as probably hostile. Care must be taken, however, to avoid

firing on own aircraft if they come within ranges while in pursuit of enemy fighters.

Long-Range A.A. Fire. 4-in. Long-Range Controlled A.A. Fire is not to be employed. Destroyers and B.P.C. may employ 4-in. barrage fire and a short fuze. In general, ships should not fire at aircraft flying above 2,000 feet as these will be dealt with by our own fighters.

Reserves
No general reserves of close range A.A. ammunition will be taken. Additional ammunition will be embarked in each ship or craft.

Recognition of Tac R Aircraft
A certain number of Mustang Tac R Aircraft are expected to fly low in the vicinity of the beaches and anchorage during the operation. This aircraft bears a marked resemblance to the German Me.109 and will be distinguished by a yellow band 12 ins. wide painted on the lower and upper surfaces of both main planes.

A.A. Readiness
Close-Range A.A. weapons are to eb fully manned from dawn on the day of the operation until return to England. Additional guns' crews will be embarked in L.C.T.s to enable this to be carried out.

Fire by H.Q. and 2nd H.Q. Ship
4-in. gunfire from either the H.Q. or 2nd H.Q. ships is most undesirable as it will probably put out of action the additional W/T sets fitted. 4-in. gunfire is not to be opened by these ships without orders from the Naval Force Commander.

Appendix N

OPERATION JUBILEE
ORDERS FOR COASTAL CRAFT

Craft to which these orders apply are:
   (*a*) Steam Gunboats.
   (*b*) Motor Gunboats ("C" type).
   (*c*) Motor Gunboats (70 ft.).
   (*d*) M.L.s

Organisation of Coastal Craft after the Assault
After the assault coastal craft are to be organised under their senior officers as follows in order to carry out certain tasks:

(*a*) 1st	S.G.B. Flotilla		Task 1.
	S.G.B. 5		
	S.G.B. 8		
	S.G.B. 3		
	S.G.B. 9		
(*b*) 14th	M.G.B. Flotilla		Spare.
	M.G.B. 316		
	M.G.B. 317		
	M.G.B. 326		
(*c*) 12th	M.G.B. Flotilla		Task 2.
	M.G.B. 315		
	M.G.B. 321		
	M.G.B. 320		
	M.G.B. 323		
(*d*) 11th	M.L. Flotilla		Task 3.
	M.L. 194		
	M.L. 191		
	M.L. 187		
	M.L. 189		

The remainder of the 11th M.L. Flotilla and M.L.s of 23rd Flotilla will not be organised as units as they are carrying out individual duties.

Task 1

Task 1 is to provide warning and cover against surface attack from the westward of Dieppe. After the Senior Officer 1st S.G.B. Flotilla has organised his craft he is to proceed to the westward parallel to the coast and at a near distance of about 10 miles from it. Starting from Dieppe he is to proceed to about 15 miles from there, then return. Speed of advance during this sweep is to be 10 knots in order to conserve fuel. Ships should be spread about 2 miles apart. On return to Dieppe S.G.B.s should concentrate and remain about 2 miles to westward of Dieppe unless otherwise ordered.

Enemy surface craft are to be reported immediately and our forces should retire on our destroyer force which will be sent to support, if in inferior strength. The S.G.B.s should not pursue the enemy further than 25 miles from Dieppe.

Task 2

Task 2 is similar to Task 1, but to the eastward of Dieppe. M.G.B.s should not normally exceed 10 knots on this patrol in order to conserve fuel.

Task 3

Task 3 is to provide an air/sea rescue service up to a distance of about 3 miles from the coast between Pointe d'Ailly and Berneval (4½ miles to the westward, and 4 miles to the eastward of Dieppe, respectively). The Senior Officer of 11th M.L. Flotilla is to dispose his M.L.s along the Northern side of this area.

Allocation of Tasks – General Policy

Although Flotillas are allocated to these tasks they must be ready to exchange duties when ordered.

The 14th Flotilla will be held in reserve and is to remain inside the area covered by the L.C.F. (L).

Miscellaneous Duties during Occupation

The various duties to be performed by coastal craft which are not formed into definite units are given briefly in Appendix C. Further details are:

(*a*) M.G.B. 312, will remain as Senior Officer of the landing at "Orange" beach. As S.G.B. 9 will join up with her flotilla after the main assault, the Senior Officer of the landing at "Orange" beach should ask the Naval Force Commander for another M.L. if he requires one.

(*b*) M.L. 190, will remain under the orders of the Boat Pool Officer throughout the operation.

(*c*) M.L. 214, will remain under the orders of the Assistant Boat Pool Officer. She is to be prepared to make smoke in accordance with J.N.O. 8.

(*d*) M.L.s 193 and 343, will remain under the orders of Senior Officers "A" and "B" L.C.T. respectively.

(*e*) M.L. 230, after Group 7 has arrived off Dieppe, M.L. 230 is to request permission of M.L. 214 to proceed to "Yellow" beach to join M.L. 346 to replace S.G.B. 5, remaining under the orders of Senior Officer of the landing at "Yellow" beach.

(*f*) M.L. 346, remains under the orders of Senior Officer of the landing at "Yellow" beach.

(*g*) M.L.s 344 and 291, are to act as despatch boats. They are to close H.M.S. *Calpe* and await orders as soon as they have completed their duties during the assault. M.L. 291 will subsequently be detached to take charge of invasion barges as they are towed out of the harbour.

(*h*) M.L. 171 and 208, orders for these two craft are given.

(*j*) M.L.s 292 and 309, are to join H.M.S. *Calpe* off Dieppe on completion of duties with M.S. 9 and M.S. 13.

Duties during Withdrawal and Return Passage
Definite orders for the employment of coastal craft during these phases cannot be laid down. In general, all craft will be required to escort the returning landing craft. Gunboats will probably be employed as distant cover and M.L.s as close escort.

Landing craft smaller than L.C.T. have been ordered to Newhaven on return, except those who sailed from Shoreham who will endeavour to return there. L.C.T. and L.C.F. (L) will return to Portsmouth by the inshore route anchoring to the eastward of the Looe until daylight if necessary.

Coastal craft are to return to the bases from which they sailed except M.L.s from Newhaven if they are in company with landing craft proceeding to Portsmouth in which case they will remain with them.

Towing Back of Invasion Barges
As there are few craft for towing back invasion barges, M.L.s must be prepared to tow one each if so required.

Coastal Craft not Proceeding to French Coast
Movements of the four 70-foot M.G.B.s and the four M.L.s all of which return to Newhaven.

All craft are to be at instant notice to sail whilst at Newhaven.

Unless otherwise ordered, 4 M.L.s as detailed by the Senior Officer M.L.s are to sail at 1200 and patrol between positions NN and DD until 2130; they are then to patrol on a line between positions (a) 50° 42.4′ N., 00° 32.4′ E. and (b) 50° 35′ N., 00° 45′ E. until daylight, when they are to carry out a sweep from DD to NN and return to Newhaven. The object of this force during daylight is to render assistance to landing craft when required, and during darkness to provide cover to the eastward.

The 70-foot M.G.B.s will be given tasks as required.

Coastal Craft Attached to Groups 1, 2, 3 and 4
J.N.O. Two, contains all orders for the sailing, forming up and general conduct of Groups 1, 2, 3 and 4, also cruising diagrams. Destroyers accompanying these groups have freedom of action to manoeuvre as necessary to repel enemy attacks. Coastal craft must therefore be prepared for such contingencies.

Duties of Gunboats when acting as Close Escort
Gunboats which form part of the escort of Groups 1, 2, 3 and 4 are to keep close in and open out if contact is made with enemy forces. This is to prevent our destroyers mistaking gunboats for E-boats.

Air Recognition of Surface Craft
All craft are to show a recognition sign consisting of yellow, red, yellow stripes extending athwartships and displayed in the most conspicuous place.

Air/Sea Rescue
Although certain craft are told off for air/sea rescue, all coastal craft must keep a good look-out for airmen who may descend in the sea and every effort is to be made to rescue them.

Medical
The medical arrangements afloat and the method of dealing with casualties are given in J.N. Medical Orders.

APPENDICES

Fuel

Great care in economy of fuel in gunboats is to be exercised. M.L.s are to work on their wing fuel tanks first, so that M.G.B.s may fuel from them if this becomes essential.

Appendix O

TABLE OF MOVEMENT OF COASTAL CRAFT AFTER THE ASSAULT

Unit	Craft	Duty during Assault	Duty during the Occupation	Duty during the Withdrawal	Duty during Return
1st S.G.B. Flot.	S.G.B. 5	Senior Officer Group 5	Carry out Task 1 under S,O, S.G.B.s S.O. Gp. 5 transfers as necessary.	Carry out Task 1	Cover & escort
1st S.G.B Flot	S.G.B. 3	With landing craft of Group 2	Carry out Task 1 under S.O. S.G.B.s.	Carry out Task 1	Cover & escort
1st S.G.B Flot	S.G.B. 8	With landing craft of Group 3	Carry out Task 1 under S.O. S.G.B.s.	Carry out Task 1	Cover & escort
1st S.G.B. Flot	S.G.B. 9	With landing craft of Group 1	Carry out Task 1 under S.O. S.G.B.s.	Carry out Task 1	Cover & escort
14th M.G.B. Flot	M.G.B. 316	Lead in landing craft of Group 3	In reserve	As required by	Cover & escort N.F.C.
14th M.G.B. Flot	M.G.B. 312	Lead in landing craft of Group 1	Remain with Group 2	Remain with Group 1	Remain with Group 1

APPENDICES

Flotilla	Vessel	Role	Task	Function
14th M.G.B. Flot	M.G.B. 317	Lead in landing craft of Group 2	In reserve	As required by N.F.C.	Cover & escort
14th M.G.B. Flot.	M.G.B. 326	Lead in landing craft of Group 4	In reserve	As required by N.F.C.	Cover & escort
12th M.G.B. Flot.	M.G.B. 315 M.G.B. 321	Escort Group 3 to QQ on return passage	R.V. with M.G.B.s 320 and 323 at QQ. The whole then proceeding to carry out Task 2 under S.O.	Carry out Task 2 Under S.O.	Cover & escort
12th M.G.B. Flot.	M.G.B. 320	Escort Group 4 M.G.B. 323 passage	R.V. with M.G.B.s to QQ on return The whole then carry out Task 2 under S.O.	Carry out Task 2 315 & 321 at QQ.	Cover & escort under S.O.
4th M.G.B. Flot.	M.G.B. 50 M.G.B. 51 M.G.B. 52 M.G.B. 57		Escort Group 4 until approx. position NN then proceed to Newhaven & remain at short notice for orders from N.F.C.	– – – –	– – – –
11th M.L. Flot.	M.L. 194	With landing craft Of Group 6	Task 3 – Air/Sea rescue	Task 3 – Air/Sea rescue	Escort
11th M.L. Flot.	M.L. 191	In charge of Group 9	Task 3 – Air/Sea rescue	Task 3 – Air/Sea rescue	Escort
11th M.L. Flot.	M.L. 187	With Group 11	Task 3 – Air/Sea Rescue	Task 3 – Air/Sea rescue	Escort

APPENDICES

Flotilla	M.L.	Role	Task	Notes
11th M.L. Flot.	M.L. 189	In charge of Group 11	Task 3 – Air/Sea rescue	Escort
11th M.L. Flot.	M.L. 190	In charge of Group 6	Boat Pool Officer	Escort
11th M.L. Flot.	M.L. 193	In charge of Group 6	S.O. "A" L.C.T.	Escort
11th M.L. Flot.	M.L. 214	In charge of Group 7	Ass Boat Pool Officer	Escort
11th M.L. Flot.	M.L. 230	With Group 7	Join Group 5 off "Yellow"	With Group 5
23rd M.L. Flot.	M.L. 346	With Group 5	With Group 5	With Group 5
23rd M.L. Flot.	M.L. 344	In charge of Group 12	Despatch boat	Escort
23rd M.L. Flot.	M.L. 291	Lead in Group 4	Despatch boat with M.G.B. 326	In charge of invasion barges outside the harbour Escort
23rd M.L. Flot.	M.L. 343	S.O. Group 8	S.O. "B" L.C.T.	Escort
2nd M.L. Flot.	M.L. 171	As laid down in J.N.M./S.2	As laid down in J.N.M./S.2	Escort
2nd M.L. Flot.	M.L. 208	As laid down in J.N.M./S.2	As laid down in J.N.M./S.2	Escort
2nd M.L. Flot.	M.L. 292	As laid down in J.N.M./S.2	Act as despatch boats	Despatch boats
2nd M.L. Flot.	M.L. 309	As laid down in J.N.M./S.2		Escort

Appendix P

OPERATION JUBILEE
INSTRUCTIONS TO CUTTING OUT FORCE

Tasks
The following tasks are to be carried out by the Cutting Out Force:
  (a) Remove for our own use about 40 German barges last seen in the Bassin de Paris and Bassin Duquesne, and craft in the outer harbour.
  (b) Destroy any barges that cannot be removed, preferably in deep water.
  (c) Blow up or destroy the floating dock in the Bassin de Paris, also all lock gates, and lock working machinery before leaving.
  (d) Remove or destroy any local craft found in the harbour.
  (e) Capture certain material.

Ships and Vessels
H.M.S. *Locust* – Carrying the Senior Officer Cutting Out Force, the Dock Master, Dock Assault Force (R.M. Commando), No 1 Dock Operating Party (R.N.) and No. 1 Demolition Party (R.M.).

H.M.S. *Alresford*
Chasseur Q14 – Carrying the Assistant Dock Master, No. 2 Dock Operating Party (R.N.) and No. 2 Demolition Party (R.M.).
Chasseurs Q43, Q42, Q13, Q10, Q41 – Carrying remainder of Dock Assault Force.
Chasseur Q5 – Carrying No. 3 Demolition Party (R.N.) and Engine Room Party.
Nos. 1 to 6 Working Parties will be landed on "Red" and "White" beaches, in Group 9 L.C.T. sailing from Newhaven.
Note. – Chasseurs are to be allocated to the duties outlined above by their Senior Officer.

The Plan

(i) H.M.S. *Locust*, after completing her preliminary task of supporting the left flank of the main landing which starts at 0520, will enter the harbour. The S.O. Cutting Out Force will decide when H.M.S. *Locust* enters the harbour; this is not to be attempted so long as an effective enemy artillery fire covers the harbour; it is hoped this fire will be silenced by 0600. The Dock Assault Force will then be landed in the Avant Port on the island. In addition to this force, the Dock Operating Party, Demolition Party, equipment and stores carried in H.M.S. *Locust* will be disembarked; these two parties will at once set about opening the lock gates and their bridges, using existing power, demolition or other means.

(ii) The Senior Officer Chasseurs is to enter harbour with his craft as soon as possible after H.M.S. *Locust*. Chasseurs on entering into harbour will berth at or near the Gare Maritime. They will then wait in the Avant Port for the barges to be brought out (*see* next paragraph). They will take them over from the L.C.P.s and tow them out of harbour. Barges are to be anchored near the L.C.F. (L) about one mile off "Red" beach and the Chasseurs are to return for another tow. H.M.S. *Alresford* will also enter harbour at the same time as the chasseurs.

(iii) L.C.P. will be sent in to the harbour after the Chasseurs. They are to enter the Bassin Duquesne and Bassin de Paris and tow out invasion barges to the Chasseurs in the Avant Port and return for more. They are to act under orders of the Naval Beach Masters at the entrance to these basins. (*See* Orders for L.C.P. Flotillas).

(iv) One hour before the final withdrawal, orders will be given to destroy lock gates, their operating gear and remaining craft in the harbour.

(v) The R.M. Commando and other parties will be re-embarked in H.M.S. *Locust*, Chasseurs, invasion craft or landing craft, depending on the circumstances. Anyone failing to get off by these means should report to the P.B.M. on "Red" or "White" beaches.

(vi) H.M.S. *Locust* will form a part of Group 4 and the Chasseurs Group 13. They will be sailed from Portsmouth area.

(vii) One L.C.F. (L) may be ordered to follow H.M.S. *Locust* into harbour if required. Orders to do this will be given either by the Senior Officer Cutting Out Force in H.M.S. *Locust* or the Naval Force Commander.

Orders for H.M.S. *Locust*

(i) *Command*. – H.M.S. *Locust* will come under the direct command of the Senior Officer Cutting Out Force who will embark in her before the operation.

(ii) The following special parties will be embarked:
Dock Assault Party (four platoons R.M. Commando).
No. 1 Dock Operating Party (R.N.).
No. 1 Demolition Party (R.M.).
(iii) H.M.S. *Locust* has the following tasks to fulfil:
- (*a*) *Bombardment.* (*See* J.N.B.) – To give support to the left flank of the landing on "Red" beach engaging targets in area A from 0510 to 0535.
- (*b*) *Entry into the Harbour.* – On completion of the assault on "Red" beach and when conditions are suitable she is to enter the harbour. Enemy positions on and in the cliff to the eastward of the harbour entrance may have to be engaged.
- (*c*) *Landing of the Cutting Out Party.* – On entering the harbour, she is to land the Dock Assault and Cutting Out Parties on the island between the Avant-Port and the Arriere-Port. She may then be required to carry out indirect bombardment of enemy Divisional Headquarters at Arques and other targets in the vicinity. Fire will be observed by F.O.O. No. 4 as laid down in J.N.B.
- (*d*) *Withdrawal.* – For the withdrawal H.M.S. *Locust* is to berth bows out at the Gare Maritime, and on leaving harbour it is the intention that H.M.S. *Locust* should cover the eastern flank.

Orders for L.C.P. Flotillas in the Harbour
(i) The 6th, 7th and 2nd L.C.P. Flotillas (Group B) will be instructed to enter the harbour after H.M.S. *Locust* and the Chasseurs. The 6th Flotilla is to proceed to the Bassin de Paris. The 7th Flotilla is to proceed to the Bassin Duquesne. These flotillas acting under the orders of the Naval Dock Masters are to tow the invasion barges out of their Basins and pass them to the Chasseurs in the Avant Port. The 2nd Flotilla is to berth near H.M.S. *Locust* in the Avant Port and await orders. they will also be required for towing later.
(ii) One hour before the final withdrawal the Senior Officer Cutting Out Force will order the destruction of remaining craft in harbour, lock gates, etc. On receipt of this order, L.C.P. flotillas are to withdraw to the Avant Port and report to the traffic controller, who will be at the junction of the Quai Henri IV and the Quai du Hable.

Control of Operations in the Harbour
(i) Acting under the orders of the Senior Officer Cutting Out Force the following officers will take charge of their separate operations as shown below:

- (a) *Officer Commanding Royal Marine Commando* will take charge of all fighting required on the dock side and the capture of all craft in harbour when resistance is offered by the crews. He will also be in charge of the final destructive demolition work.
- (b) *Naval Dock Master* is to force the lock gates into the Bassin Duquesne and remove any craft inside.
- (c) *The Assistant Dock Master* is to force the lock gates into the Bassin de Paris and remove any crat inside.
- (d) *Staff Officer Chasseurs* is to act as traffic controller in the Avant Port and assist the Second in Command R.M. Commando as shown below.
- (e) *The Second in Command, Royal Marine Commando,* will set up a Rear Headquarters at the Gare Maritime and take charge of the withdrawal.

(ii) It is the intention of the Senior Officer Cutting Out Force to set up a Naval Headquarters together with the O.C. Royal Marines at the junction of the Quai du Tonkin and the Quai Guynemer. Operations in the Arriere-Port and Basins will be controlled from this Headquarters by Loud Hailer or runner. Operations in the Outer Harbour will be controlled by the Staff Officer Chasseurs who will be acting as traffic controller and will be in a position at the junction of the Quai Henri IV and the Quai du Hable.

Landing Table
Ship: *Locust*
Name: No. 1 Dock Operating Party
Personnel: Outline Duties:
1 Dock Master (Lt.-Cdr.).   Opening the following dock gates in the
1 Lieut. (E). 1 P.O.   order mentioned –
1 Shipwright (or Blk.).   Bassin Duquesne. Bassin de Paris.
1 Stoker P.O.   Bassin de Canada.
6 A.B.s.
5 Motor Mechanics.

Ship: *Locust*
Name: Dock Assault Force
(4 Platoons)
Personnel: Outline Duties:
8 Officers.   Securing the island.
9 N.C.O.s.
145 Other Ranks.

APPENDICES

Ship: *Locust*
Name: No. 1 Demolition
Personnel:
10 Royal Marines under the orders of the Naval Dock Master.

Outline Duties:
Standing by to blow open the dock gates leading to the Bassin de Paris and Bassin Duquesne.

Ship: Chasseur Q14
Name: No. 2 Dock Operating Party
Personnel:
Asst. Dock Master (Lt.).

1 Sub-Lt. (E).
1 P.O.
1 Shipwright (or Blk.).
1 Stoker P.O.
6 A.B.s.
5 Motor Mechanics.

Outline Duties:
Opening bridges and locks, Assist No. 1 Dock Operating Party

Ship: Chasseur Q14
Name: R.M. Headquarters, No. 2 Demolition Party, R.M.
Personnel:
1 Officer.
11 Other Ranks.
10 Royal Marines under the orders of the Asst. Dock Master.

Outline Duties:
Assist No. 1 Demolition Party

Ship: Chasseur Q43
Name: Dock Assault Force (1 Platoon R.M.)
Personnel:
2 Officers.
3 N.C.O.s.
33 Other Ranks.

Outline Duties:
As detailed by Officer Commanding R.M. Commando.

Ship: Chasseur Q42
Name: Dock Assault Force (1 Platoon R.M.)
Personnel:
1 Officers.
1 N.C.O.s.
25 Other Ranks.

Outline Duties:
As detailed by Officer Commanding R.M. Commando.

APPENDICES

Ship: Chasseur *Q13*
Name: Dock Assault Force (1 Platoon R.M.)
Personnel: Outline Duties:
1 Officers.   As detailed by Officer Commanding
1 N.C.O.s.   R.M. Commando.
25 Other Ranks.

Ship: Chasseur *Q10*
Name: Dock Assault Force (1 Platoon R.M.)
Personnel: Outline Duties:
2 Officers.   As detailed by Officer Commanding
3 N.C.O.s.   R.M. Commando.
35 Other Ranks.

Ship: Chasseur *Q41*
Name: Dock Assault Force (1 Platoon R.M.)
Personnel: Outline Duties:
1 Officers.   As detailed by Officer Commanding
1 N.C.O.s.   R.M. Commando.
25 Other Ranks.

Ship: Chasseur *Q5*
Name: Engine Room Party
Personnel: Outline Duties:
1 Lieut. (E).   Starting up invasion barges and other
1 Sub-Lt. (E).   craft in harbour.
3 E.R.A.s.
11 Ldg. Stokers.
5 Stokers.

Ship: Chasseur *Q5*
Name: No. 3 Demolition Party, R.M.
Personnel: Outline Duties:
10 Other Ranks.   In reserve, reporting to H.Q.

Ship: L.C.T. 124
Name: No. 1 Working Party
Personnel: Outline Duties:
1 Lt. or Sub-Lt.   Under orders of Naval Dock Master
1 P.O.   Cutting Out invasion barges in the
2 Ldg. Sea.   Bassin de Paris, assisted by R.M.
7 A.B.s   Commandos.

APPENDICES

Ship: L.C.T. 124
Name: No. 2 Working Party
Personnel:
1 Lt. or Sub-Lt.
1 P.O.
3 Ldg. Sea.
6 A.B.s

Outline Duties:
Under orders of Naval Dock Master Cutting Out invasion barges in the Bassin de Paris, assisted by R.M. Commandos.

Ship: L.C.T. 125
Name: No. 3 Working Party
Personnel:
1 Lt. or Sub-Lt.
1 P.O.
3 Ldg. Sea.
7 A.B.s

Outline Duties:
Under orders of Naval Dock Master Cutting Out invasion barges in the Bassin de Paris, assisted by R.M. Commandos.

Ship: L.C.T. 125
Name: No. 4 Working Party
Personnel:
1 Lt. or Sub-Lt.
3 Ldg. Sea.
6 A.B.s

Outline Duties:
Under orders of Naval Dock Master Cutting Out invasion barges in the Bassin de Paris, assisted by R.M. Commandos.

Ship: L.C.T. 165
Name: No. 5 Working Party
Personnel:
1 Lt. or Sub-Lt.
3 P.O.
6 Ldg. Sea.
4 A.B.s

Outline Duties:
Under orders of Naval Dock Master Cutting Out invasion barges in the Bassin de Paris, assisted by R.M. Commandos.

Ship: L.C.T. 166
Name: No. 6 Working Party
1 Lt. or Sub-Lt.
3 Ldg. Sea.
6 A.B.s

Under orders of Naval Dock Master Cutting Out invasion barges in the Bassin de Paris, assisted by R.M. Commandos.

Appendix Q

OPERATION JUBILEE
ORDERS FOR WITHDRAWAL OF TROOPS AND RETURN PASSAGE

General
Detailed orders for the withdrawal and return passage cannot be rigidly laid down because the tactical situation during the re-embarkation of troops cannot accurately be forecast. The following instructions are issued as a general guide.

It is impressed on all concerned that large deviations from this plan must be expected.

The intention is that all tanks and the majority of the troops are re-embarked from "Red" and/or "White" beaches. Some troops will be re-embarked from the east side of the harbour and some possibly from the harbour. The method of withdrawal is basically the same for all days and varies only in the detailed timings. The time at which withdrawal is to begin, and the speed at which it will take place is governed, as far as the Navy is concerned, by the times when the tide is suitable (*i.e.* rising) for re-embarking:
(*a*) Tanks.
(*b*) Troops.

For the above reason the withdrawal on 18th to 21st August inclusive will be carried out on a "two-tide basis" and that on 22nd and 23rd on a "one-tide basis". "Two-tide basis" means that there will be a low tide between the time of landing and the embarkation of tanks. A "one-tide basis" means that the re-embarkation of tanks takes place on the same rising tide as the landing.

Executive Order to Withdraw
The executive order to withdraw will be given by the Naval and

Military Force Commanders in the form "Vanquish" (followed by a time).

This time will be known as "W" hour, and all times for withdrawal are based on this hour.

Once the operation has been launched the tables for the requisite day only should be left in the orders, the others being removed.

Delegation of Duties for Withdrawal
The Principal Beachmaster is responsible for calling in what craft he requires at the various times and to which beaches they are to go for re-embarkation. He will transmit his requirements for craft to the Boat Pool Officer, who will detail the craft required. The P.B.M. and Boat Pool Officer are to work out a programme in as much detail as possible before the operation takes place. In principle, *L.C.M., L.C.P. and L.C.T., Mk. III, should be used first, L.C.A. being left to make the final withdrawal of infantry.*

Once landing craft have been ordered to leave the beaches by the P.B.M. or his representative after loading, they come under the orders of the Boat Pool Officer.

Withdrawal from "Yellow" and "Orange" Beaches
The withdrawals from "Yellow" and "Orange" beaches are separate operations.

Return Passage
The intention is that landing craft will return to England in three main groups. The "composition" of each group is given as a rough guide only.

Assembly and Departure of each Group
Landing craft will assemble in their return groups round certain ships as follows:

Return Group 1 (Sunbeam 3) L.C.F. (L) 1
Return Group 2 (Sunbeam 4) L.C.F. (L) 5
Return Group 3 (Sunbeam 5) L.C.F. (L) 4

The approximate positions of L.C.F. (L) are shown on diagram of positions of ships and craft off "Red" and "White" beaches. L.C.F. (L) are to fly the number of their group.

Responsibility for Sailing Groups

The Boat Pool Officer is responsible for directing landing craft to assemble in their various return groups; he is also responsible for sailing the various groups. Approximate times for sailing groups and their speed of advance are given in *Appendix C*. These are only meant as a guide, and it is at the discretion of the Boat Pool Officer if he sails a group earlier or later.

Escort for Return Groups

The Naval Force Commandeer will detail destroyers to escort return groups. L.C.F. (L) other than those on which return groups are assembling will return with Return Group 3, unless otherwise ordered.

Formation of Ships in a Return Group

It is intended that vessels in a return group should proceed across the Channel in an order which will provide the best A.A. defence. Senior Officers of vessels are accordingly to form up their units as follows:
- (a) L.C.A. (with their L.C.S. and L.C.M. if in company) are to be in single line ahead and will be the centre column (or columns) of a return group.
- (b) L.C.P. flotillas are to be in single line ahead on each flank of the L.C.A.
- (c) L.C.T. are to be in single line ahead. If there is more than one column of L.C.T. in a return group, the Senior Officer of the L.C.T. present is to arrange that one column is on the starboard and one on the port flank, outside the L.C.P. flotillas.
- (d) Chasseurs with lighters in tow, are to form astern of the columns.
- (e) L.C.F. (L) are to take up positions outside the L.C.T. columns suitably spaced to provide equal A.A. fire against a flank attack.
- (f) The Senior Officer Destroyers present is to distribute destroyers, M.G.B.s and S.G.B.s ahead and astern of the columns to provide A.A. fire against an air attack from these directions.
- (g) M.L.s are to act independently in line ahead; the Senior Officer should detach any M.L.s to take stragglers in tow.

It is important that vessels do not straggle astern; the Senior Officer of a return group is to adjust the speed accordingly and order destroyers or other vessels to take craft in tow who are unable to keep up.

A destroyer will be detailed by signal to act as the guide of a return group. She is to hoist a large Black Flag where it can best be seen to indicate "I am the guide of a return group."

APPENDICES

Return of Chasseurs and Towing of Invasion Barges
Chasseurs will tow invasion barges back but it is hoped that more than the chasseurs can manage will be removed from the harbour. If this is the case, M.L.s, destroyers and H.M.S. *Locust* should take a barge in tow. The Senior Officer Cutting Out Party will order the chasseurs when to return and they may sail independently of return groups.

Return Route
All ships and craft are to return by one or other of the two swept channels. Return Groups 1 and 3 are to use the western swept channel, Return Group 2 the eastern one.

Ships and craft are then to proceed to the vicinity of position NN thence as follows:
  (a) All landing craft smaller than L.C.T.s are to proceed to Newhaven to land troops, refuel, etc., and then as directed by N.O.I.C. Newhaven. Craft which sailed from Shoreham should, however, endeavour to return there and not call at Newhaven unless it is essential to refuel.
  (b) All L.C.T.s and L.C.F. (L)s are to proceed to Portsmouth, passing to the northward of QZX 769, anchoring to the eastward of the Looe channel until dawn.
  (c) Coastal craft are to proceed in company with L.C.T.s and L.C.F. (L) unless otherwise ordered.
  (d) Destroyers will remain in company with return groups to approximate position NN and then provide cover to seaward.
  Craft with badly wounded personnel on board which would normally be proceeding to Portsmouth are to land their wounded at Newhaven *en route* if there is sufficient light for them to enter the harbour, or weather conditions permit of transfer to be made outside the harbour. When approaching Newhaven in daylight, L.C.T. are to fly a signal indicating number of wounded on board.

Air Protection
When return groups are sailed they will use the code word "*Sunbeam*" with consecutive numbers, for "help" messages. The Naval Force Commander will make a signal to the Commander-in-Chief, Portsmouth, when each group is sailed, giving time of departure and speed on passage. Thus, for example, if the 3rd group is sailed at 1335 to proceed at 8 knots, the signal will be:
Sunbeam 3 – 1335 – 8.

The Senior Officer of the return group will keep the Commander-in-Chief and the Naval Force Commander informed of any alterations which he has made in the speed or route of a group returning to England. This information will be passed to No. 11 Group by Commander-in-Chief Portsmouth.

Special Group for Evacuation of Wounded
It may be desirable to despatch some craft, probably L.C.T.s, with wounded on board earlier than with the normal groups. The decision to do this will lie with the P.B.M., Senior Medical Officers and the Naval Force Commander. This group will be referred to as *"Sunbeam O."*

Appendix R

OPERATION JUBILEE
ORDERS FOR NAVAL BEACH PARTIES

Distribution
Naval Beach parties and Beach Signal parties will be distributed as follows:

Beach.	Offs. Men.	Offs. Men.	Ship	Remarks
Yellow	1+	1 + 4	L.C.P. (L)	
Green	2 + 4* (BM)	1	P. Beatrix	(First flight.)
	1 + 4* (ABM)	3	Invicta	(To land after first flight.)
White	1 + 4 (ABM)	1	Glengyle	(First flight.)
	1 + 12 (BM)	1 + 10	L.C.T.	
Red	1 + 4 (ABM)	1	P. Charles	(First flight.)
	1 + 12 (BM)	1 + 13	L.C.T.	(Transfer to M.L.s.)
	2 + 2† (PBM)	1	P. Charles	(To land after first flight.)
		8*	S.L.C.T.	(Smoke party.)
Blue	1 + 4† (BM)	2	Q. Emma	
	2†	2	P. Astrid	
Orange	1 + 2† (BM)	1 + 4	P. Albert	
Totals	14 + 56	4 + 42	= 18 + 98	

Notes – Parties marked * and † are from the same beach party unit.

Organisation
General – (a) Since Jubilee is generally a one-flight landing, the Naval Beach parties will not be able to assist the assault except as regards craft and vehicles which may have got into difficulties, and the subsequent flights of L.C.T.

(*b*) During the military operations inland, the Naval Beach parties will prepare the beaches for a smooth and expeditious withdrawal.
(*c*) It is therefore clear that the main function of the Naval beach parties is to organise the withdrawal in such a way that changes in plan and circumstance can be readily absorbed into a simple and flexible scheme.

Duties and Movements of Naval Beach Personnel
(*a*) *The Principal Beachmaster (P.B.M.)* is the chief Naval authority on land and is responsible for the Naval organisation on the beach to implement the plan. He will work in close co-operation with the Principal Military Landing Officer (P.M.L.O.) at the Beach Headquarters which will be distinguished by a White Ensign and will be situated in the best place for controlling red and white beaches – probably near their common boundary.
(*b*) *The Beachmasters (B.M.)* are responsible for the detailed organisation of their beaches to implement the instructions received from the P.B.M. They are, under the P.B.M., the chief Naval authorities on their beaches and are to act on their own initiative in accordance with the general plan in the absence of specific instructions. They work in close co-operation with the Assistant Military Landing Officer (A.M.L.O.) on their beaches.
(*c*) *Beach Signal Officers (or Senior Ratings)* are responsible to the Beachmasters for all the communications on their beaches. They are to keep the B.M. informed of all signals made and received and of any breakdown in communications, since on the smooth working of signals depends the flexibility of the organisation.
(*d*) *Beach Provost-Marshal* is responsible that the orders given by the B.M. are carried out rapidly. He will resolve any difficulties arising from conflicting orders and see that boats are manned and despatched expeditiously and that the boat officers understand their orders.
(*e*) *Detailed Duties of Beach Parties* – (i) *"Red" and "White" beaches* – The Beach parties will land and remain throughout on these beaches.
(ii) *"Blue" and "Green" beaches* – The Beach parties will remain on their beaches until contact has been made by land with Jubilee. When the A.M.L.O. informs the B.M. that such contact has been made and that no further casualties will be sent back to the beaches, the B.M. is to withdraw his party and report to the P.B.M. The B.M. of "Green" beach will then be responsible for organising the placing and lighting of smoke generators for the final withdrawal.
(iii) *"Yellow" and "Orange" beaches* – These being self-contained operations under their own commanders, the beach parties will return to England with the troops and landing craft operating with them.
(*f*) *Chain of Command* – In the event of casualties the duties of P.B.M. on

shore will devolve as follows:

P.B.M.	Commander Lambert.
B.M. (Green)	Lt.-Commander Prior.
B.M. (Red)	Lieut. Bibby.
B.M. (White)	Lieut. Ross.
B.M. (Green)	Lieut. Oakley.
B.M. (Blue)	Lieut. Warnecke.
A.B.M.(Green)	Lieut. Miller.
A.B.M. (Red)	S/Lieut. Haslett.
A.B.M. (White)	S/Lieut. Lomas.

Withdrawal Plan

(*a*) *Casualties* – During the military operations the only withdrawal to take place will be that of wounded men. Four L.C.T. arriving with stores will be available for this duty and will take up to 250 men on stretchers in all. The P.B.M. will be informed of the numbers of wounded and will call in the L.C.T. informing the B.M. of his requirements regarding it. Casualties in small numbers arriving on the beaches may be sent off by the Beach-masters to L.C.F. The B.M. is to keep the P.B.M. informed of the numbers despatched and their whereabouts.

(*b*) The withdrawal is planned to take 3½ hours. No rigid plan can be made as it depends on the military situation inland at the time. An outline time-table is given in the next paragraph and the following principles are laid down as a guide to B.M.s:

(i) Troops and tanks will assemble under cover at the back of the beach (or in the streets leading to the sea front) and will not move towards the boats until ordered by the A.M.L.O.

(ii) L.C.T. are not to wait on the beach longer than is necessary to load.

(iii) L.C.T. are to take 200 men + 10 wounded on stretchers in addition to vehicles.

(*c*) *Outline Withdrawal Time-table* – (i) *Two-tide Plan*:
"W" Hour
The time when the Military Force Commander orders the withdrawal. (No troops or tanks may be expected for ½ hour).

	Troops.	Tanks.
W + ½ Hour	500	
W + 1 Hour	310	15
W + 1½ Hours	390	
W + 2 Hours	360	18
W + 2½ Hours	1125	
	260*	16

APPENDICES

W + 3 Hours	620	
	90*	6
W + 3½ Hours	355	3
	40*	10 Bren Carriers
W + 3¾ Hours	200	
Totals	3860	58
	390*	10 Bren Carriers

*To be embarked from *eastern* side of Harbour.

Appendix S

DETAILED MILITARY PLAN

ANNEX 2
DETAILED MILITARY PLAN

Reference Map: France
1/50000 sheets
8D/6, 9D/5.
1 in. to 0.79 miles

Intention
The 2nd Canadian Division will:
  (a) Seize "Jubilee" and vicinity.
  (b) Occupy the area until demolition and exploitation tasks are completed.
  (c) Re-embark and return to England.

Method
  Phase   Detail
  I.   Embarkation
          Part 1. Allotment of personnel, equipment and stores.
          Part 2. Movement arrangement to Ports of Embarkation.
  II.   Assault and occupation
  III.   Engineer demolition tasks
  IV.   Withdrawal and re-embarkation
  V.   Disembarkation and dispersal in England

Zero
0450 hrs.
Delay in Touch Down Main Assault
If the time is delayed at which the L.C.A. are to be lowered for the main

assault the time of the main landing will be correspondingly delayed. Therefore, the air support for the assault on "White" and "Red Beaches" must also be delayed to the same extent. Any such delay in the predicted touchdown on "White" and "Red Beaches" will be notified to all concerned as soon as wireless silence can be broken by means of the code word Suspender, followed by the amount of the delay in minutes. The tasks specified in the detailed phases of the assault and occupation will be continued in sequence without reference to zero timings.

Command of Forces Participating
Joint command of the force will be exercised as follows:

Force	Command	Location
Naval Force	Capt. J Hughes Hallet, R.N.	H.Q. Ship No. 1.
Military Force	Maj-Gen. J.H. Roberts, M.C.	H.Q. Ship No. 1.
Air Force	Air Marshal T. Leigh-Mallory C.B., D.S.O.	H.Q. No.11 Group Uxbridge.

Chain of Command – Military Force
In the event of the Military Force Commander becoming a casualty or of the severance of all communications with him, the seniority of chain of command will be as follows:

(a) Brig C.C. Mann — B.G.S. 1 Canadian Corps on H.Q. Ship No. 2.
(b) Brig. W.W. Southam, E.D. — 6 Canadian Infantry Bde.
(c) Brig. Sherwood Lett, M.C. — 4 Canadian Infantry Bde.
(d) Lt.-Col. G.P. Henderson. — G.S.O. 1 First Canadian Army on H.Q. Ship No. 1.

Distribution of Commanders and Staff on H.Q. Ships:
Appendix J
Two destroyers will be used as H.Q. Ships.
  (a) H.M.S. *Calpe* H.Q. Ship No. 1.
  (b) H.M.S. *Fernie* H.Q. Ship No. 2.

Beach Organisation and A.A. Defence Ashore – *See Appendix K*
The beach organisation will consist of:
  (a) *Naval Staff* (under P.B.M.)
    Responsible to the Naval Force Commander for the control of all landing craft and personnel in the Naval beach area.
  (b) *Military Staff* (under P.M.L.O.)
    Responsible (in collaboration with Naval Staff to the Military

Force Commander for:
(i) Control of all personnel, tanks and vehicles in Military beach area.
(ii) A.A. protection in Naval and Military beach area.
(iii) Keeping the Military Force Commander informed at all times of the situation on the beaches, and during evacuation of the numbers of personnel, tanks and vehicles re-embarked.

(c) *Beach Provost Officer*. A Provost Officer from the Royal Marines is to be detailed by the Naval Force Commander. He will be responsible to the Naval and Military Force Commanders (through P.B.M. and P.M.L.O.) for discipline and order on the beaches.

Warning Signal for Major Demolitions in Beach Area
A white or red ground flare in vicinity of target will indicate that a major demolition will be blown in approximately 30 seconds.
All personnel within 300 yards of the flare are within the danger area and must take immediate cover.

Press, Official Observers and Special Parties.
(a) Details of all special personnel who are to accompany the Military Force on the operation, and orders and instructions for them are given at Control.
(b) Any such attached personnel will be under command of the Military Force Commander and are subject to Military Law from the time at which they are attached to the Force until dispersal in England has been completed.

Identification and Recognition
(a) *Captured enemy batteries* – In order to ensure that captured enemy batteries are not fired on by our tanks or other troops, a Union Jack will be flown where it is clearly visible over the site of any enemy battery occupied by our own troops.
(b) *Enemy vehicles* – A Union Jack will be draped over any captured enemy vehicle that is being used by our own troops. In the event that a Union Jack is not available all ranks will be warned that the fact that the vehicle is being used by our troops must be advertised by prominent display of the personnel.

(c) *Officers' identity cards (AFB 2606)* – Officers will not land with identification cards (AFB 2606) in their possession.
The military officer in charge in each ship or craft is responsible for

collecting identification cards from all military officers in his ship or craft before *zero*. These will be tied up in sandbags provided for the purpose and handed to the Commanding Officer of the ship or craft for safe keeping and will be collected for re-distribution after dispersal in England has been completed.

When required, officers will show their identity discs and repeat the password.

(*d*) *Other Ranks' Pay Books (AB 64)* – All other ranks will carry pay books (AB 64). When required, they will also show their identity discs and repeat the password.

(*e*) *Pass Words* – During the operation the password will be *McNaughton*.

(*f*) *Battle Patches and Unit Badges* – Unit badges will be worn and all ranks will either:

(i) wear 2 Cdn. Div. Battle patches, or
(ii) wear none at all.

Documents and Papers Carried Ashore

(*a*) *Personal Papers* – No personal papers will be carried ashore.

The Military officer in charge in each ship or craft is responsible for collecting personal documents from all ranks in his ship or craft before zero. These will be tied up in sandbags provided for the purpose and handed to the Commanding Officer of the ship or craft for safe keeping and will be collected for re-distribution after dispersal in England has been completed.

(*b*) *Orders, Maps, Photographs and Operational Documents* – (i) Each Brigade H.Q. is authorised to carry ashore two complete copies of the Detailed Military Plan (one in each H.Q. craft). *No other copies of orders will be taken ashore* and any information required for the conduct of the operation will be carried as notes. Maps and photographs will be carried as required for operational purposes.

All ranks will ensure that no orders, maps, photographs, operational documents or notes fall into enemy hands.

(ii) On completion of the operation, all copies of orders, maps and photographs will be collected.

French Nationals

(*a*) *Evacuation of Civilians* – (i) The policy on the question of whether or not to evacuate any of the civil population is, as a principle, to avoid taking off anybody. To implement this policy, certain personnel will be supplied with posters and leaflets informing the French that no help from them is required and that it will not be possible to take any of them back to England.

(ii) Notwithstanding the distribution of such notices, men, women and children may, in the last stages of withdrawal, create scenes in their attempts to obtain evacuation. Last minute evacuation of such individuals as cannot reasonably be left behind may be made on humanitarian grounds. Should any such evacuees be men of military age they are to be warned that they will be required to serve with the Fighting French Forces. For purposes of handling requests to be taken back, there will be attached to the Force one officer and six other ranks of French nationality who will select a limited number (up to 12).

(iii) There is one other exception to this ban against bringing French personnel back and this applies to fisherfolk who have their own craft. Such persons, if indicating a desire to escape with their own craft, should be permitted to put to sea to return to England under the escort of our own forces.

(b) *French Quislings* – No action should be attempted against such persons and all denunciations should be answered by stating that the French people themselves must deal with the matter.

(c) *Conversation with civilians* – Any questions about the establishment of a second front or about action which the French should take should be dealt on the lines of "You will be told when the time for action arrives. Meanwhile, do nothing impetuous that may endanger your life or liberty but wait for the call to action. Take cover now, there is no occasion to join in in this battle"

Looting

(a) *Looting in any form is Strictly Forbidden* – The enforcement of this prohibition is a matter of great importance as the political effects of any stories of looting would be disastrous. The German occupying troops have set a high standard of individual behaviour, in spite of the organised looting of France. By this standard we shall be judged.

(b) Special passes will be signed by the Military Force Commander and issued to those individuals or parties who are authorised to bring back articles.

Reference Code Words and Special Signals

Code words have been allotted as follows:
- (a) To designate Company and Platoon localities and the most important known or suspected enemy objectives.
- (b) Special signals for use only by Force H.Q. issued as Part II of *Appendix S* with limited distribution.

APPENDICES

Synchronisation
All times quoted in this operation order and appendices are B.S.T.
All watches will be synchronised with ships' official time before *zero*.

Cancellation of the Operation
If the operation has to be cancelled after the ships have sailed the decision must be made before 0300 hours.

Appendix T

INFORMATION – ENEMY

Enemy Order of Battle.
(*a*) The Dieppe area is held by the 110th German Infantry Division, a first line division originally recruited from the Oldenburg district of Germany. It has recently seen service on the Russian front and has been sent to France to rest and refit, where it relieved the 302nd Infantry Division. Whilst the division may not be up to full strength, it has a good fighting record.
(*b*) The 110th Inf. Div. consists of the 252, 254 and 255 Inf. Regts. Its coastal front is approximately from St. Valery-en-Caux to St. Valery-sur-Somme. All three regiments hold sectors of the coast.
(*c*) *Flanks* – West of the 110th Div. the 332nd Div. hold the coast from St. Valery-en-Caux to the estuary of the Seine. East of the 110th Div. the coastal sector from (incl.) Boulogne to the R. Somme is held by 321st Div.
(*d*) *Reserves* – The 110th Div. is in 81 Army Corps. As far as is known, there are no divisions in Corps Reserve. The 10th Armoured Div. is centred on Amiens and would be available to support troops holding the Dieppe area. Tanks have been reported in Albert (just east of Amiens) and it is believed that some armoured troops are in Abbeville, 36 miles from Dieppe.
(*e*) The S.S. "Adolf Hitler" Div. was recently reported near Paris and the presence of S.S. "Reich" Div. is confirmed in Brittany. The S.S. "Adolf Hitler" is a motorised division. It possesses about 12-15 armoured cars but no tanks. In spite of continuous action in Russia it is now considered to be up to strength after refitting. It is one of the German crack divisions. Its arrival is thought to be due to the imminent departure of the 10th Armoured Division.

Enemy Dispositions.
(*a*) In the past, the town of Dieppe has normally been held by one

Infantry Battalion and ancillary troops. A number of buildings facing the sea (notably the hotels) are occupied by the military. The barracks on Rue Gambetta are about a mile from the shore and are in use.

(b) Another bn. of the same regt. is on the coast 8-10 miles west of Dieppe with H.Q. at Blosseville. The location of the third bn. is uncertain, but it is possibly held in reserve within a few miles of the coast. Its H.Q. are probably at Bacqueville.

(c) The regiment holding the coast east of Dieppe has one bn. in the Tréport-Eu area. Locations of the other two bns. are not known. One, however, is probably near Dieppe on the east side of the river Arques.

Defences.

(a) The line of the coast is held by a system of "posts" each of about 30 men with four machine-guns. On the beaches, these "posts" will be fairly close together so as to keep the whole of beach under fire.

(b) The coastguard stations are manned by German Marines.

(c) A.A. Guns – Heavy A.A. guns are sited on the cliffs about half-mile east and west of Dieppe. Another battery is situated south-west of the town about 219670.

Light A.A. guns are situated near the R.D.F. station at Caude-Côte. As these guns are readily mobile, other batteries are arranged as required.

(d) M.G.s – Numerous M.G. casemates are all along the coast, especially at the beaches. All of these, however, are not occupied at all times. It is known that some are dummies. In Dieppe itself, there are M.G. posts at many of the street junctions, so sited as to enfilade the main roads, and to cover open places. Especially to be noted are the following:
  (i)   Strong M.G. post at road junction 223683.
  (ii) Casemate at 230691 on the Boulevard Maréchal Foch, recently completed, measures 35 by 20 ft.
  (iii) M.G.s are sited on roof of barracks on Rue Gambetta.
  (iv) A pill-box, 15 ft. square, has been constructed at 237660 covering the southern approach to the town.
  (v)   At 198681 is a recently constructed casemate 16 ft. square, which appears to face east and north.
  (vi) It has not been possible to deny or confirm the existence of M.G. posts in the low cliffs to the east of the entrance to the harbour.

(e) Artillery   There are nine known battery positions which could be used in the area of operations. Latest reports state, however, that two of these are only under construction and four are unoccupied. Of the remaining three, a six-gun battery is sited south-west of Varengeville (151673), a four-gun battery is on south-west outskirts of Dieppe (220665), and a four-gun battery south of Puits (258687). It is believed the Varengeville battery is on wheels; and the battery south-west of Dieppe may be field artillery.

The Divisional Artillery (consisting normally of 48 guns plus 12 A.Tk. guns) is not permanently sited. It may be anticipated therefore that these guns are mobile and some at least can be brought into action at short notice at strategic points.

(*f*) *Strong Points, Wire etc.* – The most notable feature of the defences is the development of strong points inland and the rudimentary all-round defence of the port itself. These are shown in detail on the intelligence maps.

The wire on the beach and promenade may be electrified. No definite information, so far as Dieppe is concerned, is available, but the wire in Boulogne and other ports is known to be electrified from small transformer situated in the vicinity.

(*g*) *Obstacles* – All roads leading off "Red" and "White" beaches are blocked. Blocks appear to be masonry or concrete, are 3 to 4 ft. thick and 5 to 6 ft. high. The block on the Quai du Hable is 5 to 6 ft. thick and has a 9-ft. (approx.) gap, which can be closed. There is a 5-ft. gap in the Rue Sygogne block.

The four road blocks in 2569 (Puits) are probably wire obstacles.

(*h*) *Land Mines* – There is no evidence that the Germans have placed any land mines, either on the beach or inland, in the area of operations.

Strength of Resistance.

Up to 3 hours – One battalion in Dieppe, west of the river, supported by some 500 divisional or regimental troops. East of the river, probably a coy. of infantry, with some artillery and engineer troops.

Total (approx.) 1,700.

If 10 Armoured Div. Mechanised Recce Unit is still located in or near Abbeville (elements of 10 Armoured Div. were reported there in July) armoured cars and motor cycles could reach outskirts of Dieppe within *zero* plus 3 hours.

Rate of Reinforcement.

	Estimated strength
(*a*) *Within zero plus 5 hours* – Three coys. of infantry could be available in Dieppe from the east, plus additional divisional troops normally stationed in the regimental sector east of the area of operations.	600
	250
Should the Mechanised Recce. Unit be stationed at Amiens	<u>850</u>

it could also reach the battlefield within zero plus 5 hrs. (Normal strength is 12 heavy armoured cars, 36 light armoured cars and 130 motor cyclists)

(b) Within zero plus 8 hrs.

The reserve bn. from the south	800
Two coys. from the bn. on the west	400
Two coys. from the reserve bn. of the regiment on the east	400
	<u>1600</u>

In addition, the Tank Regiment of the 10th Armoured Divisions could reach the scene of operations within zero plus 8 hrs.

Locations of the Lorried Infantry and M/C Bn. are not certain, but are known to be based on Amiens. They are reported to be able to reinforce the forward troops within 4 hours after leaving.

(c) Within zero plus 15 hrs – Summary – By this time the whole of the 110 Infantry Division, the 10th Armoured Division and elements of the S.S. Adolf Hitler Division could be in action at the scene of the operations.

Tunnels and Caves.

(*a*) The underground reported to exist in Dieppe is said to run from the Château d'Arques, where the entrance is within the walls of the castle, to Dieppe. The entrance in the town is exactly opposite the Société Générale Bank building (south end of Rue Sygogne) and the entrance to the steps of the castle ground alongside. It is possible to make out the place by the junction of the cobbles where three roads meet, Rue Sygogne, Rue de la Barre and Rue Toustain.

(*b*) It is reported that the caves in the cliff about 237692 overlooking the east side of the harbour entrance are being used as a store for 2,300 torpedoes. It is known that E-boats which carry torpedoes are based at Dieppe.

W/T Stations.

A second RDF (Freyer) Unit has been located on the cliff edge approx. 340 yards west of the R.D.F. station at 207682.

Trawlers and E-boats.

Four trawlers, each armed with two 4-in. guns, operate from Dieppe and may be found berthed in the Outer Harbour. Up to ten E-boats are also based on Dieppe and are usually berthed at Quai Henri IV.

(*Note –* This situation is changing all the time, therefore the information could not be considered as firm.)

Appendix U

ASSAULT AND OCCUPATION

Wing Landings ("Orange" and "Yellow" beaches)
4 and 3 Commandos will destroy the enemy batteries in the vicinity of "Orange" and "Yellow" beaches, sited to cover the main beaches and the sea approaches. In the event that either commando is unsuccessful it *must* remain and pin the enemy until ordered to withdraw by the Military Force Commander.

Flank Landings ("Green" and "Blue" beaches)
South Saskatchewan Regiment must secure "Green" beach with the minimum delay to enable Camerons of Canada to pass through without opposition. "Green" beach station will only close down when it is assured that "White" and "Red" beaches are in our hands and therefore that a route for withdrawal is open to South Saskatchewan Regiment and Camerons of Canada.

Royal Regiment of Canada must secure the east headland 2369 and 2469 with the minimum delay. The attack will be supported by:
 (i) Observed fire into the face of the cliff from the bombarding destroyers, which may include smoke.
 (ii) Smoke screens and/or smoke bombs by R.A.F. from zero plus 20 to zero plus 50.
 The planes will fly very low over "Blue" beach towards the harbour, in some cases below the top of the cliff, and all ranks must be warned not to engage them.
 (iii) 3-in. mortar detachment landing at zero plus 30 on east edge of "Red" beach.

When Royal Regiment of Canada is ready for the final assault on the east headland supporting fire will be stopped.

(*a*) *Naval support* by FOO.
(*b*) *Mortar support* by wireless.

Main Landings ("White" and "Red" beaches)

It is vital to the success of the operation as a whole that "White" and "Red" beaches be in our hands with the minimum delay.

The first flight on "White" and "Red" beaches touching down at zero plus 30 will act as follows:
   (*a*) Infantry will establish a bridgehead by immediate assault.
   (*b*) Infantry, Royal Canadian Army Service Corps, Royal Canadian Ordnance Corps and Provosts will provide off-loading parties for Royal Canadian Engineers assault detachments.
   (*c*) Royal Canadian Engineers detachments will clear necessary beach roadways and remove obstacles to permit tanks to enter "Jubilee".
   (d) Tanks will support the assault. 14 Canadian Army Tank Battalion will proceed to its objectives whether "White" and "Red" beaches are clear or not.

FOO will pass success word Trawlers (*i.e.* trawlers overcome) by R/T to H.M.S. *Locust*. If the Essex Scottish Regiment in co-operation with tanks are unable to capture the trawlers they will remain in observation in a position protected from the fire of H.M.S. *Locust*, which will engage the vessels unless it is clear that they are in our hands.

Mortar Detachments – (*a*) "White" beach (Calg. Highrs.) Will engage targets of opportunity to the west of and on "White" beach.
When "White" beach has been secured the detachment will report to H.Q. 6 Canadian Infantry Brigade when it will become the Brigade Commander's mortar reserve.
(*b*) "Red" beach (R.H.C. Mortar Detachment) – Primary task to support Royal Regiment of Canada in attack on east headland – unless notified by wireless from Royal Regiment of Canada that support is not required.
Secondary tasks targets of opportunity on "Red" beach.
When "Red" beach has been secured the detachment will report to H.Q. 4 Canadian Infantry Brigade when it will become the Brigade Commander's mortar reserve.

Reporting Success on Objectives

In the following schedules only the principal objectives have been given code names. Success will be reported by the objective code name followed by the time at which it was captured and nothing else. The code names may however be used to indicate the objective for other reasons.

Units may if they so desire allot other code names to minor objectives for their own use but not for reporting to Force H.Q.

These must be within the following alphabetical series:

4 Commando, words beginning with D.
S. Sask. R., words beginning with Q.
Camerons of C., words beginning with N.
R.H.L.I., words beginning with Y.
Essex Scot., words beginning with T.
R. Regt. C., words beginning with M.
3 Commando, words beginning with A.
Fus. M.R., words beginning with B.

Hospitals

Buildings which during the operation are definitely established as being used as hospitals will be treated as follows:

(*a*) Patrols will ensure that all communications are disrupted.
(*b*) The persons in charge will be instructed to deliver up all arms and German military, naval or air personnel who are *not* patients, and will be cautioned that failure to do so will result in offensive action.
(*c*) They will be instructed also that by so doing, the patients and medical staff will be granted sanctuary and treated in accordance with the Geneva Convention, providing that no offensive action is taken against our own troops by the staff or inmates.
(*d*) Sentries will be posted outside hospitals which conform to these directions to secure them from intrusion during the occupation.

Appendix V

SCHEDULE OF TIMINGS

Serial 1
Times Zero: Zero
Times BST: -
Beach: ORANGE
Unit: 4 Commando
Principal Objectives: (*a*) 6 gun bty., 151673.
                 (*b*) Lt. A.A. gun, 149675.
                 (*c*) Lt. A.A. gun, 151671.
Code Word: (*a*) PIGEON
                 (*b*) PINCER
                 (*c*) PIEFACE
Subsequent Action: Will report to Force H.Q. as soon as tasks completed and will receive orders either to return to England or to come in to Force reserve. If bty. cannot be destroyed, Commando will remain and pin until ordered to withdraw by M.F.C. To be taken off by R.N. at Varengeville.

Serial 2
Times Zero: Zero
Times BST: -
Beach: YELLOW
Unit: 3 Commando
Principal Objectives: (*a*) 4 gun btys., 309718.
                 (*b*) Possible 4 gun Bty., 314718.
                 (*c*) Lt. A.A. guns, 305718.
                 (*d*) Possible OP., 324728.
                 (*e*) Possible Lt. A.A. & OP., 308722.

APPENDICES

Code Word:	(*a*) PATRON
	(*b*) PAPOOSE
	(*c*) PANSY
	(*d*) PAGEBOY
	(*e*) PASTIME
Subsequent Action:	Will report to Force H.Q. as soon as tasks completed and will receive orders either to return to England or to come in to Force reserve. If btys. cannot be destroyed, Commando will remain and pin until ordered to withdraw by M.F.C. To be taken off by R.N. at Berneval.

Serial 3

Times Zero:	Zero
Times BST:	–
Beach:	GREEN
Unit:	One coy S. Sask. R.
Principal Objectives:	(*a*) Two Lt. A.A. guns, 212683.
	(*b*) R.D.F. Sta. and Lt. A.A. guns, 208683.
Code Word:	(*a*) STARDUST
	(*b*) STUDY
Subsequent Action:	Consolidate. Make contact with R.H.L.I. Assist in capture of Les-Quatre-Vents Ferme 2167 with ser. below. (*Note* – One tp. tks. is co-operating with R.H.L.I.)

Serial 4

Times Zero:	Zero
Times BST:	–
Beach:	GREEN
Unit:	One coy. S. Sask. R.
Principal Objectives:	(*a*) Lt. A.A. guns, 221678.
	(*b*) Les-Quatre-Vents Ferme, 2167 (also being attacked by R.H.L.I. with one tp. of tks. co-operating)
Code Word:	(*a*) SAMBO
	(*b*) SUDDEN
Subsequent Action:	Consolidate with above serial. Select emergency landing ground in area of Les-Quatre-Vents Ferme and mark in accordance with signal instructions *Appx Q*.

APPENDICES

Serial 5
Times Zero: Zero
Times BST: -
Beach: GREEN
Unit: One coy. S. Sask. R.
Principal Objectives: M.G. 185678.
Code Word: SAUCY
Subsequent Action: Hold locality secured until Camerons of C. have landed and beach is cleared of craft.

Serial 6
Times Zero: Zero
Times BST: -
Beach: GREEN
Unit: S. Sask. R. (less 3 coys.)
Principal Objectives: Offrs. Mess – La Maison Blanche – Pourville.
Code Word: SORRY
Subsequent Action: Consolidate to secure "Green" beach. Make contact with R.H.L.I. at Les-Quatre-Vents Ferme 2167.

Serial 7
Times Zero: In accordance with developments
Times BST: n accordance with developments
Beach: -
Unit: S. Sask. R.
Principal Objectives: Cover the west flanks of the outer perimeter of Dieppe. Pt. of junc. with R.H.L.I. – bldgs. at 215671.
Code Word: -
Subsequent Action: Withdrawal in accordance with *Appx. F.*

Serial 8
Times Zero: Zero
Times BST: -
Beach: BLUE
Unit: One coy. R. Regt. C.
Principal Objectives: Possible Lt. A.A. guns, 258697.
Code Word: ROSY
Subsequent Action: Bks. At Les Glycines holiday camp are occupied and should be dealt with if located by inquiry.

APPENDICES

Coy. becomes bn. reserve and detaches one pl. for following serial.

Serial 9
Times Zero: Zero
Times BST: -
Beach: BLUE
Unit: One pl. R. Regt. C.
Principal Objectives: M.G. posts area, 268704.
Code Word: ROVER
Subsequent Action: Pl. reverts to coy. (in bn. reserve).

Serial 10
Times Zero: Zero
Times BST: -
Beach: BLUE
Unit: One coy. R. Regt. C.
Principal Objectives: (*a*) Hy. A.A. bty, 245693.
(*b*) Lt. A.A. guns, 242693.
(*c*) Lt. A.A. guns, 239693.
Code Word: (*a*) RASTUS
(*b*) RACKET
(*c*) RASHER
Subsequent Action: Mop up Marines in coast gd. houses between Puits and S/L 240692. Est. contact with Essex Scot. in vicinity of S/L 245694. Afterward reverts to bn. reserve.

Serial 11
Times Zero: Zero
Times BST: -
Beach: BLUE
Unit: R. Regt. C. (less two coys.).
Principal Objectives: (*a*) 4 gun bty. 258688.
(*b*) 3 Lt. A.A. guns, 256685.
(*c*) M.G.s area, 254679.
Code Word: (*a*) RECORD
(*b*) REDEEM
(*c*) REVEAL
Subsequent Action: Serial 15.

Serial 12
Times Zero:	Zero
Times BST:	-
Beach:	BLUE
Unit:	R. Regt. C. (Reserve party).
Principal Objectives:	Co-operation with serial 10 in capture of objectives on east headland.
Code Word:	-
Subsequent Action:	Revert to bn. reserve.

Serial 13
Times Zero:	Zero
Times BST:	-
Beach:	BLUE
Unit:	Det. 3 Lt. A.A. Regt. R.C.A.
Principal Objectives:	Co-operate with serial 10 in capture of A.A. guns on east headland.
Code Word:	-
Subsequent Action:	If guns captured intact engage enemy ground and air targets (display Union Jack).

Serial 14
Times Zero:	Zero
Times BST:	-
Beach:	BLUE
Unit:	Det. 4 Cdn. Fd. Regt. R.C.A.
Principal Objectives:	Co-operate with serial 11 in capture of 4 gun bty, 258688.
Code Word:	-
Subsequent Action:	If enemy bty. captured intact det. will engage enemy 4 Gun bty. at 249645 and targets of opportunity (display Union Jack).

Serial 15
Times Zero:	In accordance with developments
Times BST:	in accordance with developments
Beach:	BLUE
Unit:	R. Regt. C.
Principal Objectives:	Gas Works 243675 (operators should be taken alive if possible and machinery left running until R.C.E. arrive. Best destruction results will be obtained thereby).

APPENDICES

Code Word: RUTTER
Subsequent Action: Detach one coy. to cover R.C.E. party arriving to destroy gas works. R.V. with R.C.E. S.W. corner of bldg. on east side of rd. at 243675. Proceed north into bde. res., via Route de Gisors (river rd.), clearing east side of harbour.

Serial 16
Times Zero: -
Times BST: -
Beach: BLUE
Unit: One coy. R. Regt. C. (detached).
Principal Objectives: Protecting R.C.E. demolition party arriving to destroy gas works, 243675.
Code Word: -
Subsequent Action: Return with RC.E. to rejoin bn. in bde. res.

Serial 17
Times Zero: Zero + 30
Times BST: -
Beach: WHITE
Unit: One coy. R.H.L.I.
Principal Objectives: Two Lt. A.A. guns, 212683 (make contact with S. Sask. R. – one tp. tks. is to co-operate).
Code Word: STARDUST
Subsequent Action: Assist in capture of posn. At Les-Quatre-Vents Ferme 2167. Consolidate.

Serial 18
Times Zero: Zero + 30
Times BST: -
Beach: WHITE
Unit: One coy. R.H.L.I.
Principal Objectives: (*a*) Four gun bty, 220665.
(*b*) Three Lt. A.A. guns, 219668.
(*c*) Enemy posns. at Les-Quarter-Vents Ferme 2167 (also being attacked by S. Sask. R. landing at Zero). (One tp. tks. is to co-operate).
Code Word: (*a*) HEAVEN
(*b*) HADES
(*c*) SUDDEN
Subsequent Action: Consolidate with serial 17.

APPENDICES

Serial 19
Times Zero: Zero + 30
Times BST: -
Beach: WHITE
Unit: One coy. R.H.L.I.
Principal Objectives: M.G. post 225673 (one tp. and one tk. sqn. H.Q. is to co-operate).
Code Word: HOLSTEIN
Subsequent Action: Adv. to control the Rue Gambetta as far as southern edge of town. Liaise with Essex Scot. rd. junc. 236664.

Serial 20
Times Zero: Zero + 30
Times BST: -
Beach: WHITE
Unit: R.H.L.I. (less three coys.).
Principal Objectives: Res.
Code Word: -
Subsequent Action: -

Serial 21
Times Zero: In accordance with developments
Times BST: In accordance with developments
Beach: -
Unit: R.H.L.I.
Principal Objectives: Secure perimeter from incl. bldgs. at 215671. Liaise with S. Sask. R. to excl. rd. junc. 236664. Liaise with Essex Scot.
Code Word: -
Subsequent Action: -

Serial 22
Times Zero: Zero + 30
Times BST: -
Beach: WHITE
Unit: One tp. tks.
Principal Objectives: Two Lt. A.A. Guns, 212683 (co-op with R.H.L.I., *see* ser. 17)
Code Word: STARDUST
Subsequent Action: Sqn. Control.

APPENDICES

Serial 23
Times Zero: Zero + 30
Times BST: -
Beach: RED
Unit: One coy. Essex Scot.
Principal Objectives: Cross brs. north or south of Bassin du Canada, 235680-234682. 3 Lt. A.A. guns, 237688
Code Word: EGHAM
Subsequent Action: Consolidate east bank of harbour.

Serial 24
Times Zero: Zero + 30
Times BST: -
Beach: RED
Unit: One coy. Essex Scot.
Principal Objectives: Seize armed trawlers at Quayside 233687 in co-operation with tanks and det. R.M. Commando landing from H.M.S. *Locust* and Chasseurs.
Code Word: TRAWLERS
Subsequent Action: Consolidate east bank of harbour. Select suitable area on east headland to be used as emergency landing ground and mark in accordance with signal instructions, *Appx. Q*.

Serial 25
Times Zero: Zero + 30
Times BST: -
Beach: RED
Unit: One coy. Essex Scot.
Principal Objectives: (*a*) 3 Lt. A.A. guns, 239671.
(*b*) Bty. posn., 235670.
(*c*) Lt. A.A. gun posn., 235661.
Code Word: (*a*) EAGLE
(*b*) EALING
(*c*) EASTER
Subsequent Action: Liaise with R.H.L.I. rd. junc. 236664. Secure perimeter to incl. br. 240673. Select emergency landing ground in area of Racecourse and mark in accordance with signal instructions, *Appx. Q*.

Serial 26

Times Zero:	Zero + 30
Times BST:	-
Beach:	RED
Unit:	Essex Scot. (less three coys.).
Principal Objectives:	(a) Clear east side of harbour.
	(b) Clear town of Neuville.
Code Word:	(a) ESSAY
	(b) ESTEEM
Subsequent Action:	Contact R. Regt. C. Consolidate.

Serial 27

Times Zero:	In accordance with developments
Times BST:	In accordance with developments
Beach:	RED
Unit:	Essex Scot. (less one coy.).
Principal Objectives:	Consolidate to hold east side of harbour.
Code Word:	-
Subsequent Action:	(a) Remain until Phase IV.
	(b) Supply local protection for ser. 28 (up to two pls).
	(c) Liaison offr. will est. contact with R.C.E. at br. 235682 to ensure protection for R.C.E. demolition party which is to work on cranes.
	(d) Supply local protection for A.A. and fd. arty. dets. in area 4-gun bty. 258688 and pass withdrawal signal to them when received.

Serial 28

Times Zero:	Zero + 30
Times BST:	-
Beach:	RED
Unit:	Two tps. tks. (one sqn. H.Q. and one tp.) Reinforced up to sqn. as soon as possible.
Principal Objectives:	Assist one coy. Essex Scot. in subduing armed trawlers at Quayside 233687. Then cross to east bank to support Essex Scot.
Code Word:	TRAWLERS
Subsequent Action:	Dominate east side of harbour and Arques from 265663. Up to two pls. from Essex Scot. for local protection will be carried fwd. on tks. if conditions allow.

APPENDICES

Serial 29
Times Zero: Zero + 30
Times BST: -
Beach: WHITE and RED
Unit: Two pls. Fus. MR.
Principal Objectives: Land in Flight 1 of L.C.T. Act as off loading party for engineer stores and assist in building beach roadways.
Code Word: -
Subsequent Action: Report to H.Q. 6, Cdn. Inf. Bde. and become Bde. Comd.'s immediate reserve.

Serial 30
Times Zero: Zero + 30
Times BST: -
Beach: RED
Unit: "Red" beach parties.
Principal Objectives: "Red" beach.
Code Word: -
Subsequent Action: "Red" beach control main beach station.

Serial 31
Times Zero: Zero + 30
Times BST: -
Beach: GREEN
Unit: Camerons of C.
Principal Objectives: Pass through beach head secured by S. Sask. R. and move to aerodrome with best possible speed, by-passing all enemy opposition where possible. Contact tanks vicinity north edge of Bois des Vertus, 2265.
Code Word: -
Subsequent Action: Capture aerodrome 2263 in co-operation with 14 Cdn. Army Tk. Bn. and supported by naval bombarding destroyers controlled by FOO with Bn.

Serial 32
Times Zero: Zero + 45
Times BST: -
Beach: WHITE

Unit:	"White" beach parties.
Principal Objectives:	"White" beach.
Code Word:	-
Subsequent Action:	"White" beach control.

Serial 33

Times Zero:	Zero + 45
Times BST:	-
Beach:	WHITE
Unit:	One tp. tks.
Principal Objectives:	(*a*) 4 gun bty. 220665.
	(*b*) Les-Quatre-Vents Ferme 2067 (co-op. with R.H.L.I.).
Code Word:	(*a*) HEAVEN
	(*b*) SUDDEN
Subsequent Action:	Sqn. Control.

Serial 34

Times Zero:	Zero + 45
Times BST:	-
Beach:	WHITE
Unit:	One tk. sqn. Hq. and one tp.
Principal Objectives:	M.G. post with R.H.L.I., 225673.
Code Word:	HOLSTEIN
Subsequent Action:	Co-operate with R.H.L.I.

Serial 35

Times Zero:	Zero + 1hr. 15
Times BST:	-
Beach:	WHITE
Unit:	Tk. bn. Hq.
Principal Objectives:	R.V. with H.Q. 6 Cdn. Inf. Bde. Church 225685, Eglise St. Rémy.
Code Word:	-
Subsequent Action:	Co-ordinate subsequent action of tk. bn. Control action in support of the Camerons of C.'s attack on aerodrome and exploitation.

Serial 36

Times Zero:	Zero + 1hr. 15
Times BST:	-

APPENDICES

Beach:	WHITE
Unit:	Command Post (with three scout cars "Hunter, "Hound", "Hare".)
Principal Objectives:	Report to Hq. 6 Cdn. Inf. Bde. at Eglise St Rémy, 225685.
Code Word:	-
Subsequent Action:	Remain with Hq 6 Cdn. Inf. Bde. till all tks. re-embarked.

Serial 37
Times Zero:	Zero + 1hr. 15
Times BST:	-
Beach:	RED
Unit:	4 Cdn. Inf. Bde. Hq.
Principal Objectives:	Eglise St. Jacques, 229685.
Code Word:	-
Subsequent Action:	-

Serial 38
Times Zero:	Zero + 1hr. 15
Times BST:	-
Beach:	RED
Unit:	4 Cdn. Inf. Bde. Signal Sta.
Principal Objectives:	As above.
Code Word:	-
Subsequent Action:	-

Serial 39
Times Zero:	Zero + 1hr. 15
Times BST:	-
Beach:	RED
Unit:	4 Cdn. Inf. Bde. Beach Signal Sta.
Principal Objectives:	"Red" beach.
Code Word:	-
Subsequent Action:	Open immediate comn. To "White" Beach and "Blue" Beach.

Serial 40
Times Zero:	Zero + 1hr. 15
Times BST:	-
Beach:	WHITE
Unit:	6 Cdn. Inf. Bde. Hq.

Principal Objectives: Eglise St. Rémy, 225685.
Code Word: -
Subsequent Action: -

Serial 41
Times Zero: Zero + 1hr. 15
Times BST: -
Beach: WHITE
Unit: 6 Cdn. Inf. Bde. Signal Sta.
Principal Objectives: As above.
Code Word: -
Subsequent Action: -

Serial 42
Times Zero: Zero + 1hr. 15
Times BST: -
Beach: WHITE
Unit: 6 Cdn. Inf. Bde. Beach Sig. Sta.
Principal Objectives: "White" Beach.
Code Word: -
Subsequent Action: Open immediate comns. To "Green" and "Red" beaches.

Serial 43
Times Zero: Zero + 1hr. 15
Times BST: -
Beach: WHITE
Unit: Two tps. (of sqn. Supporting R.H.L.I.).
Principal Objectives: As ordered by sqn. leader.
Code Word: -
Subsequent Action: -

Serial 44
Times Zero: Zero + 1hr. 15
Times BST: -
Beach: RED
Unit: One tp. (of sqn. supporting Essex Scot.).
Principal Objectives: Support No. 4 Commando or other tasks as ordered by sqn. leader.
Code Word: -
Subsequent Action: -

Serial 45
Times Zero: In accordance with developments
Times BST: In accordance with developments
Beach: -
Unit: Camerons of C. with in. sp. 14 Cdn. Army Tk. Bn. (less one sqn.).
Principal Objectives: (*a*) 3 Lt. A.A. guns, 224639.
(*b*) 2 Lt. A.A. guns, 234640.
(*c*) 3 Lt. A.A. guns, 233635.
Code Word: (*a*) CURFEW
(*b*) CURTAIL
(*c*) CURZON
Subsequent Action: -

Serial 46
Times Zero: In accordance with developments
Times BST: In accordance with developments
Beach: -
Unit: Camerons of C. with in. sp. 14 Cdn. Army Tk. Bn. (less one sqn.).
Principal Objectives: (*a*) Aerodrome, 2263.
(*b*) 4 gun Bty., 249645.
(*c*) H.Q. 110 Inf. Div. Arques 260636, or in chateau nearby.
(*d*) Hy. A.A. gun posn., 239653.
Code Word: (*a*) CABHORSE
(*b*) CAISSON
(*c*) CATSMEAT
(*d*) CANNIBAL
Subsequent Action: Return to Dieppe when withdrawal ordered.

Serial 47
Times Zero: In accordance with developments
Times BST: In accordance with developments
Beach: -
Unit: 14 Cdn. Army Tk. Bn. (lees one sqn.).
Principal Objectives: Co-operating with Camerons of C.
Code Word: -
Subsequent Action: Return to Dieppe when withdrawal ordered.

APPENDICES

Serial 48
Times Zero: Zero + 1hr. 15
Times BST: -
Beach: GREEN, WHITE or RED
Unit: Fus. M.R. (less two pls. landing in L.C.T.).
Principal Objectives: (3 miles off-shore at Zero plus 1 hr. 15. Can be landed by about Zero plus 2 hr.)
Code Word: -
Subsequent Action: On arrival at anchorage, O.C. Fus. M.R. will report on board H.Q. ship No. 1 (H.M.S. *Calpe*) to receive orders. Rear gd. on the westward side of the harbour covering re-embarkation.

Serial 49
Times Zero: Zero + 1hr. 55
Times BST: -
Beach: RED
Unit: Three tps. (of sqn. supporting Essex Scot.).
Principal Objectives: Cross to east side of river d'Arques and join C. sqn. unless otherwise ordered by Bn. Comd.
Code Word: -
Subsequent Action: -

Serial 50
Times Zero: Zero + 1hr. 55
Times BST: -
Beach: WHITE
Unit: Sqn. H.Q. (A. Sqn.).
Principal Objectives: R.V. bn. H.Q.
Code Word: -
Subsequent Action: Recce. and prepare for landing of floating reserve.

Serial 51
Times Zero: Zero + 2hrs. 15
Times BST: -
Beach: WHITE or RED
Unit: Up to 16 tks
Principal Objectives: R.V. bn. H.Q.
Code Word: -
Subsequent Action: Mobile reserve, probably exploit to Arques-la-Bataille.

Appendix W

DETAILED AIR PLAN

General
Operation "Jubilee" is a combined operation against occupied territory. A combined plan has been prepared and issued jointly by the three Force Commanders. The combined plan is being issued to Sector Commanders only in the case of the Air Forces.

The following is a very brief outline of the operation to serve as an introduction to the more detailed Air Force orders attached hereto.

Operation "Jubilee" involves landings by two Commandos on the outer flanks, together with simultaneous inner flank landings and a main frontal assault against the town of "Jubilee".

The operation is planned so that it can take place on any morning from 18th to 23rd August, 1942, inclusive. It will take place on the first day when weather conditions are suitable.

Outward Passage
The expedition will sail from the Portsmouth area and will make passage to the enemy coast. The greater part of the voyage will be completed in darkness.

Return Passage
The return route for all ships and craft will be via the swept Channel direct to Beachy Head and thence via the South Coast swept channels to Newhaven and Portsmouth.

All outgoing and returning Fighter sorties will follow this route. This will facilitate Air/Sea rescue and will provide Fighter cover for our surface craft proceeding to and from "Jubilee".

APPENDICES

Air/Sea Rescue

The Naval Force Commander will be responsible for Air/Sea rescue within a radius of three miles of "Jubilee" whilst our forces are in the vicinity of "Jubilee". All ships will keep a look-out for aircraft crews in distress. Special Air/Sea rescue arrangements are being made within the normal Air/Sea rescue organization at home.

Recognition of Surface Craft

Friendly surface vessels employed on this operation will show a recognition sign consisting of Yellow, Red, Yellow stripes extending athwartships. In destroyers the mark will be on the foreward and aft gunshields; in other vessels the mark will be on a painted canvas strip on the most conspicuous part of the vessel.

Recognition of our Own Ground Forces

Ground forces will not carry any special recognition markings. The area occupied by friendly forces will be notified periodically to Air Force units by No. 11 Group Operations. Attacks on ground targets will be confined to territory outside the area so defined.

During their time ashore our troops may seize and employ enemy guns. To aid recognition a Union Jack will be exposed at each gun position taken over.

Emergency Landing Grounds

Two suitable grounds for crash landing aircraft have been selected close to "Jubilee" within the area to be occupied by our forces. The most suitable of the two appears to be the racecourse to the south of the town of "Jubilee". The other is on the high ground south-east of the entrance to "Jubilee" harbour. Both these emergency landing grounds will be marked with ground strips by our forces during their occupation of "Jubilee". The direction of the wind, together with the most suitable landing lane, will be indicated. Pilots forced to crash land on these grounds are to ensure that their aircraft are destroyed before being abandoned. Pilots forced to land on these emergency grounds are to proceed to Brigade Headquarters situated in the Square near the two churches in the centre of the town of "Jubilee". As our troops withdraw from the area of these emergency landing grounds they will withdraw the ground strips. Pilots are then to bale out or force land as applicable into the sea alongside a friendly vessel if in distress.

The word "McNaughton" has been adopted as a pass-word for use by all ground personnel during the occupation. All pilots should know this in case they require to use the pass-word after force landing.

A.A. Danger Zone
The A.A. guns will have freedom to fire up to a height of 2,000 ft. Our own aircraft will not fly below 3,000 ft. except in pursuit of the enemy in the immediate vicinity of "Jubilee". Aircraft flying low or diving on our ships in the area occupied by our troops at "Jubilee" will be regarded as hostile. The same restrictions will apply to all aircraft during the return passage.

Selected ships in the expedition may fly balloons for protection against low flying attack. The operational height of these balloons will not exceed 1,500 ft. A small number of balloons may be flown also on the cliffs flanking the main beaches during our occupation of "Jubilee". These balloons will not be flown at a greater height than 700 ft. above sea level – that is 500 ft. above the cliff.

During our occupation of "Jubilee" extensive demolition will take place. These may constitute a danger to low-flying aircraft. Before any major demolition is exploded a white or red flare will be exposed at the exploder control 30 seconds before the main charge is due to explode. Low-flying aircraft should keep a sharp look-out for such warnings.

Communications
A Headquarters Ship and a Reserve Headquarters Ship carrying the Force Commanders and their deputies will accompany the expedition. These two ships will be equipped with the necessary signals facilities for communicating with aircraft and with their base at Portsmouth. These facilities will include VHF R/T for communication with aircraft. Detailed Signals Instructions are contained in *Appendix J*.

      T. Leigh-Mallory,
      Air Marshal,
13th August, 1942.   Air Force Commander.

SEQUENCE OF EVENTS

Timings of Landings – The assaults will be made as follows:
 (i) At 0450 on "Yellow" Beach – No. 3 Commando (450).
 (ii) At 0450 on "Orange" Beach – No. 4 Commando (250).
 (iii) At 0450 on "Blue" Beach – Royal Regiment of Canada (500).

APPENDICES

(iv) At 0450 on "Green" Beach – South Saskatchewan Regiment (500).
(v) At 0520 on "Red" Beach – Essex Scottish Regiment (500).
(vi) At 0520 on "Red" and "White" Beaches – 18 Tanks, 14th Canadian Army Tank Battalion.
(vii) At 0520 on "White" Beach – Royal Hamilton Light Infantry (500).
(viii) At 0520 on "Green" Beach – Camerons of Canada (500).

Air Programme
(i) A pair of Intruder Aircraft engage each of two gun batteries to the south of "Jubilee" with bombs and machine guns. (code word "Hitler" and "Goering") – 0445/0450.
(ii) Fighter cover – Two Squadrons patrol in vicinity of "Jubilee" – 0450/0520.
(iii) Six Bostons bomb battery position "Rommel" (If smoke curtain is to be laid) – 0509.
(iv) Fourteen Bostons and eight Blenheims lay smoke screen over East Cliff Headland to the east of "Jubilee" Harbour – 0510/0540.
(v) One flight of Hurricane bombers attack four-gun battery position approximately 1½ miles south of "Jubilee" (Code word for battery "Goering") – 0515.
One flight of Hurricane bombers attacks enemy Divisional Headquarters in the town of A..... – 0515.
One Squadron of Hurricane bombers attack enemy gun positions (Code word "Hitler") – 0515.
(vi) Five close support Fighter Squadrons attack the Beach area between the sea wall and the frontal buildings on the water front at "Jubilee" to cover our main landings at "White" and "Red" Beaches. The fighters will first engage enemy positions on the Beaches during the approach of and until the touchdown of our landing craft. The attack will then be switched to the buildings along the front which overlook the Beach from the time that our first troops step ashore.
A proportion of this Fighter effort will, at the same time, attack enemy defensive positions on the West Headland overlooking the beaches. (The code word allotted to this headland is "Hindenberg") – 0515/0525.
(vii) Fighter Cover – Six Squadrons patrol in the vicinity of "Jubilee" – 0520/0550.
(viii) Tactical Reconnaissance of roads converging on "Jubilee" by

APPENDICES

        aircraft in pairs as necessary by Army Co-operation aircraft – 0515 onwards.
- (ix) Two Squadrons of Day Bombers available (*i.e.* at 60 minutes notice) – 0530.
- (x) Fighter cover in vicinity of "Jubilee" reduced to four Squadrons – 0550/0650.
- (xi) One Squadron Cannon Fighters (Spitfires) attack "Hess" in support of Commando landing at "Orange" Beach – 0620.
- (xii) Fighter cover reduced to three Squadrons – 0650/until withdrawal starts.
- (xiii) If R.A.F. Force Commander fails to receive information of enemy reinforcements moving towards "Jubilee" by 0800 hours, a Close Support Squadron will be despatched to the area, on call to the Military Commander – 0830/0900.
- (xiv) Two Squadrons of Day Bombers at "Readiness" + with appropriate Fighter escort (*i.e.* 30 minutes notice) – 0900.
- (xv) Fighter Cover increased to six Squadrons from start of withdrawal and maintained until Force is 3 miles off shore on return passage – 1030/1330 (approximately).
- (xvi) Close Support Fighter Squadrons will be despatched to report to Headquarters Ship to attack targets in support of the withdrawal. Squadrons will be despatched at 20-minute intervals unless the Close Support Squadrons are already fully engaged in attacking previously selected targets.
- (xvii) Fighter Cover as necessary to cover return passage.

OPERATION INSTRUCTION FOR THE EMPLOYMENT OF CLOSE SUPPORT SQUADRONS

The Assault

The Close Support Fighter Squadrons will be employed against centres of resistance likely to interfere with the progress of our troops. They will operate also against the enemy reinforcements which approach the area of "Jubilee".

It is vital during the assault to concentrate every effort on getting our forces ashore. The success or failure of the whole expedition will probably depend on results achieved during this critical period.

All close support squadrons with the exception of one which is to be retained at readiness will be directed against targets the neutralisation of which will directly assist the assault. During attacks in support of the assault our troops will be already ashore on the flanks of "Jubilee" and the attention of the whole of the German defences will probably be focused on countering our frontal and flank assaults. The batteries behind "Jubilee" will be in action against our ships and the lighter armament along the front will be likewise engaged. Our close support squadrons will be attacking, therefore, when the enemy troops are fully occupied and in action, with shells from our bombardment ships falling amongst them, and with their attention diverted from our fighters. Our fighters should therefore be able to press home their attacks on the objectives allotted to them without serious interference from enemy ground defences.

Tasks
0515. 175 *Squadron*:
One flight to attack "Goering" battery.
One flight to attack divisional headquarters in A...... using 250lb. bombs.

0515. 174 *Squadron*.
To attack "Hitler" battery using 500lb. bombs.

Squadrons to attack the frontal buildings at "Jubilee" with cannons and machine guns from 0515 to 0525. This attack is to cover the final approach landing. The first attack to be delivered when the landing troop-carrying craft are ½ mile from shore. The landing craft should take approximately 5 minutes to cover the ½ mile to the shore. During this 5 minutes of the final approach fighters should attack the whole front overlooking the beaches, *i.e.* the area between the sea wall and the houses. A proportion of these attacks is to be directed also to the near edge of the western cliff overlooking the front of "Jubilee". As soon as the leading landing craft has touched down, the close support fighters are to attack houses along the water front. The attacks are to be continued against the western cliff during this second phase of the general attack along the front.

Occupation
As soon as the assault has taken place tactical reconnaissance aircraft will be despatched to reconnoitre for enemy movements towards "Jubilee". Targets located in this way will be engaged as follows:
(i) Against small bodies of troops on points more than 10 miles inland – a flight or squadron of Hurricanes covered by a flight or squadron of Spitfires, both going in low.

(ii) Against large enemy columns located some 20 miles distant from "Jubilee" – a mixed force of Bostons and Hurricanes with Spitfire squadrons to cover. When bombers are so employed the low attack fighter squadrons are to deliver their attack shortly after the bombs have burst so as to increase the confusion caused by the bombing.

Withdrawal
It is impossible to forecast the type of target which will be attacked during the withdrawal, as it will depend upon the situation. Targets will, however, be attacked at the request of the Military Force Commander.

Close Support Squadrons "On Call"
Whenever the situation demands it a flight or squadron will be despatched "on call" at the disposal of the Military Force Commander.

If no enemy troop movements are reported by 0800 hours, a close support squadron will be despatched to patrol in the vicinity of "Jubilee" "on call" to the Military Force Commander as from 0830 hours, to attack any suitable targets which he may select.

OPERATION INSTRUCTION FOR EMPLOYMENT OF FIGHTER COVER SQUADRONS

General Role
The duties of the Fighter Cover Squadrons will commence at first light when two squadrons of Spitfires will be required to patrol in loose fours and pairs in the vicinity of "Jubilee" with the object of giving cover to our landing craft. Later, when light permits, fighter cover will be increased to six squadrons.

Once our forces are established ashore and when the situation permits, fighter cover will be reduced to four squadrons and subsequently to three. The primary task of this fighter cover will be to protect landing craft in the vicinity of the beaches.

The fighter cover will again be increased to six squadrons as from the beginning of the withdrawal and will then be gradually reduced in strength, if the situation permits, as the expedition proceeds towards the English coast.

Probable Enemy Air Action

There are several courses open to the enemy, but as our forces are limited and we cannot protect ourselves adequately against every possibility, it is only proposed to consider the courses which would most seriously prejudice the operation, and which will, therefore, be the most likely courses for him to adopt.

The two most dangerous periods of the operation are the landing and the withdrawal. During these periods our light craft will be close in shore, with troops either disembarking or re-embarking with very little A.A. to cover them.

Once our forces are established ashore they will offer a very poor target to the enemy air force, but the landing craft grouped about the beaches are most likely to be attacked by enemy fighters. The most likely courses of enemy action are as follows:
(i) Low front gun attacks against our troops and landing craft, during the landing and withdrawal.
(ii) Low altitude bombing attacks (by fighters, bombers or twin-engined day bombers), against our ships during the re-embarkation and their return to the English coast, particularly in the early stages of the return voyage.

In any event he will undoubtedly endeavour to draw off our fighter cover with his fighters, and he will probably coincide attacks against our fighters with the bombing attacks against our ships.

It is considered that the bombing attacks will be made at sea-level, and the approach will probably be from north to south, i.e., from sea to shore, so that he can retreat rapidly inland to France without having to turn after dropping his bombs.

In order to counter these probable attacks by the enemy it will be necessary for our patrols to work in very loose manoeuvrable formations, as close to the sea as possible without interfering with the freedom of action of our own A.A. forces, and, when in the vicinity of the beaches, without coming within range of the light A.A. defences. At the same time, it will be necessary for them to cover themselves against attack by enemy fighters.

The general system of providing fighter patrols will be for the lower squadrons to patrol in pairs and fours between approximately 3,000 and

5,000 ft., in the neighbourhood of the town and beaches, or the convoy of ships according to the phase of the operation in progress. When three or more squadrons are being employed, the top squadron will act as high cover at a convenient distance to the north-west of the target area. It is essential that the high cover should be in R/T touch with the top squadron doing the lower patrol. Should at any time the cover drop to two squadrons, one flight only will act as high cover.

It is expected that the high cover will act as a deterrent to the enemy in attacking our aircraft patrolling the beaches and ships. Should a strong attack be put in, the intervention of the high squadron should make it possible to break up the German attack and to destroy their aircraft. The top cover squadron should patrol between 10,000 and 12,000 ft.

Detailed sequence of patrols by fighter cover squadrons are as follows:

Station	*Squadrons*	*Time of Patrol*
Lympne	No. 65	
	No. 111	0450-0520
Hornchurch	4 Squadrons (1 squadron high cover).	0520-0550
Debden	2 Squadrons	0520-0550
Kenley	2 Squadrons (1 squadron high cover).	0550-0620
Northolt	2 Squadrons	0550-0620
Tangmere	2 Squadrons (1 squadron high cover).	0620-0650
Biggin Hill	2 Squadrons	0620-0650
North Weald	3 Squadrons (1 squadron high cover).	0700
Debden	2 Squadrons (1 squadron high cover).	
North Weald	1 Squadron	
Kenley	2 Squadrons (1 squadron high cover).	
Biggin Hill	1 Squadron	

Note – Reliefs to take place in the air over the patrol area.

OPERATION INSTRUCTION FOR EMPLOYMENT OF TACTICAL RECONNAISSANCE AIRCRAFT

It will be the object of our reconnaissance to discover movements of enemy reinforcements towards the area in which our Army is operating.

It would appear that the earliest reinforcements will arrive from the coastal districts between St. Valery and Fécamp. The likely routes in this area (including Abbeville) are to be reconnoitred every half-hour from

0515. (Negative information is just as positive and is therefore to be passed).

Outside the coastal area it would appear that reinforcements may arrive from Amiens, Rouen or Le Havre. In this connection it has recently been reported that an Armoured Division has been moved up to Amiens in the last fortnight, although this report has not definitely been confirmed. The roads approaching Dieppe from these three places are to be reconnoitred every hour from 0630 hours.

Reconnaissance aircraft will be in touch with the Headquarters Ship by R/T. In addition, reports are to be sent to 11 Group Headquarters as soon as possible after each sortie lands.

OPERATION INSTRUCTION FOR EMPLOYMENT OF ANTI-SURFACE VESSEL RECONNAISSANCE PATROLS

Coastal Command

Coastal Command aircraft will maintain anti-surface vessel patrols with A.S.V. aircraft from 2300 hours until first light, with the object of locating any enemy surface craft proceeding from the Cherbourg and Havre-Fécamp areas in a northerly or north-easterly direction, and from the area Gris Nez-Le Touquet in a westerly or south-westerly direction. Reports from these patrols will be passed by normal W/T channels to the Coastal Group concerned, and thence to No. 11 Group. Details of any enemy vessels will then be passed by No. 11 Group via Portsmouth to the Headquarters Ship.

"Jim Crow" (Fighter) Reconnaissance Patrols

Fighter aircraft of No. 91 Squadron will maintain patrols during daylight hours to search for enemy-armed surface craft approaching either from Le Havre or Boulogne to threaten our naval forces.

Reports of any enemy-armed surface craft sighted will be passed to the Headquarters Ship by No. 11 Group through Portsmouth W/T Channel.

On the night of the withdrawal many British craft will be in the area to the south and south-west of Beachy Head and proceeding along the inshore route to Selsey. An A.S.V. patrol is required on a line from 30 miles south of Beachy Head to 15 miles south of Selsey from first dark to first light. Reports will be made by the same means as on the previous evening.

OPERATION INSTRUCTION FOR EMPLOYMENT OF SMOKE-LAYING AIRCRAFT

Smoke will be used in this operation to screen off the German defences on the Eastern Cliff overlooking the main front of "Jubilee", where the principal landings will be made.

The neutralization of these defences by smoke is required from 0510 to 0540 hours.

The method of laying the smoke will depend upon the direction of the wind. With the wind from 240 degrees clockwise to 090 degrees the smoke will be laid by means of an S.C.I. smoke curtain (this will be known as Scheme "A"). With the wind between 090 degrees clockwise to 240 degrees, the smoke screen will be laid by dropping 100-lb. phosphorous smoke bombs. (This will be known as Scheme "B".)

Scheme "A"
If the mortars landed in the initial attack with the Battalion at "Blue" Beach can be got into action in time, they will fire smoke projectiles in and around the battery positions. They will also fire a certain percentage of H.E. projectiles on these batteries at the same time. They are due to open fire at 0505 hours. In case this party gets held up, and to ensure that there is some smoke in the battery areas before the original S.C.I. smoke curtain is laid, two Bostons will drop sticks of 100-lb. phosphorus smoke bombs on the battery areas and the cliff end at 0509 hours. At the same time six Bostons will bomb "Rommel" battery. The object of this is to divert the attention of all A.A. gunners in a southerly direction at the time when the first two Bostons are going in to lay the smoke curtain just to the north of them. By this diversion, and the smoke which has been put down in and around the battery positions, it is hoped that the original smoke curtain will come as a complete surprise, and the aircraft laying it get away while the attention of the gunners is otherwise fully occupied.

The programme for Scheme "A" is as follows:
0505	Mortars commence fire with smoke and H.E.
0509	Two Bostons drop 100-lb. smoke bombs on batteries and along the cliff.
0509	Six Bostons bomb "Rommel" battery.
0510	Two Bostons flying below the cliff top lay the initial smoke curtain.
0511	Three Bostons lay a smoke curtain, starting from two miles

away from the headland, the actual direction of the curtain depending on the direction of the wind.

0516   Three Bostons lay an additional smoke curtain.
0521   Three Bostons lay an additional smoke curtain.
0526   Three Blenheims lay an additional smoke screen.
0531   Three Blenheims lay an additional smoke screen.
0536   Three Blenheims lay an additional smoke screen.

The programme for Scheme "B" is as follows:
0505   Mortars commence fire with smoke and H.E.
0510   Two Bostons drop sticks of 100-lb. phosphorus smoke bombs in the area selected according to the direction of the wind. This is to be repeated at three-minute intervals up to 0537, the Bostons carrying on up to 0525 and the Blenheims carrying on from 0528 to 0537.

OPERATION INSTRUCTION FOR EMPLOYMENT OF DAY BOMBERS

Day Bombing

Two Boston Squadrons of No. 2 Group will be located at Ford for this operation. These squadrons will be employed to attack any German M.T. columns despatched to reinforce the "Jubilee" area after our landing has taken place. These attacks will take the form of small "Circuses", the bombers diving to about 5,000 ft. to attack the columns, while cannon fighters go down to shoot up the columns. Fighter escort will be provided for the bombers as necessary. A third Bomber Squadron will be available in No. 2 Group on call to the Air Force Commander for operation "Jubilee" throughout the period of the operation.

The necessary maps for Day Bomber Squadrons will be available at Ford, where all arrangements for briefing will be made.

Six Bostons from this Force will be employed in the pre-arranged programme to bomb battery posts to the east of "Jubilee" (code word for the battery posts "Rommel"). This attack will be required only if conditions are suitable for laying a smoke curtain.

AIR FORCE ORDER OF BATTLE

Day Fighter Force   56 squadrons.
Day Bomber Force   3 squadrons.

Army Co-operation Force   5 squadrons.
Disposed in sectors and operating from aerodromes as follows:

Kenley Sector (7 squadrons)	Kenley 4.
	Redhill 3.
Northolt Sector (5 squadrons)	Northolt 2.
	Heston 2.
	Redhill 1.
Tangmere Sector (20 squadrons)	Merston 2.
	W. Hampnett 1.
	Thorney Island 2.
	Tangmere 6.
	Shoreham 2.
	Friston 2.
	Ford 4 (2 Hurricane Bomber and 2 Day Bomber).
	Thruxton 1. (Boston aircraft for smoke).
Debden Sector	(5 squadrons)
	Gravesend 3.
	Hawkinge 2.
North Weald Sector (6 squadrons)	Southend 2.
	Manston 4.
Hornchurch Sector (8 squadrons)	Hornchurch 3.
	Fairlop 2.
	W. Malling 3.
Biggin Hill Sector (8 squadrons)	Biggin Hill 3.
	Lympne 2.
	Eastchurch 2.
	Hawkinge 1.
Army Co-operation Squadrons	Gatwick 3.
	Thruxton 2 (Smoke laying aircraft).

SIGNALS ORGANISATION

R.A.F. Communications in Headquarters Ships

The Naval and Military Commanders will be located in a Headquarters Ship. Owing to the extent of their communications requirements two ships will be employed to accommodate the necessary equipment and will be known as Ship No. 1 and Ship No. 2 respectively. Communication between these ships, which will remain in company throughout the operation, will be provided by two VHF R/T links, one for the joint use of the Military Commander and Air Force Commander's representative and the other as a standby.

The R.A.F. signals facilities in the ships will be as follows:
  (i) *Ship No. 1* – (a) A VHF R/T watch on Tangmere Ops. 2 frequency (Channel A in ships VHF set). This channel will be at the disposal of the Fighter Controller for communication with Close Support Fighters. This VHF set will also be fitted with No. 11 Group Guard No. 1 frequency in Channel B to enable the Fighter Controller to communicate with the lowest squadron of the Fighter Cover and to warn them of the approach of enemy aircraft if necessary. This set will be adjusted and maintained by a corporal wireless mechanic provided by Headquarters No. 11 Group.
  (b) An HF R/T listening watch on 2,620 Kcs. for the reception of Tactical Reconnaissance Reports. A Type 19 set manned by R.A.F. operators will be provided for this watch by Headquarters, Army Co-operation Command.
  (ii) *Ship No. 2* – (a) A VHF set tuned to the same frequencies as that in Ship No. 1 as a standby against failure of that set. Continuous watch is to be kept on No. 11 Group Guard No. 1 (Channel B) on which frequency the Fighter Controller may, if necessary, warn the lowest squadron of fighters of the approach of enemy aircraft. This set will be adjusted and maintained by a corporal wireless mechanic provided by Headquarters No. 11 Group.
  (b) An HF R/T watch on 2,620 Kcs. for the reception of Tactical Reconnaissance Reports and the answering of calls from aircraft. This set will be manned by R.A.F. operators provided by Headquarters, Army Co-operation Command.
  (c) A W/T Link with Portsmouth to be known as the R.A.F. Base wave to be manned by Naval Operators. This link is provided for the transmission and reception of the following:
    (i) Transmission of requests for Air Support.
    (ii) Transmission of Military Situation Reports for the Air Force Commander.
    (iii) Transmission of any necessary message from the Air Force Commander at Uxbridge to the Military or Naval Commanders.

Messages from the Air Force Commander for the Military or Naval Force Commanders or for the Air Force Commander's representative in the Headquarters Ship are to be passed to the M.I.L.O. at Uxbridge for transmission by direct telephone line to the Portsmouth W/T Room

for onward transmission on the R.A.F. Base Wave to the Headquarters Ship. All such messages will be addressed:
"To *Calpe* from Uxbridge."

Arrangements for the distribution of R/T and W/T messages in the two ships will be made by the Senior Naval Signals Officer. The R.A.F. Signals Officer is to ensure that all messages are passed without delay to the Air Force Commander's representative on board and from this Officer to the Air Force Commander at Uxbridge.

Requests by Military Force Commander for Air Support
(i) The Naval or Military Force Commander may transmit calls for Air Support by W/T on the R.A.F. Base Wave to the C.-in-C. Portsmouth for onward transmission to Headquarters No. 11 Group who will also maintain a listening watch on this frequency. Code words will be used in messages to denote pre-arranged targets, other targets being described by use of the Reconnaissance Code. Requests for air support which will be transmitted in the form detailed in Part I, Section 6 of the Combined Operations Signals Book are to be given priority over all other calls on the R.A.F. Base Wave.
(ii) Close Support Fighters are to call the Headquarters Ship when within 15 miles of the French coast on the outward journey on Tangmere Ops. 2 frequency (Channel B in aircraft) using the R/T callsign "Crowfoot". The Leader of the lowest squadron of the Fighter Cover operating on No. 11 Group Guard No. 1 frequency is to establish communication with the Headquarters Ship on arrival in the vicinity of "Jubilee".

R.A.F. Base Wave
(i) Messages for transmission by R.A.F. Base Wave to the Air Force Commander are to be addressed to Uxbridge and passed from No. 1 Ship to No. 2 Ship via the R/T link for onward transmission. When passing the messages by the R/T link each word is to be spelt out in the phonetic alphabet to ensure that they are correctly received.
(ii) The R.A.F. Base Wave will be manned in No. 2 Ship and at Portsmouth by Naval Operators. The Port Signals Officer, Portsmouth, will be responsible for ensuring that insofar as is possible this vital link functions without interruption whilst the operation is in progress and for clearing all traffic without delay. He will also be responsible for ordering any necessary frequency changes and in emergency for clearing traffic by any W/T channel available if communication on the R.A.F. Base Wave fails.

(iii) The Port Signals Officer, Portsmouth, is to inform Chief Signals Officer No. 11 Group of any change of frequency of the R.A.F. Base Wave.

(iv) It is to be impressed upon all personnel who handle messages on the R.A.F. Base Wave that speed in the handling of these messages is of vital importance.

Control of Fighters

(i) No. 10 group Wing will operate on No. 10 Group Guard No. 2 frequency under control of Tangmere.

(ii) No. 12 Group Wing will operate on No. 12 Group Guard No. 1 frequency under control of Hornchurch.

(iii) Close Support Fighter Squadrons will operate on Tangmere Ops. 2 frequency (Channel B, in aircraft) under control of Tangmere. This frequency is for the use of Close Support Fighter Squadrons *only*.

(iv) Sector Wings, other than the lowest squadron of the Fighter Cover will operate on Sector Ops. 1 frequencies (Channel A, in aircraft) under control of their parent Sectors.

(v) The lowest squadron of the Fighter Cover will operate on No. 11 Group Guard No. 1 frequency. The Group Controller when issuing the Form A. is to include instructions as to which squadron will operate on Group Guard No. 1.

(vi) No. 91 Squadron aircraft will operate on 5,750 kc/s. (Channel A, in aircraft) under Biggin Hill control. A listening watch on this frequency is to be maintained by Tangmere. For the period of the operation this frequency is *not* to be used by any other squadrons during daylight hours.

(vii) Fighters escorting Day Bombers are to operate on No. 11 Group Guard No. 1 frequency (Channel C, in fighter and bomber aircraft).

Incoming Squadrons

Incoming Fighter Squadrons are to maintain R/T silence during their move. Immediately on arrival in No. 11 Group the VHF sets in aircraft are to be tuned to the appropriate Sector frequencies. R/T callsigns are to be allotted to these squadrons from the block of R/T callsigns in use in the Sector.

(ii) After the arrival of additional squadrons, R/T traffic is to be strictly controlled and kept down to the level existing prior to reinforcement.

(iii) No. 11 Group Squadrons moving to forward aerodromes are to do so at low heights maintaining R/T silence en route.

(iv) No. 2 Group Squadrons are to maintain W/T and R/T silence during their move to Ford.

Day Bombers

(i) No. 2 Group Bombers are to keep continuous listening watch on No. 2 Group Operational Control frequency. Operational callsigns will be allocated by C.S.O. No. 2 Group, who will inform all concerned. If it is necessary to divert the Bombers after they are airborne, No. 2 Group may be instructed to pass the message by W/T on the No. 2 Group Operational frequency or the Leader of the Close Escort Fighters may be instructed to pass the message to the Bomber Leader by VHF R/T on No. 11 Group Guard 1.

(ii) Bomber sorties will be ordered off direct from No. 11 Group by landline. W/T and R/T silence is to be maintained until the French coast is crossed.

(iii) Formation Leaders will be fitted with VHF R/T sets tuned to No. 11 Group Guard 1 frequency in Channel C, and Tangmere Ops. 2 frequency in Channel D. Bomber aircraft will normally operate on No. 11 Group Guard No. 1 frequency (Button C in aircraft), but when necessary will communicate with Close Support Fighters on Tangmere Ops. 2 frequency (Button D in aircraft).

(iv) Homing can be obtained from Tangmere Flying Control on 5,190 kc/s. if required. Details of callsigns, etc., will be notified to all concerned by C.S.O. No. 2 Group.

(v) Local flying control is to be effected on the "Darky" frequency using TR 9 D sets in the aircraft and in the Flying Control Office at Ford.

(vi) Test transmissions by aircraft after arrival at Ford are to be confined to an absolute minimum for security reasons.

Army Co-operation

(i) Army Co-operation aircraft will operate on a frequency of 2,620 kc/s. When approaching the French coast two way communication is to be established with the Headquarters Ship prior to proceeding on reconnaissance. This reconnaissance, however, will *not* be abandoned if the aircraft fails to establish communication with the Ship. Pilots should be instructed that the R/T range from the Headquarters Ship is likely to be restricted, and that they should endeavour to return to the vicinity of the Ship to pass their messages.

(ii) Reconnaissance Reports are to be passed by R/T to No. 2 Headquarters Ship. A watch will also be kept in No. 1 Headquarters Ship and if the operator of this set hears an aircraft call twice without reply, he is to answer the call using the control callsign in accordance with normal procedure.

(iii) The operators keeping watch in Nos. 1 and 2 Headquarters Ships on

2,620 kc/s. are to make three copies of all signals received which will be distributed by Naval runner as follows:
- (*a*) In No. 1 Ship, one copy to the Military Commanders and one copy to the Air Force Commander's representative.
- (*b*) In No. 2 Ship, two copies to the Military Commander's representative. If necessary this Officer will transmit each message to the Military Commander and Air Force Commander's representative in No. 1 Ship.

(iv) After the move of aircraft to Gatwick, the following test procedure is to be strictly observed:
- (*a*) Any testing required prior to the change over to the operational frequency is to be carried out by aircraft using their normal frequencies and callsigns and working with their parent stations.
- (*b*) On changing to the Operational frequency, tests are to be as brief as possible and kept to an absolute minimum.
- (*c*) All tests on the Operational frequency by Nos. 400 and 414 Squadrons are to be carried out below 1,000 ft.
- (*d*) The ground station used for tests on the Operational frequency is to be a Type 19 set supplied by No. 26 Squadron at Gatwick. In order to prevent interference to the Control Station the use of medium power equipment is forbidden except by Gatwick HF D/F Station when passing homing bearings.

Smoke Aircraft

Three Squadrons of Smoke aircraft will operate from Thruxton on a frequency of 4,365 kc/s. using callsigns as detailed in para. 905. Communication between No. 11 Group and Thruxton will be provided by setting up a long duration call over the G.P.O. network with a voice-operated relay at Thruxton. Telephone number Andover 2321.

Homing

(i) A Homing watch on No. 11 Group Guard 1 frequency is to be maintained at Ford for the purpose of homing No. 11 Group Fighters in an emergency. Pilots are to be warned only to use this frequency if absolutely essential, as its use is likely to cause interference with operations.

(ii) Homing watch for the No. 10 Group Wing is to be maintained at Tangmere on No. 10 Group Guard No. 2 frequency.

(iii) Homing watch for the No. 12 Group Wing is to be maintained at West Malling on No. 12 Group Guard No. 1 frequency, and emergency homing at Manston on No. 12 Group Guard No. 2 frequency.

(iv) Homing watch for Army Co-operation aircraft is to be maintained at Gatwick and Friston on 2,620 kc/s.

(v) Homing watch for Day Bomber aircraft operating from Ford is to be maintained by Tangmere Flying Control on Tangmere Regional Control frequency. Callsigns will be detailed by C.S.O. No. 2 Group.

Air/Sea Rescue

(i) For Fighter aircraft Air/Sea Rescue Fixer Layouts are allocated to Fighter aircraft as follows:
- (a) Biggin Hill No. 2; 12 Group Wing on 12 Group Guard No. 2 frequency.
- (b) Tangmere; 10 Group Wing on 10 Group Guard No. 1 frequency.
- (c) Kenley No. 1; Debden Wings.
- (d) Kenley No. 2; North Weald Wings.

(ii) For Army Co-operation Aircraft P4 D/F Stations will be stationed at Friston and Shoreham, and will maintain watch on 2,620 kc/s. Bearings obtained on aircraft in distress are to be passed to Kenley by telephone prefaced by the words "Aircraft Distress Message". These messages are to include the callsign of the pilot, the bearing and the time the last bearing was taken. On receipt of such a message Kenley is to initiate Air/Sea Rescue action. All Army Co-operation pilots are to be instructed to use Fighter Command R/T procedure when making distress calls.

(iii) Bomber aircraft in distress are to transmit SOS calls on MF D/F Section "P".

E-Boat Reconnaissance

Reports of enemy E-Boats transmitted by No. 91 Squadron are to be passed immediately by Tangmere and Biggin Hill to No. 11 Group Controller by telephone, for appropriate action and onward transmission to Portsmouth.

R.A.F. Landline Communications

(i) In addition to existing landline communication, operational landline communications are being arranged as follows:
- (a) Debden to Gravesend via H.Q. No. 11 Group Ops. P.B.X.
- (b) Debden to Hawkinge via H.Q. No. 11 Group Ops. P.B.X.
- (c) North Weald to Manston – Direct line by plugging up Circuits No. PW. 6565 and PW. 17237.
- (d) Northolt to Croydon – Direct line by plugging up Circuits No. PWLR. 47047 and PW. 7602.
- (e) Hornchurch to West Malling via Biggin Hill.

APPENDICES

(f) H.Q. No. 11 Group to Gatwick.
(g) H.Q. No. 11 Group M.I.L.O. to Portsmouth W/T Room – Direct line.
(ii) Circuits will be plugged up on receipt of instructions from C.S.O. No. 11 Group.

Callsigns for Use with Air Forces

(i) *W/T Callsigns*

    (a) Day Bombers Squadrons   To be detailed by C.S.O. 2 Group
                                 Squadrons   To be detailed by C.S.O. 2 Group
    (b) Smoke Aircraft 13 Squadron   H 5 P
                           614 Squadron   1 O S
                           226 squadron   To be detailed by C.S.O. 2 Group.
    (c) Tangmere   HF/DF   H G 8
    (d) H.Q. Ship   To be detailed later.
    (e) Portsmouth   M T N
    (f) H.Q. No. 11 Grp.   V Y 6
    (g) Thruxton   H/F D/F Q 3 W

(ii) *R/T Callsigns*

    (a) Army Co-operation Aircraft:
    No. 26 Squadron   J
    No. 400 Squadron   K
    No. 414 Squadron   M
    (b) Wartling HF D/F Station   D S
    (c) Gatwick HF D/F Station   Elephant
    (d) H.Q. Ship HF R/T   Control   A T
                                  Listening C Y
    (e) Fighter Squadrons –   As detailed by Sector Commanders. Fighter Controller in H.Q. Ships to use "Fighters" as Fighter call sign.
    (f) H.Q. Ship No. 1 VHF R/T   Crowfoot
    (g) H.Q. Ship No. 2 VHF R/T   Crowfoot Two
    (h) H.Q. No. 11 Group VHF R/T   Cocktail
    (i) Ford "Darky"   Ronny
    (j) Thruxton HF D/F   Furlong

Frequencies for Use with Air Forces

(i) *W/T Frequencies*

    (a) R.A.F. Base Wave   3,000 kc/s (Alternative 4,850 kc/s)
    (b) Admiral's Wave   2,000 kc/s
    (c) Port Wave   2,300 kc/s

APPENDICES

 (d) Day Bombers   No. 2 Group Operational frequency
 (e) Smoke Aircraft   4,365 kc/s
 (ii) *R/T Frequencies*
 (a) Tactical Reconnaissance Aircraft   2,620 kc/s (Alternative 2,920 kc/s if ordered by C.S.O. No. 11 Group)
 (b) No. 11 Group Guard No. 1
 fundamental frequency   6537.5 kc/s
 (c) Tangmere Ops. 2 frequency   5912.5 kc/s

Times of Opening R/T and W/T Watches

(i) R.A.F. VHF and HF R/T Watches in the two Headquarters Ships will be opened at the time detailed by the R.A.F. Signals Officer on board Headquarters Ship No. 1.

(ii) Watch will be set on 2,620 kc/s at the D/F Stations at Wartling, Gatwick and Shoreham, from 0500 hours on the day of the operation until closed down by C.S.O. No. 11 Group.

(iii) Watch will be set on the R.A.F. Base Wave from the time of sailing of the Headquarters Ships until their return to Portsmouth. W/T silence will be maintained until 0515 hours except for the transmission of any messages authorised by the Force Commanders.

R/T Discipline

All pilots are to be specially warned of the importance of restricting R/T traffic on No. 11 Group Guard No. 1 and Tangmere Ops. 2 frequencies to the minimum.

Appendix X

OFFICERS IN COMMAND

Naval Forces

Naval Force Commander   Captain J. Hughes Hallett, R.N.

Ship   *Commanding Officer*
Destroyers
H.M.S. *Calpe*   Lt.-Cdr. J.H. Wallace, R.N.
(Headquarters Ship)

H.M.S. *Fernie*   Lt. W.B. Willett, R.N.
(2nd Headquarters Ship)

H.M.S. *Brocklesby*   Lt.-Cdr. E.N. Pumphrey, D.S.O., D.S.C., R.N.
H.M.S. *Garth*   Lt.-Cdr. J.P. Scatchard, R.N.
H.M.S. *Albrighton*   Lt.-Cdr. R.J. Hanson, R.N.
H.M.S. *Berkeley*   Lt. J.J.S. Yorke, R.N.
H.M.S. *Bleasdale*   Lt. P.B. North-Lewis, R.N.
O.R.P. *Slazak*   Cdr. R. Tyminiski.

Sloop and Gunboat
H.M.S. *Alresford*   Cdr. R.E.C. Dunbar, R.N. (Ret.).
H.M.S. *Locust*   Lt.-Cdr. W.J. Stride, M.B.E., R.N., (Ret.).

Minesweeper Flotillas
H.M. 9th   Cdr. H.T. Rust, D.S.O., R.N.
Minesweeper Flotilla
H.M. 13th   Cr. L.J.S. Ede, D.S.O., R.N.
Minesweeper Flotilla

APPENDICES

Landing Ship, Infantry (Large)
H.M.S. *Glengyle*   Captain D.S. McGrath, R.N. (Ret.).

Landing Ships, Infantry (Medium)
H.M.S. *Queen Emma*   Captain G.L.D. Gibbs, D.S.O., R.N. (Ret.)
H.M.S. *Princess Beatrix* Cdr. T.B. Brunton, R.N. (Ret.).

Landing Ships, Infantry (Small)
H.M.S. *Prince Charles*   A/Cdr. S.H. Dennis, D.S.C., R.N. (Ret.).
H.M.S. *Prince Albert*   Lt.-Cdr. H.B. Peate, R.N.R.
H.M.S. *Prince Leopold*   Lt.-Cdr. W.S. Byles, R.D., R.N.R.
H.M.S. *Princess Astrid* A/Lt.-Cdr. C.E. Hall, R.N.R, (Ret.).

Landing Ships, Infantry (Handhoisting)
H.M.S. *Invicta*   Cdr. A.I. Robertson, R.D., R.N.R.
H.M.S. *Duke of*   Lt.-Cdr. J.F.H. Coombes, R.D., R.N.R.
Wellington

Group
5 (Senior Officer   Cdr. D.B. Wyburd, R.N.
Landings,"Yellow" Beach)
6   Cdr. H.V.P. McClintock, R.N.
7   Lt.-Cdr. J.H. Dathan, R.N.
8   Lt.-Cdr. Earl Beatty, R.N.
9   Ty. Lt. H. Leslie, R.N.V.R. (Q.O.).
10   Lt.-Cdr. G.H. Stevens, R.N. (Ret.).
11   Act. Lt. N.B.H. Lloyd, R.N.V.R.
12   Ty. Lt. L.E. Barker, R.N.V.R.
13 7 Chasseurs   Lt. M. Buist, R.N.

Senior Officer Landings
"Orange" Beach   Lt.-Cdr. H.H.H. Mulleneux, R.N.
"Green" Beach   Lt.-Cdr. R.M. Prior, D.S.C., R.N.
"Blue" Beach   Lt.-Cdr. H.W. Goulding, D.S.O. R.N.R.
"White" Beach   Lt.-Cdr. C.W. McMullen, R.N.
"Red" and "White"   Cdr. G.T. Lambert, R.N.
Beaches and Principal
Beach Master.
Officer Commanding   Cdr. R.E.D. Ryder, V.C., R.N.
Cutting-Out Party.

APPENDICES

Landing Craft

Commanding Officer's Name	L.C.(P.) No.
First Flotilla	
Lt. D.R. Stevens R.N.V.R. (Flotilla Officer).	1
Sub-Lt. H.A. Hancock, R.N.V.R.	80
Sub-Lt. B.K. McCosh, R.N.V.R.	81
Sub-Lt. A.M. Button, R.N.V.R.	85
Sub-Lt. R.E.D. Fenning, R.N.V.R.	86
Sub-Lt. N.W. Dunn, R.N.V.R.	87
Lt. G.W. Holt, R.N.V.R.	95
Sub-Lt. A.L. Oates, R.N.V.R.	118
Sub-Lt. J. Rutherford	128
Sub-Lt. M.V. Nicholl, R.N.V.R.	145
Sub-Lt. K. Child, R.N.V.R.	157
Second Flotilla	
Lt. G. Byerley, R.N.V.R. (Flotilla Officer).	19
Sub-Lt. Franklin, R.N.V.R.	88
Sub-Lt. M. Easton, R.N.V.R.	94
Sub-Lt. D.H. Botly, R.C.N.V.R.	119
Sub-Lt. R.M. Smith, R.C.N.V.R.	124
Sub-Lt. D.L. Marchant, R.N.V.R.	125
Sub-Lt. J.E. O'Rourke, R.C.N.V.R.	129
Sub-Lt. D. Masson, R.N.V.R.	147
Sub-Lt. J.D. Nisbet, R.N.V.R.	156
Fourth Flotilla	
Lt.-Cdr. W.L.N. Wallace, R.N.V.R. (Flotilla Officer).	186
Lt. J. Hawkes, R.N.V.R.	195
Lt. F. Lock, R.N.V.R.	187
Lt. R.A. Durham, R.N.V.R.	212
Sub-Lt. S.G.P. Walker, R.N.V.R.	175
Sub-Lt. W.E. Ibell	170
Sub-Lt. D.B. Corcoran, R.N.V.R.	188
Sub-Lt. C.T. Kitching, R.N.V.R.	192
Sub-Lt. R.C.A. Barnes, R.N.V.R.	174
Sub-Lt. C.H. Lindfoot, R.N.V.R.	173

Sub-Lt. G.W. Lindfoot, R.N.V.R.   199
Sub-Lt. G.M. Doaman, R.N.V.R.   172
Sub-Lt. N. Sparks, R.N.V.R.   53
Sub-Lt. J.H. Vellacott, R.N.V.R.   28

Fifth Flotilla
Lt.-Cdr. N.C. Roulston, R.N.V.R.
(Flotilla Officer).   163
Lt. R.F.H. Morgan, R.N.V.R.   164
Lt. A Wilson, R.N.V.R.   165
Lt. E.R.C. Hunt, R.N.V.R.   166
Lt. C. Newman, R.N.V.R.   167
Lt. C. Tymms, R.N.V.R.   209
Lt. K.D. Cox, R.N.V.R.   210
Sub-Lt. J. Vaughan, R.N.V.R.   208
Sub-Lt. T. Williams, R.N.V.R.   155
Lt. R.F. McRae, R.N.V.R.   45
Sub-Lt. G.E. Evans, R.N.V.R.   31
Sub-Lt. D.B. Rogers, R.C.N.V.R.   163

Sixth Flotilla
Lt. J. Murray, R.N.V.R.
(Flotilla Officer).   127
Lt. P. Moss, R.N.V.R.   130
Lt. D.R. Tride, R.N.V.R.   131
Sub.-Lt. L.C. Breeze, R.N.V.R.   132
Sub.-Lt. J. Whiting, R.N.V.R.   134
Lt. C.W.R. Cross, R.N.V.R.   135
Sub.-Lt. A.D. Waters, R.N.V.R.   136
Sub.-Lt. T.L. Rankin, R.N.V.R.   153
Sub.-Lt. J. Murts, R.N.V.R.   158

Seventh Flotilla
Lt.-Cdr. H. Garrard, R.N.V.R.
(Flotilla Officer).   101
Sub.-Lt. H.A. Carter, R.N.V.R.   83
Sub.-Lt. B.T. Heath, R.N.V.R.   84
Lt. J. Mattinson, R.N.V.R.   99
Lt. C. Lawrie, R.N.V.R.   102
Lt. J. Cassidy, R.N.V.R.   104
Lt. E.N. Russel, R.N.V.R.   110
Sub.-Lt. R.G. Holmes, R.N.V.R.   113

APPENDICES

Lt. M.L. Bateson, R.N.V.R.	159
Lt. G. O'Keefe Wilson, R.N.V.R.	160

Twenty-fourth Flotilla

Lt.-Cdr. C.L. Corke, R.N.V.R. (Flotilla Officer)	42
Sub.-Lt. A.D.H. Kelly, R.N.V.R.	3
Sub.-Lt. B. Burden, R.N.V.R.	4
Sub.-Lt. Plummer, R.N.V.R.	13
Lt. H.T. Duckee, R.N.V.R.	15
Sub.-Lt. R. Hough, R.N.V.R.	23
Sub.-Lt. G.E. Green, R.N.V.R.	34
Sub.-Lt. P.J. Record, R.N.V.R.	40
Sub.-Lt. D.H. Spring, R.N.V.R.	41
Lt. G. Brown, R.N.V.R.	43
Sub.-Lt. B. Faragher, R.N.V.R.	44
Sub.-Lt. M.S. Pilkington, R.N.V.R.	115
Midshipman A.B. Potter, R.N.V.R.	L.C.P. (Navigational)
Lt.-Cdr. H.P. Brownell, R.A.N.V.R.	1st L.C.F. (L) and 2nd L.C.T. Flotilla Officer.

L.C.T. No.

Lt. C. Brookes Hill, R.N.V.R.	121
Lt. G.H. Reynolds, R.N.V.R.	145
Lt. L.A. Gwinner, R.N.V.R.	124
Lt. T.A. Robertson, R.N.V.R.	125
Lt. A. Cheney, R.N.V.R.	126
Skpr. B.D. McPherson, R.N.R.	127
Sub.-Lt. W.H. Cooke, R.N.V.R.	159
Skpr. T.A. Cooke, D.S.C., R.N.R.	163
Skpr. C.L. Barber, R.N.R.	165
Sub.-Lt. S. Alanson, R.N.V.R.	166

L.C.F. (L)

Lt. E.L. Graham, R.N.V.R.	2
Lt. N.R. Woodeson, R.N.V.R.	4
Lt. H.C. Trickey, R.N.V.R.	6
Lt. T.M. Foggitt, R.A.N.V.R.	1
Lt. E. Arundale, R.N.V.R.	3
Lt. C. Grantham, R.N.V.R.	5

APPENDICES

Lt.-Cdr. C. Masterman, R.A.N.V.R. 4th L.C.T. Flotilla Officer.

	L.C.T. No.
Lt. F.F. Appleton, R.A.N.V.R.	305
Lt. P. Dew, R.N.V.R.	304
Lt. P. Bull, R.N.V.R.	303
Sub.-Lt. S. Carr-Smith, R.N.V.R.	302
Lt. D.J.B. Morris, R.A.N.V.R.	306
Lt. L. Bailey, R.N.V.R.	308
Lt. R.M. Thacker, R.N.V.R.	376
Lt. K.B. Porteous, R.N.V.R.	361
Lt. F.F. Welcome, R.N.V.R.	309
Sub.-Lt. R. Dewhurst, R.N.V.R.	310
Skpr. E.J. Brown, R.N.R.	360
Skpr. C.D. Powdrall, R.N.R.	307
Lt. R.E. Green, R.N.V.R.	318
Skpr. A.C. Tavandale, R.N.R.	325

Escorting Craft

	M.G.B. No.
T. Sub.-Lt. L.H. Ennis, R.N.V.R.	50
T. Sub.-Lt. G. Clarke, R.N.V.R.	51
T. Lt. W.B.G. Leith, R.N.V.R.	52
T. Sub.-Lt. C.C.P. Broadhurst, R.N.V.R.	57
T. Lt. A.R.H. Nye, R.N.V.R.	312
T. Lt. J.L. Lloyd, R.N.V.R.	315
T. A. Lt.-Cdr. T.M. Cartwright, R.N.V.R., (Q.O.C.F.)	316
T. Lt. J.H. Coste, R.N.V.R.	317
T. Lt. N.W, Hughes, R.N.V.R.	320
T. Lt. B.L. Bourne, R.N.V.R.	321
T. Lt. G.C. Fanner, R.N.V.R.	323
T. Lt. R.D. Russell-Roberts, R.N.V.R.	326

	S.G.B. No.
T. Lt. G.H. Hummel, R.N.R.	5
T. Lt. H.C.T. Bradford, D.S.C., R.N.V.R.	6
Lt. I.R. Griffiths, R.N.	8
T. Lt. P.M. Scott, R.N.V.R.	9

	M.L. No.
T. Sub.-Lt. G.F. Bayne, R.N.C.V.R.	114

T. Lt. E.K. Jones, R.N.V.R. (Q.O.C.F.) 120
T. A. Lt.-Cdr. R.N. Wood, R.N.V.R. 123
T. Lt. (Q.O.C.F.) C.J. Jerram, R.N.V.R. 171
T. Lt. G.N. Johnstone, R.N.V.R. 187
Lt. B.H. Lloyd, R.N.V.R. 189
T. Lt. R.W. Ball, R.N.V.R. 190
T. Lt. H. Leslie, (Q.O.C.F.) R.N.V.R. 191
T. Lt. J.F. Humphreys, R.N.V.R. 193
A. Lt.-Cdr. W. Whitfield, R.N.R.(Q.O.C.F.) 194
T. Lt. J.S.E. Page, R.N.V.R. 208
T. Lt. I.D. Lyle, R.N.V.R. 214
T. Lt. H.M. Nees, R.N.V.R. 230
T. Lt. D.H. Titcombe, R.N.V.R. 246
T. Lt. J.B.C. Lumsden, R.N.V.R. 291
A.T. Lt.-Cdr. G. Shaw-Brundell, R.N.V.R. 292
T. A. Lt.-Cdr. F. Hellings, R.N.V.R. 309
T. Lt. G.A. Wright, R.N.V.R. 343
T. Lt. L.E. Barker, R.N.V.R. 344
T. Lt. A.D. Fear, R.N.V.R. 346

Chasseurs

Lt. W.H.P. Loftie, R.N. A-14
Lt. de Vaiseau Y.J. Boja, F.N.F.C. B-43
Officier des Equipages, J. Parc, F.N.F.C. C-42
Lt. E.G. Egerton, R.N. D-13
Lt. J.E. Syms, R.N. E-41
Enseigne de Vaiseau Chanlieau, F.N.F.C. F-10
Officier des Equipages M. Ibarlucia, G-5
　　F.N.F.C.

MILITARY FORCES
2nd CANADIAN DIVISION

Major-General J.H. Roberts, M.C.

Regiment	*Commanding Officer*
4th Canadian Infantry Brigade	Brigadier W.W. Southam, E.D.
6th Canadian Infantry Brigade	Brigadier Sherwood Lett, M.C., E.D.
Royal Hamilton Light Infantry	Lt.-Col. R.R. Labatt.
Essex Scots	Lt.-Col. F.K. Jesperson.
Queens Own Camerons	Lt.-Col. G.W. Gostling.
Royal Regiment of Canada	Lt.-Col. D.E. Catto.

APPENDICES

South Saskatchewan Regiment   Lt.-Col. C.C.I. Merritt.
Les Fusiliers Mont-Royal   Lt.-Col. D. Menard.
Calgary Regiment (14th Canadian
    Tank Battalion)   Lt.-Col. J.G. Andrews.
2nd Canadian Light Field
    Ambulance, R.C.A.M.C.   Lt.-Col. K.A. Hunter.

COMMANDOS

No. 3 Commando   Lt.-Col. J.F. Durnford-Slater, D.S.O.
No. 4 Commando   Lt.-Col. The Lord Lovat, M.C.
Royal Marine Commando   Lt.-Col. J.P.P. Philipps, R.M.

ROYAL AIR FORCE

Air Marshal T. Leigh Mallory, C.B., D.S.O.

Fighter Squadrons   *Leaders of Squadrons*
No.
611 R.A.F.   Squadron Leader D.H. Watkins, D.F.C.
402 C.R.A.F.   Squadron Leader N.H. Bretz, D.F.C.
350 Belgian   Squadron Leader D.A. Guillaume.
306 Polish   Squadron Leader J. Czerwinski.
302 Polish   Squadron Leader J. Kowalski, D.F.C.
131 R.A.F.   Wing Commander M.G.F. Pedley.
412 C.R.A.F.   Squadron Leader J.C. Fee.
129 R.A.F.   Squadron Leader R.H. Thomas, D.F.C.
111 R.A.F.   Squadron Leader P.R.W. Wickham, D.F.C.
43 R.A.F.   Squadron Leader LeRoy du Vivier, D.F.C.
3 R.A.F.   Squadron Leader A.E. Berry.
32 R.A.F.   Squadron Leader E.R. Thorn, D.F.M.
174 R.A.F.   Commandant F.E. Fayolle, D.F.C.
71 Eagle   Squadron Leader C.G. Peterson, D.F.C.
124 R.A.F.   Squadron Leader T. Balmforth, D.F.C.
616 R.A.F.   Squadron Leader H.L.I. Brown.
416 C.R.A.F.   Squadron Leader L.C. Chadburn, D.F.C.
121 Eagle   Squadron Leader W.D. Williams, D.F.C.
331 R. Norge   Major H. Maehre, D.F.C.
332 R. Norge   Major H. Mohr, D.F.C.
64 R.A.F.   Squadron Leader W.G.G.D. Smith, D.F.C.
122 R.A.F.   Squadron Leader J.R.C. Killian.
340 F. French   Commandant B. Duperier, D.F.C.

81 R.A.F.	Squadron Leader R. Berry, D.F.C.
154 R.A.F.	Squadron Leader D. Carlson.
133 Eagle	Flight Lieutenant D.J. Blakeslee.
401 C.R.A.F.	Squadron Leader K.L.B. Hodson, D.F.C.
165 R.A.F.	Squadron Leader H.J. Hallowes, D.F.M.
65 R.A.F.	Squadron Leader D.A.P. MacMullen, D.F.C.
242 R.A.F.	Squadron Leader T.C. Parker.
91 R.A.F.	Squadron Leader J.E. Demozay, D.F.C.
609 R.A.F.	Squadron Leader P.H.M. Richey, D.F.C.
56 R.A.F.	Squadron Leader H.S.L. Dundas, D.F.C.
266 R.A.F.	Squadron Leader C.L. Green
485 R.N.Z.A.F.	Squadron Leader R.J.C. Grant, D.F.M.
610 R.A.F.	Squadron Leader J.E. Johnson, D.F.C.
411 R.C.A.F.	Squadron Leader R.B. Newton, D.F.C.
253 R.A.F.	Squadron Leader D.S. Yapp, D.F.C.
303 Polish	Squadron Leader J.E.L. Zumbach, D.F.C.
307 U.S. Air Corps Pursuit Sq.	Major M.L. McNickle.
308 U.S. Air Corps Pursuit Sq.	Major F.M. Bean.
309 U.S. Air Corps Pursuit Sq.	Major H.R. Thyng.
232 R.A.F.	Squadron Leader A. McDowall, D.F.M.
403 R.C.A.F.	Squadron Leader L.S. Ford, D.F.C.
310 Czech	Squadron Leader F. Dolezal.
312 Czech	Squadron Leader J. Cernak.
130 R.A.F.	Squadron Leader P.J. Simpson, D.F.C.
66 R.A.F.	Squadron Leader R.D. Yule, D.F.C.
118 R.A.F.	Squadron Leader E.W. Wootten, D.F.C.
501 R.A.F.	Squadron Leader J.W. Villa, D.F.C.
87 R.A.F.	Squadron Leader D.G. Smallwood.
245 R.A.F.	Squadron Leader H.H.B. Mould.
175 R.A.F.	Squadron Leader J.R. Pennington-Legh, D.F.C.
19 R.A.F.	Squadron Leader P.B.G. Davies.
41 R.A.F.	Squadron Leader G.C. Hyde.
317 Polish	Squadron Leader S. Skalski, D.F.C.
222 R.A.F.	Squadron Leader R.W. Oxspring, D.F.C.

Bomber Squadrons
No.

88 R.A.F.	Wing Commander J.E. Pelly-Fry.
107 R.A.F.	Wing Commander L.A. Lynn, D.F.C.

APPENDICES

226 R.A.F.   Wing Commander W.E. Surplice, D.F.C.

Army Co-operation Squadrons
No.
26 R.A.F.   Wing Commander T.W.G. Fazan.
239 R.A.F.   Wing Commander P.L. Donkin.
400 R.C.A.F.   Wing Commander R.C.A. Waddell.
414 R.A.F.   Wing Commander R.F. Begg.

Appendix Y

REPORT BY NAVAL FORCE COMMANDER

Generally speaking, the assembly of the force and the passage were carried out in accordance with the plan and without any major incident. After clearing the gate, H.M.S. *Queen Emma* (Captain G.L.D. Gibbs, D.S.O., R.N. (Ret.)), leading Groups 1, 2 and 3, appeared to me to be proceeding at an excessive speed, and H.M.S. *Calpe* (Lieut.-Commander J.H. Wallace, R.N.) and the destroyers had some difficulty in taking station ahead. At 0016, when H.M.S. *Calpe* was abeam of H.M.S. *Queen Emma*, a signal was made informing her that she was ahead of station and instructing her to reduce to 18 knots. After this the destroyers formed ahead, and shorty afterwards altered course for the western passage through the minefield. The dan buoys and the M.L. marking the entrance to this channel were only sighted about 2 minutes before H.M.S. *Calpe* entered the channel, no signals from the Type 78 beacon being received on account of a breakdown of H.M.S. *Calpe's* R.D.F. However, H.M.S. *Calpe* and the destroyers of the 2nd Division successfully passed through the western channel, but H.M.S. *Queen Emma* with Groups 1, 2 and 3 in company, lost touch with the destroyers and passed through the eastern channel, overtaking H.M.S. *Fernie* (Lieutenant W.B. Willett, R.N.) and certain groups of L.C.T. and L.C.P., but fortunately without any collisions.

A word of praise is due to the 9th and 13th M/S Flotillas (Commander H.T. Rust, R.N., and Commander L.S.J. Ede, D.S.O., R.N.), who carried out the task allotted to them with efficiency and precision.

After passing through the minefield, H.M.S. *Calpe* stopped in accordance with the plan, and subsequently signalled her position to H.M.S. *Queen Emma*, H.M.S. *Prince Albert* (Lieutenant-Commander Peate, R.N.R.), and H.M.S. *Glengyle* (Captain D.S. McGrath, R.N.), as these vessels respectively came in sight. H.M.S. *Calpe* then proceeded and stopped about 1 mile to seaward of the position in which H.M.S. *Glengyle* with Group 4 had stopped to lower their boats.

At about 0350, gunfire was observed to the E.S.E., which, it was realised, must be in the immediate vicinity of Group 5. At the time I considered this might be caused by an E-Boat attack, but with the knowledge that O.R.P. *Slazak* (Komandor Podporueznik, R. Tyminski) and H.M.S. *Brocklesby* (Lieutenant-Commander E.N. Pumphrey, D.S.O., D.S.C., R.N.) were within about 4 miles of Group 5 and that H.M.S. *Calpe* was the only ship in the immediate vicinity of H.M.S. *Glengyle* and Group 4, it was decided to keep Group 4 in sight.

Actually Group 5 had made a chance encounter with some armed trawlers. The Naval Force Commander, Commander D.B. Wyburd, R.N., in S.G.B. 5 (Lieutenant G.H. Hummel, R.N.R.) maintained a steady course and speed in order that his L.C.P. should remain in company, but S.G.B. 5 was soon disabled, and the L.C.P. disorganised. Commander Wyburd's persistence in remaining the guide of the slow L.C.P., while himself under heavy fire, showed great gallantry and determination. Nevertheless, I am of the opinion that he would have done better to use the speed and smoke-laying capabilities of S.G.B.s in order to protect the L.C.P.s. L.C.F. (L) 1 (Lieutenant T.M. Foggitt, R.A.N.V.R.) also in company with Group 5, successfully engaged the German vessels, setting one on fire and claiming to have sunk a second. In the course of this engagement her fire control was unfortunately put out of action.

During the action, O.R.P. *Slazak* with H.M.S. *Brocklesby* in company, was approximately 4 miles to the N.N.E., but did not intervene. The Commanding Officer of O.R.P. *Slazak* has since informed me that he considered the firing came from the shore and therefore thought it best to continue with his patrol. I consider this was an error of judgment, observing that the sole reason for his patrol was to provide support for vessels engaged in the landing in the event of a contingency such as this. In future operations of this complexity it would be better to ensure, if possible, that British officers are in command of all detached units.

It will be convenient at this stage to complete the story of "Yellow" Beach landings, which were frustrated by this encounter.

Five L.C.P. effected a delayed landing on "Yellow I" Beach. Heavy opposition was encountered and the troops made no progress.

Subsequent attempts were made by the L.C.P. to withdraw them, but it proved impossible to close the beach on account of machine-gun fire, and eventually only the Naval Beach Party, who swam off to the boats, were taken off. During this period, a small German tanker was set on fire and driven ashore by M.L. 346 (Lieutenant A.D. Fear, R.N.V.R.), whose conduct throughout the operation was outstanding.

One L.C.P. effected an unopposed landing at "Yellow II" Beach. The troops on board, under the command of Major P. Young, M.C., succeeded in approaching the coast defence battery at Berneval and in sniping it for about 2 hours. Subsequently they were successfully withdrawn. I have little doubt that the failure of the coast defence battery at Berneval to play an effective part in the operation was largely due to the action of Major Young.

Subsequently, on the extreme western flank, H.M.S. *Prince Albert's* landing craft, carrying No. 4 Commando, were successfully landed according to plan. This part of the operation, which was under the joint command of Lieutenant-Commander H.H.H. Mulleneux, R.N., and Lieutenant-Colonel the Lord Lovat, M.C., went through without a hitch from beginning to end. The troops were very fortunate in that they blew up an ammunition dump at their objective by a chance mortar hit early in their attack. They were subsequently withdrawn at approximately 0815 and returned to England without incident.

Reverting to the main landings, that at "Green" Beach took place punctually and according to plan, and only encountered slight opposition. Subsequently Group 6, under the command of Commander H.V.P. McClintock, R.N., and carrying the Camerons of Canada, effected a landing at "Green" Beach according to plan about 30 minutes late. The reason for the delay lay partly in the anxiety of the Senior Military Officer not to be landed ahead of time, and partly due to navigational difficulties occasioned by smoke during the final approach. This landing met with a certain amount of opposition, but the troops were successfully put ashore. It is interesting to note that at this stage the enemy fire on the approaches to "Green" Beach was slight, but steadily increased throughout the operation, and resulted in very heavy casualties being suffered during the eventual withdrawal. This was because the force landed proved insufficient to hold an adequate bridgehead.

The landing on "Blue" Beach was delayed for 15 minutes, on account of time lost when the boats were forming up. This was due to M.G.B. 315

(Lieutenant J.I. Lloyd, R.N.V.R., whose role was to remain with H.M.S. *Queen Emma* and escort her back) going ahead and getting mixed up with the landing craft from H.M.S. *Princess Astrid*. They mistook her for M.G.B. 316 (Acting Temporary Lieutenant-Commander T.N. Cartwright, R.N.V.R.), whose role it was to lead in these landing craft. Although the landing subsequently took place according to plan, I fear that the 15 minutes' delay must have been partly responsible for the very heavy opposition which the troops immediately encountered after landing, and which apparently pinned them down on the beach area throughout the day. Subsequently H.M.S. *Duke of Wellington's* Flotilla of L.C.A. landed additional troops on this beach according to plan. This landing took place at about 0545 and encountered no abnormal opposition. Subsequently, at about 0530, I was informed that a signal had been received stating that no landing had taken place on "Blue" Beach and I reported this in my situation report made at 0612. Actually, there is some reason to suppose that this report was of German origin, but the whole of the events that took place ashore at "Blue" Beach were obscure, although it was clear from the very outset that the troops were held up. There is little doubt that this was the chief cause of the failure of the Military Plan, and in view of the uncertainty about what really happened, I have since requested the Commanding officer, H.M.S. *Queen Emma*, to conduct a close enquiry with all the boat officers concerned.

Meanwhile the main landings on "Red" and "White" Beaches took place punctually and according to plan, with the exception that the leading wave of three L.C.T. approached from too far to the westward and were about 10 to 15 minutes late in touching down.

The air support, and the smoke-making aircraft on the East Cliff, were accurately synchronised, and the destroyer's fire, both on the houses along the front while the boats were going in, and subsequently on the east and west cliffs, appeared to be as effective as could be expected. No losses of landing craft took place during the initial landing, but it did not appear to the officer in charge that the troops were able to capture the strong points along the front after landing. However, the L.C.T. on going in encountered very heavy opposition, and I consider that theirs was a notable achievement in landing 28 out of 30 tanks dry-shod. The heavy damage and casualties in the L.C.T. were undoubtedly due in a large measure to the relatively long periods they remained on the beach, waiting for the miscellaneous troops that they were carrying in addition to the tanks to disembark.

The work of L.C.F. (L) 2 (Lieutenant E.L. Graham, R.N.V.R.) in supporting the main landing, calls for special mention. This vessel closed in to point-blank range, and gave most effective support. She was soon disabled, and her Captain killed, but her guns were fought until one by one they were put out of action and the ship herself was finally sunk.

Lieutenant-Commander J.H. Dathan, R.N. (Senior Officer of Group 7), carrying reserve troops in L.C.P., reported on board H.M.S. *Calpe* within 5 minutes of the time laid down in the plan. At the request of Major-General Roberts, I instructed him to land his force on "Red" Beach, and the landing was successfully effected by 0700. This landing, which was shielded by smoke until the last moment, encountered very heavy fire just off the beaches, but all boats effected a landing although in most cases the troops sustained heavy casualties immediately afterwards. Two out of the 26 boats were destroyed.

Up to this point the Naval part of the plan had proceeded very much as was intended, with the exception of the frustration of the "Yellow" Beach landing. Furthermore, there had been remarkably little opposition from shore batteries, and apparently none from enemy aircraft. Nevertheless, it was clear that the military operations were not proceeding according to plan, and that the opposition ashore was considerably greater than had been expected. In view of the failure of the "Blue" Beach landing and hence of the plan to capture the East Cliff, I felt doubtful whether H.M.S. *Locust's* proposed entry into the harbour would be either practicable or profitable. Commander R.E.D. Ryder V.C., R.N., who was signalled to come on board H.M.S. *Calpe* at about 0645, shared this view, and informed me that H.M.S. *Locust* had already suffered damage and casualties whilst closing the East Cliff earlier on. Major-General Roberts was consulted and agreed that no attempt should be made to enter the harbour. It was decided instead to transfer the Royal Marine Commando to armoured landing craft and to land them as reinforcements. The General asked that they should be sent to "White" Beach, and this operation was entrusted to Commander Ryder, all L.C.F. (L) being ordered to close H.M.S. *Locust* and give support. Actually, owing to communication difficulties, only two L.C.F. (L) responded, but all the Chasseurs backed them up and gave good support. The landing was effected in face of very heavy opposition at about 0840. Judging from the reports of the landing craft who took part, it is doubtful whether the Royal Marines were able to achieve anything.

About this time Commander Wyburd came aboard H.M.S. *Calpe* and informed me of what had occurred to the best of his knowledge to Group 5. He was instructed to embark in M.G.B. 317 and to proceed to the vicinity of "Yellow" Beaches to round up what L.C.P. he could fine.

Lieutenant-Commander H.W. Goulding, D.S.O., R.N.R., also came on board about this time and informed me of the landing at "Blue" Beach, an account of which is given earlier. He was instructed to proceed to "Blue" Beach with four L.C.A. to endeavour to withdraw any troops which were there. Lieutenant-Commander C.W. McMullen, R.N., in an M.L., proceeded with him to provide support. I received a report later to the effect that Lieutenant-Commander Goulding was unable to close "Blue" Beach owing to heavy opposition and that no one could be seen on the beach.

Commander H.V.P. McClintock, R.N., also reported on board H.M.S. *Calpe*, and I instructed him to proceed to investigate "Green" Beach and inform the Beachmaster that he should not evacuate the beach, as it might be necessary to withdraw all the troops from "Green" Beach. Commander McClintock was unable to approach close to "Green" Beach owing to heavy and well-directed fire of the enemy.

At about 0750, I received information that ten E-Boats were approaching from Boulogne. Accordingly, H.M. Ships *Brocklesby*, *Bleasdale* and O.R.P. *Slazak* were ordered to proceed to the north-eastward, and all available M.G.B.s were also ordered to patrol to the eastward. (My 0752 and 0816 refer.) Nothing more was heard of the E-Boats, and it is remarkable that at no time during the entire operation was there any organised opposition from German naval forces. While detached on this service, O.R.P. *Slazak* was damaged by near misses, and later had to return to England.

Throughout the period which followed, enemy fire from the shore steadily increased, and the destroyers were forced constantly to shift their positions in order to avoid damage and keep under cover of smoke. Periodically requests were received from the shore for supporting fire against strong points, but in no cases was an F.O.O. in a position to observe this fire. The requests were met by detailing destroyers in succession, but I felt very doubtful of the efficacy of their support under the conditions which prevailed.

H.M.S. *Calpe's* appearance during most of this period must have resembled that of a Fleet Flagship on regatta day, as there were seldom less than from six to ten craft alongside. They came to transfer wounded, bring reports, or seek instructions, and their presence was rather an embarrassment to the Commanding Officer when he wished to manoeuvre to avoid gunfire. Lieutenant-Commander Wallace remained imperturbable, however, throughout the operation, and by his coolness set an excellent example.

My general impression during this phase of the operation, from the Naval point of view, was a feeling of inability to give the troops effective support. The military situation was completely obscure, and the large quantities of smoke drifting inshore made it impossible to see what was happening. On the other hand, had it not been for the smoke, it would have been impossible for the destroyers and landing craft to remain as close inshore as they did.

Immediately after the landings, the landing craft had withdrawn to seaward of the destroyers. This was on accordance with the instructions they had received in the event of their finding that the approaches to the beaches remained under heavy fire. It was this fact, more than anything else, that indicated to me from the outset that things ashore were not going according to plan.

At about 0900, H.M.S. *Garth* reported that her ammunition was nearly exhausted. I accordingly ordered her to escort H.M.S. *Alresford*, which had a damaged L.C.T. in tow, and Nos. 10 and 11 Groups, whose tanks and troops the General had decided not to land, back to England.

By 0900 it had become clear to me that the troops ashore were in difficulties and were unlikely to gain possession of the east and west cliffs, which dominated the main beaches. I learned later that even some of the buildings on the front were still in enemy hands. It was obvious therefore that the military situation was serious, and that it was becoming steadily more difficult for ships and craft to close the beaches. Accordingly, I advised the General that the withdrawal should take place with as little further delay as possible, and should be confined to personnel. I considered that 1030 would be the earliest practicable time, as it was necessary to warn the Air Officer Commanding 11 Group and to pass instructions to the landing craft. The General agreed, subject to confirmation nearer to time.

Accordingly, Commander McClintock was summoned on board H.M.S. *Calpe*, and it was decided that all A.L.C. and M.L.C. should be instructed to proceed into the same beaches as those on which they had originally landed and should ferry troops off on to L.C.T. who should remain about 1 mile from the shore. All possible support was to be given by destroyers and L.C.F. (L). (I considered it out of the question to send L.C.P. or L.C.T. inshore, in view of the volume of enemy fire.)

To give effect to this plan, Commander McClintock proceeded in M.L. 187 and gave necessary instructions to the landing craft, and a signal, similar to that later sent at 0950, save that the time for the withdrawal was given as 1030, was coded and prepared for despatch. Later on, however, the General informed me that he would prefer to wait until 1100. The signal thus amended was then despatched and Commander McClintock was informed of the later time. At about 1022, the destroyers were ordered to form on a line to bear 070° to 250° and to follow the landing craft in. All vessels suitably placed were instructed to make smoke. The wind was on-shore and slightly from the west, and an effective screen of smoke prevented the landing craft from being fired upon until they were close inshore. Unfortunately, the smoke also hid the beaches from the destroyers and it was very difficult to see what was going on, or to offer effective support by gunfire. Nevertheless, without the smoke it is doubtful whether any withdrawal would have been possible.

During these events H.M.S. *Calpe* steered for the western end of "Green" Beach, as it was thought that no supporting fire would be necessary in this area, and both the Military Force Commander and the Air Liaison Officer were extremely averse to H.M.S. *Calpe's* guns being fired, on account of the risk to the special wireless apparatus that had been installed. Actually, however, it soon became apparent that the western cliff at the end of "Green" Beach was held by the enemy, and H.M.S. *Calpe* came under small arms and machine-gun fire, necessitating her opening the range. It is interesting to record that when subsequently both H.M.S. *Calpe* and H.M.S. *Fernie* were obliged to open fire with their main armament, much of the wireless apparatus remained intact.

It soon became virtually impossible to know how the withdrawal was proceeding but, at about 1130, H.M.S. *Calpe* embarked two landing craft loads of troops, mostly wounded, from whom it was learned that there were still men waiting to come off at "Green" Beach. At about the same time the General asked for the ship to proceed to the main beaches and ascertain the position there. Accordingly, M.L. 194 (Act. Lieut.-

Commander W. Whitfield, R.N.R.) was hailed and instructed to round up the landing craft in the area and send them in again. At about the same time, a signal, originator unknown, was received to the effect that there were no more troops on "Green" Beach, and was immediately contradicted by my 1147. H.M.S. *Calpe* then proceeded off the main beaches and closed L.C.T. 9, to whom troops were being transferred by landing craft. Some of these troops were embarked in H.M.S. *Calpe* in order to save time. Slightly later I closed A.L.C. 185 and 188, who had just come off the main beach. Both gave it as their opinion that the conditions ashore precluded further evacuation.

At about 1220, a signal was received from Commander McClintock indicating that no further evacuation was feasible. However, the Military Force Commander asked that a further effort should be made, and although I felt that this might well result in greater losses to troops already embarked, than in the embarkation of additional troops, I decided to give Commander McClintock discretion whether to make a further effort. Accordingly, the following signal was made:
"If no further evacuation possible withdraw."

Actually, the signal as reported to Commander McClintock omitted the word "if", and from that time onwards H.M.S. *Calpe* was unable to get into touch with him. I supposed at the time that his M.L. must have been sunk, but actually he was able to order the withdrawal of all landing craft to a pre-arranged position, 4 miles 330° from Dieppe. Consequently L.C.A. 185 and 188, with H.M.S. *Calpe*, were soon the only craft left close inshore, but owing to the low visibility I was not aware of this at the time.

Throughout the whole operation, Commander McClintock, R.N., was of the greatest service in his capacity of "Boat Pool Officer". He was ably seconded by Lieut.-Commander Dathan, and Lieut.-Commander McMullen. The fact that over a thousand troops were evacuated, under conditions which can seldom have been equalled, must be attributed largely to the work of these officers.

At about 1250 I decided to close the beach again for a final personal view, and keeping A.L.C. 185 and 188 on either bow, H.M.S. *Calpe* steered for the eastern end of "Red" Beach, at the same time opening fire from the foremost guns at the breakwaters, on which machine-gun posts were reported to be preventing the troops on "Red" Beach from reaching the water. When about 9 cables from the beach, H.M.S. *Calpe* came under heavy fire, and no sign of troops or landing craft, other than derelicts, could be seen on the beach. Accordingly, H.M.S. *Calpe* manoeuvred to gain the cover of smoke, and I felt convinced that any further attempt to take off troops would be unlikely to succeed. Before finally giving up however, I proceeded to seaward to close H.M.S. *Locust* and ascertain Commander Ryder's views, as it seemed possible that with H.M.S. *Locust's* shallow draught he might be more aware of the situation on the beaches. Whilst this interchange of signals was in progress, however, the General informed me that the larger body of the troops on the beach had surrendered. At almost exactly the same time H.M.S. *Berkeley* (Lieutenant J.J.S. Yorke, R.N.) received a direct hit with a heavy bomb. The ship's back was broken, her forecastle awash, and the engine and boiler-rooms were flooding. Fortunately, the loss of life was small, partly owing to the promptitude with which S.G.B. 8 proceeded alongside to take off her crew and partly owing to the presence of A.L.C. 185 and 188, who were able to pick up survivors in the water. I instructed H.M.S. *Albrighton* to sink her, which she did by torpedo fire. At much the same time a fighter attack was made on H.M.S. *Calpe's* bridge, causing several casualties, including Air Commodore Cole, who was severely wounded. The destroyers in the vicinity of H.M.S. *Berkeley* then proceeded to seaward to join the main convoy of landing craft and coastal craft, who had formed up in accordance with instructions, approximately 4 miles to seaward of Dieppe and were now heading slowly north.

H.M.S. *Fernie* was instructed to take Guide, and shortly afterwards I unwisely instructed H.M.S. *Calpe* to proceed to the eastward to pick up a British pilot who was reported in the water. This resulted in two bombing attacks by dive bombers on H.M.S. *Calpe* both of which secured near misses, causing damage and casualties.

Subsequently H.M.S. *Calpe* re-joined the convoy which proceeded without incident, other than some ineffectual air attacks, through the western swept channel, and to a position approximately 20 miles from Newhaven. At this point I was joined by Captain D. (16) with H.M.S. *Mackay* and H.M.S. *Blencathra*, and I requested him to escort the small craft into Newhaven thus releasing H.M.S. *Calpe* and the other destroyers and H.M.S. *Locust* to proceed direct to Portsmouth with their wounded, who totalled over 500. The coastal craft and landing craft reached Newhaven without further incident, and the destroyers and H.M.S. *Locust* berthed alongside at Portsmouth shortly after midnight.

Before closing this narrative, a word of praise is due to the medical officers with the force. An exceptional strain was thrown upon them, partly by the very large proportion of casualties among the troops, and partly because the organisation carefully prepared by Surgeon-Commander W.B.D. Miller, D.S.C., M.B., Ch.B., R.N.V.R., was upset by the turning back of Group 12. This group, comprising four spare L.C.T.s, carried an important proportion of the available medical parties. It was a mistake on my part not to bring them on, despite the fact that they were no longer required for an evacuation as originally planned.

A detailed account of the work of the medical parties has been made separately, but the services performed by Surgeon-Lieutenant M.P. Martin, M.R.C.S., L.R.C.P., R.N.V.R., deserve special mention. This officer was embarked in L.C.F. (L) 2, and took charge of her when her other officers became casualties. Subsequently he was rescued from the water, after L.C.F. (L) 2 had sunk, and transferred to H.M.S. *Calpe*. Although himself injured, he was untiring in helping H.M.S. *Calpe's* medical officers, who had to compete with casualties to over a quarter of the crew, plus 278 wounded soldiers.

J. Hughes Hallett,
Captain R.N.,
Naval Force Commander.

Appendix Z

REPORT BY MILITARY POLICE COMMANDER

This report covers the operation from the commencement of the movement to embarkation points until the return to ports in England.

Assembly
The assembly from the ordinary accommodation areas took place in accordance with the plans and without hitch. The stores and equipment were found to be allotted in accordance with the plans and were in satisfactory condition when taken over by the military personnel. It is, however, considered that this could be done more smoothly if the added risks from the security aspect were accepted by having unit officers and small parties at the vessels in advance. They would be able to carry out such tasks as the cleaning of weapons, fusing of grenades and a more detailed stowage related to the tactical requirements. At Newhaven it was noticeable that a considerable number of civilians were in observation of the embarking process. It is considered that this situation should not occur in future if it is possible to seal the area without thereby disclosing the intention to carry out an actual operation.

The Passage
The passage took place in accordance with the plan and was without incident with the exception of the unfortunate encounter with an enemy convoy, which it may be assumed disclosed our intention to the enemy.

Landings
"Orange" Beach – 4 Commando, under command of Lieutenant-Colonel The Lord Lovat, captured and destroyed their main objective, an enemy battery, in addition to which they disposed of its ammunition dump, withdrawing successfully.
"Green" Beach – The South Saskatchewan Regiment, under command

of Lieutenant-Colonel C.C.I. Merritt, landed unopposed at 0450 hours, as planned. This regiment established a bridgehead and captured its immediate objectives. Strong opposition was met from the area Les-Quatre-Vents Farm and during the morning a reserve enemy battalion appeared on the west side of the River Scie, causing some difficulty.
The Camerons of Canada, under command of Lieutenant-Colonel A.C. Gostling (who was killed immediately he stepped ashore), passing through the South Saskatchewan Regiment, exploited some 2 miles inland on the west side of the River Scie – a change from the original plan necessitated by the opposition met by the South Saskatchewan Regiment.

Before the Camerons of Canada were able to reach their objective (the aerodrome), the withdrawal order necessitated their return. During their penetration a considerable number of the enemy were accounted for with little loss to themselves.

Although the withdrawal to the beach area was accomplished with small loss, the embarkation stage resulted in heavy casualties from enfilade machine-gun fire, observed mortar and artillery fire.

"White" and "Red" Beaches – The frontal attack was made by the Royal Hamilton Light Infantry under command of Lieutenant-Colonel R.R. Labatt, on the right, and Essex Scottish Regiment, on the left, closely followed by the first wave of tanks from 14 Canadian Army Tank Battalion, under command of Lieutenant-Colonel J.G. Andrews. Although the beach had been heavily engaged prior to the assault by Naval bombardment and close support attacks bombing by the Air Force, the troops came under heavy fire from concealed posts in the two headlands to the west and east of the beaches and also from artillery sited under cover of the first line of buildings, which was able to fire directly into the assault craft as they landed. The first wave of tanks came under direct fire as soon as they came out of the L.C.T. and, in consequence, some failed to get in. About one hour after touch down, information received indicated that "Red" Beach was sufficiently cleared to permit the landing of the floating reserve. The Fusiliers Mont Royal, under command of Lieutenant-Colonel D. Menard, therefore were ordered to land and, moving to the west, establish themselves on "White" Beach and on the edge of the town of Dieppe.

Unfortunately, the assault demolition parties of engineers, which were designed to enable the tanks to penetrate through the crust of the enemy's defences were unable to carry out their task owing to heavy casualties. Many of their stores were set on fire before landing.

This resulted in all prospect of successful penetration being foredoomed to failure.

"Blue" Beach – The Royal Regiment of Canada, under command of Lt.-Col D.E. Catto, landed in two waves and immediately came under very heavy fire from prepared posts on the cliff and pill-boxes on the beach. They were unable to secure the beachhead and to climb the cliff to capture the east headland, which was essential to the success of operations on the main beaches ("White" and "Red"). Consequently, in spite of continuous Naval bombardment from destroyers and gunboats, and close support bombers, the heavy and light guns sited on this headland and in the face of the cliff were never permanently neutralised and this considerably affected the success of the landings on the main beaches.

"Yellow" Beach – 3 Commando, under command of Lieutenant-Colonel J. Durnford-Slater, had been dispersed in their previous engagement with the enemy coastal craft and only five L.C.P. were able to touch down. This reduced party, however, while unable to destroy the coast defence battery, which was its main objective, was able to prevent it from taking part in the main action throughout the operation. The party withdrew successfully.

Withdrawal
At 0930 hours, about 4½ hours after the initial landings, the enemy had moved up a number of mobile batteries, mortars and additional infantry, which made it clear that not only was the capture of the planned objectives now impossible, but also that it had become necessary to make immediate plans for withdrawal.

The decision was made to withdraw at 1100 hours, which necessitated abandoning any tanks that had been landed in order to re-embark personnel. At the same time the craft carrying the remaining tanks and some 700 men, which had not attempted to land, were ordered to return to England. Full support was given by the Air Force and the ships' guns to cover the withdrawal, but by this time the enemy had organised very heavy fire on both the beaches and the sea approaches which made it practically impossible for the landing craft to approach. In addition, dive bombers attacked the ships and the assault craft lying off Dieppe.

In spite of heavy casualties to both personnel and craft, the Navy went in again and again to every beach until it was heard that our men on "White" and "Red" Beaches were either killed or overwhelmed, when any further attempts would have been to no avail.

Every possible effort was made by the Navy to get the assault craft into the beaches, including the Force Commander's destroyer which closed the beach until it almost grounded, in an effort to support the withdrawal by fire and to pick up survivors. The expedition returned to England under an umbrella of Air Force fighter cover, which prevented any serious interference to the return journey. The dispersal arrangements in England were most efficiently organised by 1 Canadian Corps and all returning personnel were given hot food on arrival, the wounded being despatched to hospital immediately and the remainder returned to unit areas.

General
Air cover and bombing which, during the whole operation involved 2,892 sorties, was magnificent. The close support effort was directed in the area by a controller in the Force Commanders' ship whilst the fighter cover was similarly directed from No. 2 Headquarters Ship. This is the first time that this method of control had been used and it proved to be most satisfactory. Throughout the operation the Air Force provided smoke screes by use of smoke-laying aircraft and 100-lb. phosphorus bombs, both of which were very effective.

The conduct of all ranks and their determination to capture their objectives was beyond praise. Although coming under the heaviest form of shell and machine-gun fire, there was no hesitation on the part of anyone to get to grips with the enemy.

All the men who returned are in wonderful spirits and have expressed their desire to go back at the enemy again as soon as possible.

Intelligence.
(i) *Enemy Troops* – Despite previous Intelligence reports, no evidence was obtained to indicate the presence of 110 Division. All prisoners stated that 302 Division was still in the area and had received no orders to move.

The garrison appears to have been from 302 Division and elements of 571 Regiment, an *Ersatz* low category unit composed of Poles only recently drafted into service. 571 Regiment appears to have arrived in Dieppe on 10th August and to have been mainly trained for observation.

In addition, at least one battalion of the Todt Organisation had been employed for some time in the improvement of coastal defences.

(ii) *Interrogation of Prisoners* – Interrogation of prisoners indicates that a special "Stand to" with troops, sleeping fully clothed (*Hoechstalarmbereitschaft*), had been in effect for the whole Channel coast since 1st August, 1942. This same special stand-to had already once been ordered, end of June to 25th July, 1942, and was apparently not based on specific information, but was a normal precaution taken during periods when tide, weather, and general conditions were favourable for sea landings. No special precautions such as re-doubling of picquets, etc., had been taken on the night of 18th/19th August, 1942, nor did this occur during the first week of July, 1942.

(iii) *Defensive Walls* – As revealed by air photographs and by reports from the operation itself, the enemy has been actively improving his defences along the whole coast and in the Dieppe area. These have been completed to the point where they were ready for use.

(iv) *Defensive Armament and Employment* – The enemy's defence consisted of a skilfully co-ordinated fire plan employing field artillery, anti-aircraft and anti-tank guns, mortars, and machine-guns.

Considerable high velocity artillery was sited where it could bear on the landing craft, using positions in the cliffs and in the houses on the front of the promenade. Undoubtedly many anti-aircraft guns were sited for a dual anti-aircraft/anti-tank role and it is certain that some of these guns were able to pierce and knock out the Churchill tanks.

The enemy's use of mortars which were liberally dispersed over the front, was excellent in the extreme and devastating to our troops. They were sited in covered positions with fixed lines of fire and additional control by Forward Observation Officers who were in communication by telephone. In fact, they were employed similarly to a light howitzer. Mobile batteries, as was expected, were sited to fire on beaches, and additional batteries and horse-drawn mortars were quickly brought into action. Machine-guns were well sited in caves, pill-boxes and houses.

Some were able to fire directly into the landing craft as soon as the doors were lowered. Extensive use was made of cross-fire, and the enemy was quick to cover with fire any gaps which were made in the wire.

The enemy also employed grenade pits sited behind the sea wall, from which he was able to deal with troops attempting to scale the wall. Access to these pits was by crawl trench.

The enemy's snipers were numerous and well trained, and concentrated on officers and on personnel carrying equipment such as wireless sets, etc.

A prisoner reports that in pill-boxes covering 900 yards from the cliff edge near the *Casino* westwards there were:
Four 3.7-cm. anti-tank guns.
One 4.7-cm. anti-tank gun.

It has been reported that the enemy employed concealed anti-tank traps on the beach behind the wire and there are some unconfirmed reports of the use of anti-tank mines.

The wire used was of Dannert type, but of heavier gauge than ours and backed by an ordinary apron fence. There is no proof that the wire was electrified.

An outstanding point was the enemy's extensive use of tracer ammunition of all natures and for all purposes.

Own Weapons
Six-pounder Gun – Confirmed reports show that the six-pounder was able to deal with pill-boxes successfully.

Boys Anti-Tank Rifle – Proved its usefulness time and time again against the enemy behind any light defences.

Sten Gun – Numerous reports indicate that the Sten gun was very subject to jamming. This principal failure is in the ejection. This should be rectified at once.

Air Support
(i) *Close Support Attacks* – The close support on the main beaches, although pressed home, was of necessity of short duration and, owing

to the troops being unable to reach the houses before the enemy had recovered, he material effect of this support was to a great extent lost. It is difficult to assess the value of the bombing attacks made by the Hurricane bombers, but it was noticeable that such attacks were constantly called for.

(ii) *Smoke* – The S.C.I. proved to be extremely valuable and efficient, but the resources in this equipment were inadequate to meet the demands under the circumstances.

Naval Support

The Naval fire support was of considerable value. In the circumstances Forward Observation Officers were unable to establish themselves in suitable Observation Posts, but nevertheless were able to bring fire to bear on a number of targets, including pill-boxes on the jetty which were successfully engaged.

Recommendations

(i) *Tanks* – The employment of tanks in a raid of short duration is not recommended and it is considered that a bridgehead must be established prior to the disembarkation of tanks.

(ii) *Landing Craft* – All landing craft should have heavier armament, which should be shielded and so positioned that it can support the assaulting troops.

(iii) *Landing Craft Support* – Some form of heavily armoured and heavily armed support craft is necessary. This should be a shallow draft craft, so that if necessary it could be beached.

(iv) *Tracer Ammunition* – All automatic weapons should have a high proportion of tracer and in the case of medium machine-guns this should be factory loaded.

(v) *Bomber Support* – The effect on the population of coastal towns of heavy bombing as a preliminary to a landing must be accepted.

When a suitable measure of air superiority is attained, Bomber Command should be prepared to employ accurate and heavy day bombing on targets such as towns and heavily defended beaches.

This appears to be the only way of obtaining the equivalent of heavy artillery concentrations in land operations.

Air Recognition

A much higher standard of air recognition is required in combined operations. There were numerous occasions when our own aircraft were engaged.

(vii) *Intercommunication* – It is recommended that a signals control room is required on each headquarters ship.

(viii) *Flexibility* – It is considered that in all operations of this nature the initial assault should be made by light forces to feel out the soft spots, with strong and flexible reserves quickly available.

J.H. Roberts,
Major-General,
Comd. 2 Cdn. Div.

Appendix AA

REPORT BY THE AIR FORCE COMMANDER

General Outline
Operation "Jubilee" was a raid against occupied territory with the purpose of capturing, by assault, and occupying for a limited period, the town of Dieppe. Military tasks in the area of Dieppe included the destruction of local defences, power stations, dock installations – the capture of prisoners and the destruction of the aerodrome installations near the town. It was also intended to capture and to remove German invasion barges and other craft in the harbour.

The operation was planned to take place on the first suitable morning for such a landing between the 18th and 23rd August. The expedition sailed from the area of the Portsmouth Command in a succession of groups starting at civil twilight on the evening of 18th August.

The plan prepared jointly by the three Force Commanders involved a landing on the outer flanks of Dieppe at "Orange" and "Yellow" Beaches by Nos. 4 and 3 Commandos, whose tasks were to neutralise enemy battery positions 6 miles to the east and west of Dieppe. At the same time a Regiment of the 2nd Canadian Corps was to be landed to secure "Green" Beach, 3 miles to the west of Dieppe, and to attack objectives on the west outer perimeter of the town, "Hindenburg". Simultaneously, the Royal Regiment of Canada was to secure "Blue" Beach, 1½ miles to the east of Dieppe, and objectives on the east flank of the outer perimeter, i.e. "Bismark". Half an hour later the Royal Hamilton Light Infantry and Essex Scottish Regiment with the Camerons of Canada, were to make frontal assaults on "Red" and "White" Beaches in front of the town of Dieppe. This frontal assault was to have been supported by an armoured detachment of 18 tanks. Later a Royal Marine Commando was to land near the Harbour of Dieppe to demolish objectives in the Dock area. A further echelon of tanks was then to be landed, making a total force of 58 tanks. It was intended, when the tasks ashore had been completed to withdraw the whole force for re-embarkation at about 1100 hours.

Air Support

Air support was to be provided throughout the operation as follows:

(i) *Fighter Cover.*

Fighter cover and general protection for the expedition throughout the hours of daylight. The primary task of this cover was to protect the expedition against air attack. It was considered that the two most dangerous periods in regard to attack from the air would be the landing and withdrawal. It was, therefore, decided that the strength of this fighter cover should vary from two to 6 squadrons during the different phases of the operation, with such reinforcement as might prove necessary.

(ii) *Close Support.*

(a) Close support, bombing and low-flying fighter attacks on selected targets were to be made in direct support of the assault, occupation and withdrawal.

(b) Smoke-laying aircraft were t be used to neutralise defences, both in accordance with the pre-arranged plan and subsequently as required at the request of the Military Force Commander.

(c) Day Bomber Squadrons were to be employed to attack both pre-arranged targets and requested targets.

(iii) *Reconnaissance.*

(a) Tactical Reconnaissance was to be made over the area of the operation, including the lines of approach of any enemy reinforcement.

(b) Coastal A.S.V. reconnaissance from Cherbourg to Boulogne was to be maintained throughout the night prior to the assault.

(c) Fighter anti-surface vessel reconnaissance patrols were to be maintained throughout daylight hours.

(iv) *Strategical Bombing.*

It had been agreed between the three Force Commanders not to lay on any preliminary or diversionary effort with bombers prior to the assault in order not to jeopardise surprise. A strategical bombing attack was, however, planned against the enemy aerodrome of Abbeville-Drucat, with a view to interfering with the operation of his defending fighters. This attack was to coincide with the main withdrawal from the beaches at which time considerable interference was anticipated from fighters operating from the Abbeville area.

Disposition of the Air Forces in No. 11 Group

The following forces were available:

Day Fighter forces	50 Squadrons Cover.
	6 Squadrons Close Support.
Day Bomber forces	2 Squadrons
Hurricane Bomber forces	2 Squadrons
Army Co-operation forces	4 Squadrons
"Smoke" forces	3 Squadrons

These forces were disposed as set out in the Order of Battle at Appendix A to this report.

The assembly of these forces involved internal moves of Squadrons within No. 11 Group and the reinforcement of the Group by 15 Squadrons from outside. These extensive movements were carried out on the 14th and 15th August. Details of the Squadron and necessary maintenance unit moves were as follows:

	Intake of Units into No. 11 Group.	*Internal Movements in No. 11 Group.*
Fighter Squadrons	17	17
Servicing Echelon	–	8
Squadron Transports	4½	9½
Petrol Tankers	7	12
Starter Trolleys	32	116
Echelons without air lift	–	6
Squadrons without air lift	–	6
Squadrons with air lift	–	11

The following supplies of ammunition and petrol were accumulated at Stations in No. 11 Group immediately prior to the Operation:

Ammunition

20-mm. Ball.	20-mm H.E./1.	.303 A.P.	.303 Incend.	20-mm Links.
727,200	727,200	7,484,400	2,474,800	1,454,400

Petrol – 100 Octane gallons – 712,000.

Enemy Dispositions

The German Air Force had approximately 260 front-line single-engined aircraft between Brest and Texel. These were disposed as follows:

Holland	40
Pas de Calais	125
Brest to Fécamp	95

The German policy since June this year has been to concentrate these air forces on a few aerodromes along the western front. The German system of reinforcement is flexible up to a point, with extreme mobility of units from one place to another. On the other hand, he finds difficulty in adapting his control areas quickly to these reinforcements.

Apart from the reconnaissance units and a small number of aircraft used for anti-shipping, the whole of the German bomber force on the western front has been in use by night only. This force was disposed mainly in the Dutch bases at *Eindhoven, Soesterberg, Gilze Rijen* and *Deelen*. It numbered some 120 long-range bombers, with a further 100 at *Beauvais, Creil, Châteaudun, Chartres* and *Rennes*. Reports from pilots during the Operation "Jubilee" indicate that a small number of bombers from reserve training units were brought into action. It was considered unlikely that the enemy would be able to bring his fighters from as far west as Brest or as far north as Holland early in the operation. Thus, the Fighter forces likely to oppose us in the early stages were from the *Abbeville* area – 50, *Beaumont-le-Roger* area – 50, *Cherbourg* area – 20, together with possible reinforcements from *St. Omer* and *Courtrai*; approximately 30 and 45 respectively.

Operational Control

Control of all air forces was exercised direct by the Air Force Commander from his operational Headquarters at Uxbridge. Aircraft were despatched on instructions issued from No. 11 Group Operations Room through the normal Group to Sector, Sector to Squadron Dispersal Point channels. The Force Commanders afloat were able to ask at any time for special air support from bombers or fighters by means of the W/T link provided between Portsmouth and the Headquarters Ship, and a listening watch maintained at No. 11 Group Headquarters.

The lowest Squadron in the Fighter Cover operated on No. 11 Group Guard No. 1 frequency so that the Fighter Controller in either of the

Headquarters Ships could communicate with the Squadrons of the Fighter Cover.

All outgoing Close Support Fighter sorties called the Headquarters Ship by V.H.F. R/T when approaching the enemy coast. The Fighter Controller in the Headquarters Ship then, at the request of either the Military or Naval Commanders re-directed Fighter sorties to attack any suitable alternative target which the situation demanded.

Despite the fact that a very large number of Squadrons were being used throughout the operation (over 60 Squadrons), this method of control worked admirably. During the whole course of this very gruelling test of the normal ground control organisation in No. 11 Group there was no breakdown.

This proved conclusively that the existing Fighter ground control organisation, although primarily designed for defensive purposes, provides all the facilities required for the direction of offensive operations within normal fighter range. The co-ordination of the Air Force effort from a central point is essential. The Group Operations Room, with its extensive network of communications augmented by advanced W/T and R/T communication with local Commanders in the expedition proved to be ideal.

The local control by the Headquarters Ships proved equally successful. The bottom Squadron of all Fighter Cover formations operated on No. 11 Group Guard 1 frequency, and were directed on to enemy aircraft by a Controller in Headquarters Ship No. 2. Close Support Squadrons operated on a Tangmere Sector Operational frequency and were directed on to targets as required by the Military Commander by a Controller in Headquarters Ship No. 1. Thus, the two Headquarters Ships accompanying the expedition were used to assist in the control of air forces as would an A.A.S.C. during a land battle.

In the majority of cases Close Support fighter pilots had been briefed, as to the targets to be attacked, before leaving the ground, but experience gained during the operation showed conclusively that it was possible to re-direct Fighters or to give them assistance in finding their target by local direction. Similarly, Fighters were frequently assisted in sighting enemy aircraft by the running commentary given by the Controller in Headquarters Ship No. 2. There is no doubt that this local control was largely responsible for the high percentage of interceptions made on enemy aircraft, thus greatly minimising the effectiveness of enemy air attacks on ships and troops.

977. To summarise – the system of control from the Group, through Sectors, and through the Headquarters Ships, adequately met all requirements. The excellent communications and flexible control facilities of the normal Fighter organisation at home proved most efficient for such combined operations.

Tactical Reconnaissance

Tactical Reconnaissance units suffered a higher casualty rate than any other type. This was due to the deep penetration required of them which necessitated their patrolling well beyond the area of Fighter Cover. The coast roads leading to Dieppe were reconnoitred every half hour, and those from Amiens, Rouen, Yvetot and Le Havre, places from which reinforcements might be expected, every hour.

Aircraft took off from Gatwick, flew to the Dieppe area via the Beachy Head route, made contact with the Command Ship, and then proceeded on their allotted tasks. On completion of each sortie Tactical Reconnaissance pilots flew sufficiently near to the ship to ensure satisfactory R/T transmission of any information they had. They then returned immediately to Gatwick and passed their information by telephone to the Air Force Commander.

The only movement worthy of note was that of about five light tanks approaching Dieppe reported at 1210 hours.

The range of the H.F. fitted in the Tactical Reconnaissance aircraft proved inadequate.

A.S.V. Reconnaissance Patrols

Aircraft of Coastal Command maintained A.S.V. search patrols throughout the hours of darkness on the flanks of the expedition during the passage. No sightings were made.

General Narrative

The operation is conveniently divided into five distinct phases. The first covers the outward passage and the landings on various beaches. The second covers the period when progress was being made towards the pre-determined objectives ashore. The third phase covers the withdrawal of landing parties to their beaches. The fourth period

APPENDICES

extends to the time when the withdrawal was complete. The fifth phase covers the return passage to England.

Time.

2000 The expedition sailed from the area of the Portsmouth Command in a succession of Groups on the evening of 18th August, headed by the destroyer *Calpe*.

2130 Shortly before dark the convoy which consisted of 217 craft in all, steamed past the *Calpe* (Headquarters Ship No. 1) to be checked.

0115 In the early hours of 19th August, H.M.S. *Calpe* led the way through an enemy minefield, which had already been swept by a flotilla of minesweepers from Newhaven. A quarter of an hour later the whole convoy was safely through the minefield, but it was noticed that the L.C.T. had lagged some way behind.

0300 Shortly after 0300 hours the first landing craft were lowered from their parent ships. The lighthouse on the cliff outside Dieppe was then visible. Up to this time the outward passage was comparatively uneventful, but a misfortune now occurred.

0320 The landing craft conveying No. 3 Commando, which had been detailed to attack "Yellow" Beach (6 miles east of Dieppe) came into contact with an enemy convoy which included armed trawlers, and a number of our small craft were sunk. These losses resulted in the failure to subdue coast defence batteries to the east of Dieppe.

here was no other enemy activity throughout the night and no attempt was made by the enemy to reconnoitre for our approaching expedition. It would seem, therefore, that the force was assembled and dispatched without disclosure. It would have achieved complete tactical surprise if No. 3 Commando had not unfortunately been intercepted by the enemy trawlers *en route*.

Narrative, Phase 1, 0445-0550

Despite the chance contact with enemy ships *en route*, the forces arrived at Dieppe approximately on time, and the initial Naval bombardment of selected objectives was carried out as arranged.

In the opening attack, escort was provided for smoke-carrying aircraft of Bomber and Army Co-operation Commands laying a smoke screen over the cliff headland to the east of Dieppe Harbour. This was most effective, lasting from 0510 to 0600 hours. Intruder aircraft engaged each of the two-gun Batteries to the south of Dieppe with bombs and machine-guns. Hurricane Bombers, Fighters and Spitfires attacked the coastal emplacements and beach defences. Cannon fighters provided direct support to our troops as they landed at "Red" and "White" Beaches in front of Dieppe and were successful in centralising enemy fire along the front from 0515 to 0525. During the landings there was little opposition from enemy aircraft.

0538 In Phase 1, our surface forces kept to their time-table despite shelling by enemy shore batteries. Batteries situated to the south of the town were slow to commence firing, but when they did were particularly destructive. Further smoke screens were requested to cover our landings, a necessity which had already been anticipated and additional smoke aircraft were already on their way to the scene of action.

Phase 2, 0550-0730

By the second phase landings had been effected successfully on "Yellow" (East Commando), "Green" (West Flank) and "Orange" (West Commando) Beaches, and progress had been made towards the surrounding houses.

0640 The western Commando had been completely successful in overcoming the battery position at "Hess" and killing all the personnel. The final assault on this position was assisted by a Squadron of Spitfires, which attacked "Hess" Battery at 0620 just before our men were due to attack. This assistance was successful and the attack was made immediately our aircraft had finished. The Observation Post of this Battery was in a Lighthouse close by, which had been attacked by two Spitfires at first light. The landing on the beach 1½ miles to the west of Dieppe ("Green" Beach) was also successful, capturing the R.D.F. station and destroying their other objectives.

986. The eastern flank ("Blue" Beach) initial attack had, however, failed. A second attack made at approximately 0740 resulted in a small penetration which, however, did not succeed in silencing the guns on the eastern headland. In the main landing on "Red" and "White" Beaches the tanks were held up by the inability of the Engineers to land the explosives necessary to blast a passage through the promenade wall, with the result that the majority of the tanks were stranded, and the infantry were disembarked, whilst the tanks were still immobilised. Large white houses overlooking the beaches gave considerable trouble and bombardment by destroyers was requested from our troops ashore.

APPENDICES

0605   In view of these difficulties, a further smoke screen was called for on the eastern headland "Bismarck", but no aircraft were immediately available for this. The smoke-carrying aircraft were at once ordered to load up with smoke bombs and take off as soon as they were ready.

0621   Earlier attacks had failed to silence the eastern headland defences and the gun positions ("Hitler" and "Goering") south of Dieppe, continued to shell the beaches.

0605- Twelve Bostons had already been ordered off to bomb "Hitler"
0615   and were quickly airborne.

0640-"Rommel" was also still giving trouble and the landing on
0645   "Blue" Beach had in consequence failed. The only remaining Bostons were, therefore, detailed to attack "Rommel", followed by a further six when they became available.

0723   All these batteries continued to harass our troops and an attack was called for on "Bismarck". A Squadron of Cannon Hurricanes had already been despatched to be "on call" to the Headquarters Ship by 0740, and a second Squadron of Cannon Hurricanes was despatched to be "on call" to Headquarters Ship 20 minutes later.

987. Thus, at the end of the second phase, the R.D.F. Station, five light A.A. positions had been captured and the gun battery behind the "Orange" Beach had been demolished. Throughout this period air cover was afforded to the troops against moderate enemy fighter opposition; the number of enemy aircraft patrolling the area at any one time during this period did not exceed one squadron.

Phase 3, 0730-1050
This third phase covers the withdrawal to the beaches.
0750
At 0752, two Cannon Hurricane Squadrons were ordered to engage enemy E-Boats which had been reported proceeding south from Boulogne. Two fighter cover Squadrons accompanied these Hurricanes.

0740   At the same time a message was received cancelling the support on "Bismarck" and "Rommel". The Air Force Commander was always doubtful whether this latter message was genuine, but had to act on it as information was received within a few minutes that a second landing on "Blue" beach had been successful. At this time one Bomber Squadron was on its way to bomb

"Rommel" and was beyond range of recall. Aircraft were also on their way to drop smoke bombs on the eastern headland; these were recalled.

0830 The situation had meanwhile deteriorated on the western flank. Heavy opposition was also coming from the western headland and the houses behind the beach.

0916 Machine-gunning and shelling continued undiminished from the headland and from "Hindenburg".

0926 A Squadron of Hurricane Bombers and a Squadron of Cannon Fighters covered by two Spitfire Squadrons were ordered to attack these positions.

0940 The situation in various areas continued to grow critical and due to various delays, the time scheduled for the evacuation was deferred from 1030 hours to 1100 hours.

0956 At 0956, the following reply was received to the Air Force Commander's request for a situation report:
"Situation too obscure to give useful report. Air co-operation faultless. Enemy air opposition now increasing. Have you any questions?"

1004 A few minutes later a request was received for a 30-minute smoke screen along "Red" and "White" Beaches from 1100 to 1130 hours; Thruxton was ordered to prepare as many aircraft as possible with S.C.I. and as many aircraft as could be fitted were ordered off for this purpose. 1010
The Military Commander gave "Green" Beach third priority after "Red" and "White" Beaches for smoke, and three Blenheims with an escort Squadron were detailed to this task.

1039 A request was made for maximum fighter support against machine-gun positions on both headlands.

1039 Four Close Support Squadrons were ordered to these attacks with two Squadrons as cover.

1047 A further call for support against the headland came in 20 minutes later, by which time Squadrons were already on their way. At this time, it appeared that the L.C.A. were arriving at "White" Beach ready to re-embark the forces on shore. Thus, at the beginning of this third period the right wing of our landing forces had made progress, but those in the centre, including the tanks, were held up.

Enemy air opposition had by now increased considerably, 20 to 30 fighters being seen continuously in the area until 1000 hours, when enemy bombers appeared, escorted by fighters.

The enemy employed a considerable number of bombers from aerodromes in Holland, in addition to small numbers from Beauvais.

1050   To counter this increase of enemy activity, and in order to cover re-embarkation, which was about to commence, the strength of fighter cover over Dieppe was increased from three to six, and at times to nine squadrons. Heavy casualties were inflicted on the enemy bombers, who were now concentrating on shipping and landing craft.

Phase 4, 1050-1410

The fourth phase marks the withdrawal from the beaches. During this time the gun batteries "Bismarck" and "Hindenburg" on the east and west headlands continued their intense bombardment, and in many areas the situation was more than critical.

Until the expedition had safely withdrawn, frequent and urgent requests were received for bombing and close support attacks on enemy gun positions, and calls for smoke screens were made.

At 1030 hours, a most successful pre-arranged attack was made by 24 Fortress Bombers, escorted by four Spitfire IX Squadrons, on the enemy Fighter aerodrome at Abbeville-Drucat. Some 25 tons of high explosives and a large number of incendiaries were dropped. Many bursts were seen in the north-west dispersal areas and on the runways, whilst fires were started in woods adjoining the dispersal areas. Bursts were also observed on storage sites and clouds of black smoke were seen rising from the whole target area. This very accurate bombing of dispersal areas and runways – bombs fell near to at least 16 aircraft in these areas – caused considerable confusion to the enemy, and he was denied the use of his aerodrome for probably 2 hours, his aircraft being instructed to land at alternatives. The Abbeville control was out of action until the evening, when a new and unfamiliar voice came on the air.

This attack on Abbeville was followed by a diversionary feint made towards Ostend by a Typhoon Wing in an endeavour to draw enemy Air Forces away from Dieppe.

1100   The enemy air activity by 1100 had increased and he had altered his form of attack. The tactics of our fighter cover were changed to meet this situation by adding a high Squadron of Spitfire IXs. at 23,000 ft.

1200   During this period bombing attacks were made by Boston Squadrons on "Bismarck" and "Hindenburg".

Further attacks were also made by three Close Support Squadrons and smoke was laid between the east and west headlands across the port of Dieppe to cover the final withdrawal.

The constant requests for bombing, close support and smoke were met to the limit, demands frequently bring anticipated as a result of the clear picture available in the Fighter Control Room at Uxbridge. All types of Squadrons were called on to operate a shuttle service.

It was decided that Tactical Reconnaissance aircraft could serve no further useful purpose and their operational flights were discontinued.

In the final withdrawal a maximum effort was directed to protect our re-embarking forces from both ground and air attack.

1310 By 1310, it appeared doubtful whether any more troops could be evacuated. An hour later the last craft was reported 3 miles from the French Coast. The withdrawal from Dieppe had been completed.

Phase 5, 1410-2245

As our forces cleared the enemy coast, smoke-laying aircraft laid a protective screen between them and the enemy's defences.

The Typhoon Wing was then reinforcing our Spitfires in intercepting enemy bombers coming from the direction of Holland.

1428 Fighter Cover was maintained throughout the long voyage home.

1545 There was considerable deterioration in the weather, and the enemy took advantage of the increasing cloud cover to send out single bombers to attack our ships as they neared the English coast. One or two formations of F.W. 190.s were also employed for this purpose. In addition, to standing cover over the returning convoy, 86 interception sorties were made.

Appreciation of the Enemy's Air Effort

The enemy reacted almost as had been foreseen, at first, he did not appear to appreciate the scale of our effort and he used only 25/30 fighters in each sortie. As the day went on the strength of his sorties increased to between 50/100 aircraft. At first fighter bombers, and later, when the moves from Holland had been effected, night bombers in increasing numbers were used until all his resources on the Western Front were in action.

Early in the day, enemy air effort was confined entirely to fighters patrolling the area in small numbers. Occasionally, dive attacks on our ships were made from height. The German control merely instructed his aircraft to go to the Dieppe area, where large numbers of British bombers and fighters were operating.

It was not until about 1000 hours, some six hours after our assault, that our patrols encountered enemy bombers. It would seem, therefore, that these had not been at a high state of readiness.

The first bombers came in small numbers and were escorted by F.W. 190.s. Later, larger formations up to 15 in number operated under the main German Fighter Force, which was engaging our cover patrols. Reports from pilots indicate that a small number of reserve training bombers were included.

The German Bomber Force throughout confined its attention to our convoy, and did not harass out troops ashore. A bomber jettisoning its bombs crippled H.M.S. *Berkeley* shortly before 1300 hours. She was later sunk by our own forces.

The attack on Abbeville-Drucat at 1030 hours was undoubtedly successful in striking at the enemy's most congested aerodrome at a critical period in the operation. This attack was timed and pre-arranged to this end and it undoubtedly succeeded in considerably reducing the efforts of the G.A.F. against our expedition.

Casualties
Details concerning air effort, serviceability of aircraft, casualties to aircraft and personnel, and results achieved by the Air Forces during operations at Dieppe are shown in Appendix F to this report.
The very low rate of casualties suffered in all types of Squadrons during such intensive daylight operations in close support of a combined expedition are of particular interest.

The concentration and re-disposition of Air Forces in No. 11 Group was for security reasons undertaken as a reinforcing exercise, under the title of "Venom".
No serious administrative difficulties were experienced throughout the operation, though the shortness of the period of activity did not perhaps bring to light some of the difficulties which might have arisen had it been more prolonged.

Communications

Communications on the whole were excellent. Signals were promptly and clearly received at Uxbridge. The majority of outgoing messages from Uxbridge to the Headquarters Ship re-transmitted by Portsmouth, did not reach the Military Commander afloat, so that requests for Close Support from the Ship were often repeated unnecessarily.

The Control organisation in the Ships worked very efficiently and this system is capable of further expansion and development.

Additional land line links to Uxbridge for the operation worked fairly satisfactorily, although some of the temporary lines were not up to the high standard necessary.

The Operations and Intelligence Teleprinter Operators worked at high pressure, but were able to handle the traffic without serious delays.

Conclusions

(i) This operation showed that such expeditions can be successfully supported and protected by home defence Fighters operated by the normal Home Defence Fighter Organisation, assisted by forward direction through R/T in ships. This efficient organisation is fully capable of so operating Air Forces to the limit of present fighter range and is bound to be superior to any alternative forward control scheme which could never provide anything like equal facilities.

(ii) Landings on such a scale in occupied territory in daylight effectively pin the enemy air forces to an area enabling our supporting Fighters to operate at height and in conditions best suited to them. In existing circumstances, the enemy is forced to employ his night bombers in daylight, at times unescorted by fighters, thus sacrificing an appreciable part of his limited bomber resources.

(iii) Close Support attacks by Cannon Fighters are effective only whilst they are engaging their targets, but they have no lasting material effect on well-protected defensive positions. They are extravagant, in as much as each aircraft is in action for a few seconds only. To achieve any lasting moral effect would demand such a large expenditure of these Fighters that our efforts in other directions would eb reduced to unacceptable proportions.

(iv) A very much higher standard of interservice recognition is essential in combined operations. As modern aircraft are all so alike, it is imperative that all personnel have a very thorough knowledge of and frequent practice in recognition.

(v) Airborne smoke is extremely valuable in combined operations. Smoke is often likely to have better effect than bombing, particularly if it is intended to protect surface forces against well placed gun positions. It is essential however, to speed up the present rate of turn round for smoke carrying aircraft, and to be able quickly to alternate between S.C.I. and bombs, and to change over from one to the other on the ground in the shortest possible time.

(vi) Some difficulty was experienced at times in obtaining detailed target requirements from the Headquarters Ship. This problem of locating and selecting suitable targets for Air Attacks, together with methods for defining to the Air Force Commander, requires careful interservice study so that the Air effort is always profitably employed. Certain major conclusions together with my recommendations for awards are being forwarded by me in a separate letter.

T. Leigh-Mallory,
Air Marshal.
Air Force Commander.

Appendix BB

ORDER OF BATTLE OF THE ROYAL AIR FORCE

Sector Type	No. of Squadrons		Units	Operating from
Kenley	4	111	Kenley	Spitfire V
		611	Kenley	Spitfire IX
		308 US.A.	Kenley	Spitfire V
		402	Kenley	Spitfire IX
	3	350	Redhill	Spitfire V
		310	Redhill	Spitfire V
		312	Redhill	Spitfire V
Northolt	4	306 (P)	Northolt	Spitfire V
		317 (P)	Northolt	Spitfire V
		308 (P)	Heston	Spitfire V
		302 (P)	Heston	Spitfire V
	1	303 (P)	Redhill	Spitfire V
Tangmere	2	131	Merston	Spitfire V
		412	Merston	Spitfire V
	1	309 U.S.A.	W. Hampnett.	Spitfire V
	2	129	Thorney Island	Spitfire V
		130	Thorney Island	Spitfire V
	4	66	Tangmere	Spitfire V
		118	Tangmere	Spitfire V
		501	Tangmere	Spitfire V
		41	Tangmere	Spitfire V
	2 Close Support	43	Tangmere	Hurricane
		87	Tangmere	Hurricane

APPENDICES

	2 Close Support	3	Shoreham	Hurricane
		245	Shoreham	Hurricane
	2 Close Support	32	Friston	Hurricane
		253	Friston	Hurricane
	2 Hurricane Bomber	174	Ford	Hurricane bomber
		175	Ford	Hurricane bomber
	2 Bomber	88	Ford	Boston
		107	Ford	Boston
	3 Smoke	13	Thruxton	Blenheim
		614	Thruxton	Blenheim
		226	Thruxton	Boston
Debden	3	232	Gravesend	Spitfire V
		71	Gravesend	Spitfire V
		124	Gravesend	Spitfire VI
	2	616	Hawkinge	Spitfire VI
		416	Hawkinge	Spitfire V
North Weald	2	121	Southend	Spitfire V
		19	Southend	Spitfire V
	4	242	Manston	Spitfire V
		331	Manston	Spitfire V
		332	Manston	Spitfire V
		403	Manston	Spitfire V
Hornchurch	3	64	Hornchurch	Spitfire IX
		122	Hornchurch	Spitfire V
		340	Hornchurch	Spitfire V
	2	81	Fairlop	Spitfire V
		154	Fairlop	Spitfire V
	3	485	West Malling	Spitfire V
		610	West Malling	Spitfire V
		411	West Malling	Spitfire V
Biggin Hill	3	602	Biggin Hill	Spitfire V
		307 U.S.A.	Biggin Hill	Spitfire V
		222	Biggin Hill	Spitfire V
	2	165	Lympne	Spitfire V
		401	Lympne	Spitfire IX
	2	65	Eastchurch	Spitfire V
		133	Eastchurch	Spitfire V
	1	51	Hawknige	Spitfire V

APPENDICES

Gatwick	4	26	Gatwick	Mustang
		239	Gatwick	Mustang
		400	Gatwick	Mustang
		414	Gatwick	Mustang
Duxford	2	266	Duxford	Typhoon
		56	Duxford	Typhoon

Appendix CC

ANALYSIS OF BOMBING ATTACKS

Target	Squadron	No. of A/craft	Bombs dropped	Result
"Rommel"	No. 2 Group	14	55 x 500 48 x 40	Not observed but believed "target area and to E"
	174	10	12 x 250 6 x 250	Bursts in target area Houses s. of "Rommel"
	175	18 10	16 x 250 20 x 250	Six bursts in target area Direct hits on emplacements
"Bismarck"	No. 2 Group	12	48 x 500	Target straddled and entire area covered with smoke
	Army Co-op Smoke Laying	14	156 smoke bombs	Objective reached
	174	12	18 x 500 6 x 250	No target seen on landfall. Targets selected were 2 miles east of Dieppe (houses and woods)
"Hitler"	No. 2 Group	13	39 x 500 92 x 40	South and east of target overshot
	174	12	18 x 500 4 x 250	Many bursts in target area
	605	1	10 x 40	Results not observed

"Goering"	No. 2 Group	1	3 x 500 8 x 40	South and east of target. Unobserved
	418	3	30 x 40	Target located and bombed
"Hindenburg"	No. 2 Group	12	36 x 500 92 x 40	Most bombs in target area
Road Dieppe / Rouen	No. 2 Group	6	–	Bombed railway at Ouville
"Red, White Beaches"	Army Co-op. Smoke Laying	4	36 smoke bombs	Effective screen
		2	-	-
		2	-	Successful. Mole w. headland
		4	-	Successful screen. East and w. headland
		3	-	Did not attack target
		3	-	Task successfully completed
"Green Beach"	Army Co-op. Smoke Laying	6	60 smoke bombs	Smoke screen good
		6	72 smoke bombs	Task completed
W. Headland	175	-	24 x 250	Bursts on houses and church used as flak post

Appendix DD

AN ESTIMATE OF ENEMY AIRCRAFT SEEN OVER DIEPPE DURING THE ACTION

Time	First Estimate 20th August		Second Estimate 15th September	
	Fighters	Bombers	Fighters	Bombers
0000-0400	2	–	2	–
0400-0600	39	–	36	–
0600-0800	44	–	40	–
0800-1000	129	21	120	28
1000-1200	151	67	140	62
1200-1400	70	44	65	40
1400-1600	87	29	88	20
1600-1800	94	8	80	7
1800-2000	4	8	4	4
	620	177	575	160

Appendix EE

REACTIONS OF THE GERMAN AIR FORCE

German Air Force Order of Battle
1010. *Disposition* – At the date of this operation, it is estimated that the German Air Force Disposition of I.E. aircraft in France, Belgium and Holland was as follows:

	France W. of Seine.	N. of Seine.	Belgium	Holland	Total	Estimated I.E. + Serviceable Strength a/c	
L.R. Bombers	47	50	–	120	217	280	+ 170
B. Recce	54	9	–	3	66	85	+ 50
Dive Bombers	–	–	–	–	–	–	–
S.E. Fighters	87	78	45	45	255	330	+ 250
T.E. Fighters	–	–	–	(156)*	(156)*	(200)*	+ (175)*
Army Co-op.	–	–	–	–	–	–	–
Coastal	9	–	–	–	9	12	+ 7
	197	137	45	168	547	707	+ 477

*These Defensive Night Fighters were, naturally, not engaged during this operation and are not included in the totals.

State of Readiness
There is reason to believe that, at the time of the raid, one of the enemy's periodical states of alert was in operation. However, no unusual state of readiness was displayed by the German Air Force during our attack, nor had any special disposition apparently been taken up. Our first sweep covering landings at dawn encountered no enemy air opposition. The manner in which the German Air Force units were controlled showed that operational plans probably exist to meet an emergency

such as that created by the Dieppe raid. The enemy was forced to make use of all available operational units within immediate range, but, since the air operations did not last longer than the daylight hours of 19th August, he was not compelled to bring in other units from outside the area which included Belgium and Holland. He might well have had to do so, had the air attack been continued on subsequent days.

Operations
(*a*) *Types of Aircraft Engaged* – The German Air Force aircraft employed were all of well-known types and consisted of Ju.88s, He.111s, Do.217s used as L.R. Bombers and B. Recce, the latter may also have included a few Me.210s; and F.W.190s and Me109F fighters and fighter bombers.
A report by pilots refers to one or more Me.210s having been seen in the target area at about 1400 hours, but no engagement took place. In view of the probable equipment of at least part of a Bomber Recce. unit in the Low Countries with this type it is likely that a few of these aircraft may have taken part.
The great majority of the fighters encountered were F.W.190s, but some 20 Me.109s were also sighted.
There is no reason to believe that any L.R. Bomber training units were engaged during the operation.
(*b*) *Reconnaissance* – Normal reconnaissance flights in other areas were not modified as a result of the attack. Over the English Channel and to the east and west of it there was more activity by Recce. Units. One unit operated 5 aircraft over the Channel in areas Portland, S.E. of St. Catherine's Point and Dieppe. Another made five flights over the S.W. approaches between 0800 and 1920 hours. Four aircraft of a different recce. units made flights over the eastern English Channel between 0900-1715 hours. Another 9 aircraft from two additional units carried out flights off the east coast and in the eastern English Channel.

The total effort by L.R. reconnaissance types during the daylight hours on the 19th August over all Western Front areas is estimated at 30 sorties.

Bomber Operations
From the evidence available, it is estimated that L.R. Bombers made a total of 125 sorties during the operation. All serviceable aircraft of the L.R. Bomber units based in France and the Low Countries took part, with the exception of the F.W.200s based at Bordeaux; there appear to have been only two to three aircraft (of K.G.2) which made a second sortie.

Most of the aircraft based in Holland returned to their bases, but a few made use of the aerodromes at St. André-de-l'Eure, where they landed after completing their tasks.

Bombers were not actively engaged over the scene of the operation before 1000 hours, but from then onwards an average of about 20 L.R. Bombers kept up harassing attacks mainly directed against our shipping standing off Dieppe. Formations varied in size from 3 aircraft to 12. There are no specific instances of them receiving special fighter escort, but fighters in the target area provided local protection to their bombers as far as possible and received warning of their proximity in certain instances.

This activity lasted until approximately 1500 hours, after which the enemy employed a total of 30 L.R. Bombers operating singly at a rate of 4 aircraft per hour, in attacks from cloud cover on our returning ships. Deterioration in the weather during the afternoon considerably assisted enemy aircraft in these operations.

Fighter Operations
The opposition by single-engine fighters was mainly provided by I and II/J.G.2, and the whole of J.G.26 which occupied both the sectors immediately concerned, namely Abbeville and Beaumont-le-Roger, also Courtrai. The Courtrai wing was moved down and became engaged during the afternoon.
Throughout the operation, aircraft remained under the control of their respective sectors, but those from the Beaumont-le-Roger sector were probably mainly engaged on free-lance interception patrols.
Patrols were recalled after 1½ hours and the intensive effort periods were roughly as follows:
From 0830-0930 *hours*, when the Abbeville and St. Omer aircraft were operating up to 40 aircraft.
From 0930-1130 *hours*, when strong cover was being provided for bombers. At one time during this period there appears to have been up to 100 fighters in action.
From 1200-1300 *hours*, when cover of up to 50 was again provided for bombers.
From 1415-1500 *hours*, when special attention was given to intercepting our own attacks.
By 1730 hours activity had practically ceased, except for sporadic attacks by the fighter-bombers on our ships during withdrawal.
With the exception of the identified fighter bomber Staffel, fighters appeared to concentrate nearly all their efforts on intercepting British

aircraft, and they do not appear to have turned their attacks against our troops or landing craft.

Defensive Patrols
Defensive patrols were flown as follows:
   (i) *Dutch Area* – At Dunkirk at 0730 hours, from 0928 to 0950 hours between Flushing and Ghent, from 1053-1135 hours over the Flushing area.
   (ii) *Cherbourg Area* – From 0637 to 0720 hours, again from 0941 to 0949 hours, at 1159 hours, from 1530 to 1547 hours, between 1827 and 1835 hours.
   (iii) *Brest Area* – From 1725 to 1903 hours, and from 2003 to 2022 hours a routine patrol was maintained in an unidentified area.

Sorties by Types
In the course of the operation, from the evidence available it would appear that the following effort was put up by bombers and fighters:

	I.E. Available	Serviceability Per cent.	A/C Serviceable	Sorties
L.R. Bombers	217	60	130	125
S.E. Fighters	170/205*	75	130/155	600

*In the preceding paragraph, under Defensive Patrols (i) Dutch Area, it will be seen that patrols in the Flushing Area appear to have ceased after 1135 hours, which leads to the possibility of these aircraft being brought in to operate over Dieppe in the afternoon. This would bring down the number of sorties per serviceable S.E.F. aircraft over Dieppe from roughly 4.6 to 3.8, which seems more probable.

Casualties – German Air Force
Exact figures of enemy losses are difficult to obtain for an operation of this nature where the scale of effort is intense and casualties occur either over the sea or on enemy territory.
However, from all available evidence, the final assessment of casualties is accepted at:

	Destroyed	Probably Destroyed	Damaged
L.R. Bombers	43	10	56
S.E. Fighters	<u>49</u>	<u>29</u>	<u>84</u>
	<u>92</u>	<u>39</u>	<u>140</u>

During the operation, W/T reports show that some 31 bombers were called in vain. Of these only 14 have since been heard. This may point to an increase in the casualties over and above the figures given.

The reliability of casualty assessments of L.R. Bombers is greatly assisted by W/T reports, but assessment of fighter losses is almost exclusively based on pilots' reports. The reliability in this case is more difficult to establish, but due allowance has been made for possible duplication in reports.

Conclusions

From a close study of all reports available the following conclusions are reached:

(*a*) that, from an air point of view, the operation was highly successful, because it forced all available German Air Force aircraft to operate and thus enabled the Royal Air Force to inflict considerable casualties on the enemy's forces on the Western Front, and draw on his already depleted reserves;

(b) that, although the operation was satisfactory, it was not of sufficient duration to deplete the enemy to a point where he was no longer able to make good his losses from his reserves.

Had the operation been extended over a period of two or three days, or been followed up immediately by a second similar raid in the same or some other area, the damage inflicted on the German Air Force Western Front forces might have been far reaching; the effect would have gone a long way towards expending the forces available and would, no doubt, have necessitated the withdrawal of units from probably the Russian Front or, possibly, the Mediterranean theatre.

As it was, the wastage inflicted on the German Air Force on the Western Front by Fighter Command during the operation, was greater than during a normal month of recent offensive sweeps.

Appendix FF

MEDICAL ARRANGEMENTS FOR CASUALTY EVACUATION

The backbone of the medical organisation during this operation consisted of four L.C.T., Mark 3, specifically allotted for the task. These four craft were manned by two Medical Officers, one Sick Berth Petty Officer and ten Sick Berth Ratings. They carried an M.S. Unit of Medical Stores, 50 Mark II, Army Pattern stretchers and 150 blankets. The intention was to ground them on the beaches an hour before the evacuation, load them up to capacity, which was 100 stretcher cases and 60 walking wounded each, and return them to the hards at Stokes Bay where liaison had been made with the Assistant Director of Medical Services of the Second Canadian Division. Here the seriously wounded were to be evacuated by ambulance convoy to R.N. Hospital, Haslar, and those fit to make the journey were to be transferred by ambulance convoy to the 15th Canadian General Hospital at Bramshott, 26 miles away.

In addition, six L.C.F. (L) were available for evacuation from craft in the neighbourhood of the beaches carrying one medical officer and three S.B.R.s with an M.S. unit of medical stores. The six destroyers had their usual medical complement and in two of them an additional three Medical Officers and ten S.B.R.s were carried as a reserve. All ships and craft carrying Medical Officers flew the Medical Flag.

Assembly
Three Medical Officers and Sick Berth Ratings were assembled in the Portsmouth area and a training exercise in carrying loaded stretchers and embarking them on an L.C.T. (3) was carried out on the two weekends prior to the operation. This exercise was carried out under instructions from C.C.O. for Section "C", R.A.P. Committee, and afforded useful cover for the training of personnel. All Medical Stores

were assembled at R.N. Hospital, Haslar, and stretchers and blankets were held by the Senior Naval Stores Officer (S.N.S.O.), H.M. Dockyard, Portsmouth.

Distribution

Distribution of personnel and stores commenced at 2100 on the night before the operation when the four "Hospital L.C.T." were loaded with their stores and personnel at the Stokes Bay Hards. At 1100 on the morning of the operation two buses and three 3-ton lorries conveyed personnel and stores to Newhaven where they were distributed to their appropriate crafts. H.M. ships *Locust*, *Alresford*, *Fernie* and *Bleasdale* received their stores and personnel that afternoon. Personnel and stores had been despatched to Southampton for the *Duke of Wellington* three days before.

Three M.G.B. had one Sick Berth Rating and a small quantity of stores put on board that afternoon.

The placing of stores and personnel on board ships and craft at Southampton, Portsmouth and Newhaven on the day prior to the operation was a task requiring the most detailed planning and timing. That this was carried out efficiently and well, was almost entirely due to the very soundest co-operation from S.N.S.O., H.M. Dockyard, Portsmouth, who provided the most prompt and willing help throughout.

Execution

Casualties during the operation began to come off about 0430 to the destroyers and L.C.F. (L). They came in a gentle stream and were at no time unmanageable. L.C.F. 2 was put out of action at 0630, the Medical Officer being the last surviving officer, ordered abandon ship and, gallantly, with his Sick Berth Ratings and 14 wounded men, took to the water. They were picked up by an L.C.A. about an hour later and ultimately transferred to H.M.S. *Calpe*, where they continued to render excellent service throughout the day.

All other L.C.F. received casualties from this time onwards and, spread out as they were in the anchorage and flying their Medical Flag, were of the greatest assistance in clearing craft of casualties and survivors. The destroyers when possible took casualties on board but both they and the L.C.F. were, of course, fighting ships and had to keep on the move with their guns frequently in action.

By 0850, when it was clear to the Force Commanders that the beaches were not securely held, the four special L.C.T. which lay well out to sea were ordered to return to port.

This information did not reach the Senior Medical Officer on board the *Fernie* until 1030.

A signal was received from H.M.S. *Albrighton* requesting medical assistance and one Medical Officer and four S.B.R.s were despatched forthwith. This party never contacted the *Albrighton* but went on board an L.C.T. which had many wounded and survivors on board and as a unit of stores was already on board they were of the greatest assistance. A repetition of the signal was later received from H.M.S. *Albrighton* and it was realised that the first party had failed to reach them. This time one Medical Officer and two S.B.R.s were despatched and they were of great assistance to the Medical Officer on board that ship throughout the remainder of the action. No other signals requesting help were received though three Medical Officers and ten S.B.R.s were on board the *Bleasdale* as a reserve.

It is realised that the S.M.O. should be in the Headquarters Ship so that he can more appropriately direct the medical resources available.

Treatment
In an operation of this kind all medical treatment must be confined to coping with the immediate problem of saving life – that is, anti-shock treatment, arrest of haemorrhage, warmth and food.

The facilities on a "Hunt" class destroyer are limited, for with the wardroom full, the after mess-deck is the only available space where cover is afforded and the capacity for efficient treatment is limited to approximately 40 cases. Later in the action several ships had more casualties than they could conveniently attend to, whilst others could have dealt with more. In particular, the *Calpe* had many survivors on board for whom there was no deck cover and casualties occurred amongst them from splinters and near misses.

Reception
The plan of reception had to be altered and four destroyers came alongside North-West Wall in Portsmouth Dockyard at approximately midnight. Many kindly and enthusiastic people were there to receive them but there was a total lack of co-ordinated effort and no

organisation was laid on to deal efficiently with the evacuation. On humanitarian grounds everybody was in favour of evacuating wounded first, but this is obvious nonsense for, with upward of 200 men on the deck of a destroyer, the collection and disembarkation of walking wounded and stretcher cases is well-nigh impossible.

It is considered that the best drill is for all non-wounded personnel to be evacuated first, walking wounded to follow and stretcher cases last. The difficulty of an evacuation of this kind is that the first wounded off are placed in the best ambulances and are driven away to an R.N. hospital, where their wounds may be found to be neither serious nor in need of urgent surgical attention. Classification is essential at a Reception Shed.

On this occasion adequate brows were not available and a large number of cases had to be transported up the companion ladder from the after deck, often at a perilous angle on a Mark II stretcher, before they could be carried ashore.

An attempt to obviate this was made by landing 80 Neil Robertson stretchers from a store in the Dockyard where a quantity of them were known to be. This was carried out by the Naval Store Night Watch personnel and two 3-ton lorries had to make a circuitous journey through the tail of the ambulance convoy and round by "D" Basin in order to deposit the stretchers where they were required. Army personnel are not familiar with the Neil Robertson stretcher and their attempts to place wounded men in them left something to be desired. The Medical Officer of Health was present with approximately 80 vehicles of one sort and another. These ambulances are unsuited to take Mark II stretchers and cases had to be transferred on the ground from a Mark II to an A.R.P. wire stretcher before being loaded. This means further delay and a considerable move for the wounded man.

The private cars for sitting cases can rarely take more than two on account of gear they carry in the front seat, and it is probably better for the A.R.P. organization to stay away from a service evacuation unless the transport situation is very bad.

In spite of all these delays and difficulties evacuation proceeded fairly well, and by 0530 on 20th August the operation was completed.

The establishment of a Clearing Station is essential, as the following will show. The Royal Naval Hospital at Haslar stated that it was prepared to take 100 surgical cases. When the ships began to arrive at Portsmouth the slightly wounded were the first ashore and were at once taken to the Royal Naval Hospital, where they filled up all the cot accommodation available. Thus, when the more severely wounded were landed, no cots were any longer available for them at Haslar. The establishment of a Clearing House would prevent such an occurrence from happening again and would ensure that the earliest possible surgical attention was available for those most in need of it.

At Newhaven, cot cases had to be hoisted by crane, which is always a slow business. Many craft with wounded on board had to lie off shore for hours, as there was no room for them in the harbour. Energetic attempts were made by Lieutenant-Commander A.D. Courage, R.N., of C.O.H.Q., to collect casualties from craft lying off, but the difficulty of hoisting still remained.

Hards should be allotted specially where landing craft can beach and have their casualties quickly evacuated to hospital.

A hospital train was available at Newhaven but it was routed to the vicinity of Birmingham. This necessitated further delay for those cases which were in urgent need of surgical attention, and a clearing house is again stressed as an essential requirement so that these cases may be transferred by ambulance convoy to the nearest Emergency Medical Service hospital.

Liaison with Canadians
Colonel C.P. Fenwick, M.C., the Assistant Director Medical Services of the Second Canadian Division, and Lieutenant-Colonel Morgan Smith, of the Royal Canadian Army Medical Corps, during the training weekend prior to the operation, had arranged to bring our four L.C.T. into the hards at Stokes Bay, where we would hand over the casualties for evacuation by ambulance convoy to the Canadians. All cases in need of urgent surgical attention, of all services, were to be admitted to R.N. Hospital, Haslar, involving a journey by ambulance convoy of some 10 minutes. The balance of the casualties were being carried by ambulance convoy to No. 15 Canadian General Hospital at Bramshott, a distance of 26 miles away.

This organization did not work, as the destroyers loaded with casualties came into Portsmouth Harbour. Colonel Fenwick switched his organization round to the Dockyard, though he received information about the transfer later than he would have wished.

Conclusions
All medical officers and sick berth ratings were kept busy throughout the action. They were widely distributed and until late in the action casualties were fairly evenly distributed. The *Calpe* took on board a large number of survivors from the *Berkeley* as well as Canadian troops from the final evacuation. She could have done with some assistance but no request was received for it, and her needs were not known. It is agreed by the Naval Force Commander that the Senior Medical Officer should, in future, be carried on the Headquarters ship.

The medical organization was satisfactory and, though reception of casualties left something to be desired, this matter has finally been covered by an organization in the Port concerned.

Appendix GG

MEDICAL EVACUATION AT A DOCKYARD

The following lessons were learnt during the evacuation in Portsmouth Dockyard after the Dieppe raid. The evacuation was unrehearsed since it had been hoped to send wounded in special medical L.C.T. to Stokes Bay, but on account of the beaches remaining under fire at Dieppe these L.C.T. were unable to close in and collect wounded, and casualties were brought back to England in ships and craft which could not discharge them across beaches.

A Control Officer of senior rank (such as the Principal Medical Officer, of the R.N. Barracks), assisted by suitable staff, is necessary to lay on the organization and be there in person to conduct and control all movements, either by loud-speakers or by employment of efficient runners.

One-way traffic should be clearly indicated by lights at night and indicator boards during the day, and guides should be available for ambulance convoys.

A clearing house should be provided for non-wounded personnel and gear. At Portsmouth South Railway jetty affords the essentials for this operation and a rehearsal would throw into bold relief all necessary adjuncts, *e.g.* telephones, lavatories and possibilities for canteen arrangements, etc.

For actual evacuation of ships it is proposed that all unwounded personnel of every service, grade and category be evacuated first; passed through a clearing house at some suitable distance away and transported from there. Walking wounded and stretcher cases could be dealt with in an orderly and efficient manner and the delay would be amply compensated.

It is recommended that vessels lie alongside the disembarkation wharf – that adequate brows be provided and that a store of Neil Robertson

APPENDICES

and Mark II stretchers should be readily available. All A.R.P. vehicles should be kept in reserve only, as the private cars for walking wounded are of limited capacity and A.R.P. ambulances are not fitted to take service stretchers.

Hospitals in the immediate vicinity should be used in preference to ones further away, even if not of the same service or unit. (Birmingham (*see* para. 1036) is 160 miles from Newhaven).

Appendix HH

SECURITY ARRANGEMENTS

General Security Plan
(1) (*a*) The routine Security Plan for Combined Operations is as follows:
Naval – The S.O.I. of the Naval C.-in-C. who is providing the escort advises on the Naval Security aspect of the operation.
Army – Home Forces troops are under G.S.O.I., Intelligence (*b*), G.H.Q., Home Forces, with appropriate local Security organisation.
Special Service Brigade – Under Commander S.S.B., with his G.S.O.3.I. (*b*) and an officer in charge of Security in each Commando.
R.A.F. – Under Air Ministry Security organisation and the local Security Officers.
(*b*) The reports from all Security sources are collated by the Security Section of C.O.H.Q., who receive reports of leakages, indiscretions, etc., and, with advice from M.I.5 and I.S.S.B., are able to assess for C.C.O. the chances of the operation having been compromised beforehand.
(*c*) C.O.H.Q. also make certain that no part of the operation has been left uncovered, that censorship of mails, telephones and telegrams is applied where necessary, that ships and personnel are sealed after briefing, and that all other Security precautions, as laid down in Force Commanders' Orders, are taken.
(ii) "Jubilee" was a re-mounted "Rutter", for which the troops engaged had been briefed; full details of the operation were, therefore, fairly widely known. For this reason, the routine security plan was modified with the Chiefs of Staff's approval; liaison with security officials in the various Services was kept to the minimum of those whose participation in the operation made them essential to its success.
(iii) In spite of the arrangements mentioned in (i) (*c*) above, disturbing reports of leakage reached C.O.H.Q. immediately before the operation. It will, however, be appreciated that, at the time of "Jubilee", information concerning "Rutter" was beginning to circulate and that

some leakages attributed to "Jubilee" may well have sprung from "Rutter". Some instances of leakages were reported.

(iv) After the operation, conversation with all ranks of the Services showed that there was a fairly general opinion that the enemy had foreknowledge of the raid. Careful examination, however, of the result of the interrogation of prisoners and of other evidence, leaves no doubt that tactical surprise was, in fact, achieved. The widespread belief that the Germans anticipated the raid on the night it occurred arose principally from three sources:

- (a) From the fact that for months we had been encouraging the Germans in the belief that we were about to invade, in order to draw off pressure from the Russian Front. Therefore, a certain degree of readiness was to be expected on any night when conditions were favourable to us.
- (b) From chance remarks in French made by civilians at Dieppe, which were wrongly interpreted to mean "We were expecting you to-day".
- (c) From unofficial statements of German prisoners to their captors, such as that 5,000 reinforcements had arrived in Dieppe a few days before. In fact, we know now that only normal replacements arrived.

(v) it is considered that the operation was not compromised to the enemy before sailing.

Naval Security

(i) The principal measure of Naval security taken was to keep the ships well dispersed while at their embarkation berths. Embarkation took place at Southampton, Portsmouth, Shoreham and Newhaven. This method of embarkation is much more secure than that adopted for "Rutter", where all the ships were concentrated off Cowes, Isle of Wight, and nearby anchorages such as Yarmouth and Southampton Water. The crews of naval craft engaged had no indication that they were putting to sea until 1900 hours on 18th August and had no detailed information about the operation.

(ii) Landing Ships (Infantry) were disguised during the departure from home waters; the material was erected just before sailing and taken off as soon as it was dark. The intention was to make L.S.I. appear as ordinary merchant ships sailing to join a convoy. The disguises were designed to deceive an observer in a fast aircraft passing over the ships at dusk; they could, however, be penetrated by aerial photographs (P.R.U.), but by the time the photographs were developed and distributed it can be assumed that the ships would be at their destination.

(iii) As a result of "Jubilee", N.O. i/c, Newhaven, proposed that Naval Officers in Charge should have authority at their discretion to inform Base Staff Officers of as much of the plan as is essential to their duties. This proposal was referred to C.-in-C., Portsmouth, and has his agreement. The degree to which initiation is desirable naturally varies with the character of each operation and the final decision on "briefing" lies with C.C.O.

(iv) *Ammunition and Stores* – All L.C.T. in Portsmouth Command irrespective of whether or not they were going on the raid were issued with increased stock with a letter saying that this scale of outfit had recently been adopted.

L.C.P. (L) – Petrol and water containers and stocks of soup were issued in bulk to N.O. i/c Newhaven and Shoreham with a letter stating that it had been decided to establish operational stocks in these ports. Nothing was consigned to the craft, except small "done-up" packets of food and ammunition for troops which were delivered at Newhaven and Shoreham half an hour before troops arrived.

L.S.I. – A letter was sent from C.C.O. saying than an increase in stores had been decided upon; all L.S.I. including those that did not take part in the operation were included. Stores were delivered after assembly by army lorries as permanent stores.

Ammunition – Destroyers were loaded at various ports before assembly. Coastal craft were loaded from a lighter moored in the stream opposite Dockyard.

Canadian Force Security

(i) The following general security precautions were taken:
- (a) The force was not concentrated before embarkation. The final move on the day prior to the operation was made under cover of a divisional movement exercises. Planning was done by as limited a staff as possible.
- (b) Suitable cover plans for the planning staff, the waterproofing of tanks, infantry, equipment and stores were arranged and took the form of preparations for exercises, demonstrations, etc.
- (c) Briefing dates were restricted as follows:

Brigadiers	1 August, 1942.
Battalion Commanders:	
In broad outline	4 August, 1942.
In detail	10 August, 1942.
Company Commanders	14 August, 1942.
Field Security Personnel	15 August, 1942.
Troops (On board or immediately Prior to embarkation)	18 August, 1942.

(ii) Orders regarding documents, identity cards, etc., were issued as follows:

Military Detailed Plan – Para. 18 (*b*) of the Detailed Plan issued by the Military Force Commander contains the following:

Each Brigade Headquarters is authorised to carry ashore two complete copies of the Military Detailed Plan (one in each Headquarters craft). *No other copies of orders will be taken ashore* and any information required for the conduct of the operation will be carried as notes. Maps and photographs will be carried as required for operational purposes. *All ranks will ensure that no orders, maps, photographs, operational documents or notes fall into enemy hands.*

    The Germans claim the capture of copy No. 37 of the Detailed Military Plan of Jubilee; they have supported their claim with published details and photographs which leave no doubt that they do in fact hold a copy or parts of a copy. Copy No. 37 was one of the two copies held by Brigadier W.W. Southam of 6th Canadian Infantry Brigade. The Germans, in their published details, stated that copy No. 37 contained 121 pages. A complete copy of the plan contains 199 pages; it is not possible to determine which pages are in German hands. Two copies were taken ashore because either Brigadier might have become the Military Force Commander if the two Headquarters ships had become casualties. The Acting Military Force Commander would then have required to be in possession of more detailed information than would otherwise have been necessary for the conduct of his own particular share in the operation. Although authorised to take their orders ashore by the Military Force Commander, orders taken were in far greater detail than was justifiable.

    After the operation two complete copies of the Operation Orders were handed in at Newhaven by a Naval Officer; he stated that one was found on the beach at Dieppe and another in a derelict landing craft.

(*b*) *Paybooks* – O.R.s were instructed to carry paybooks. As opposed to a British paybook a Canadian Militia Book, Mobilisation (M.B.M.1.) contains details of the soldier's unit, training, etc., and is a complete record of his service. This information carried by a soldier is in direct contradiction to the "name, rank and number" policy which has been taught by means of training films and security lectures.

(*c*) *Officers' Identity Cards and all Personal Papers* – Orders issued were that officers' identity cards and personal papers carried by all ranks were to be collected by the Senior Military Officer in each ship or craft and handed over to the Captain of the ship. Circumstances prevented their being collected in barracks or billets prior to embarkation. These orders were in general obeyed, but some officers' identity cards (AFB 2606) and private papers have been discovered in the pockets of discarded battle-dress blouses since the operation.

No. 4 Commando Security

The original intention was to represent the training at Weymouth as an exercise. As the training proceeded it was clear that from its nature it must be obvious that it was for an actual operation. On 13th August, therefore, two Norwegians were attached so as to suggest a raid on Norway. This second cover plan was marred by the arrival on 17th August, from the Commandos, of three Fighting French personnel, whose shoulder flashes indicated the unit to which they belonged. General Roberts had intended to visit the Commando on 6th August, but was asked not to do so on security grounds.

Press Security

On the day before the first date the raid was likely to take place the Press party were collected at Bristol and Bath. They remained at these places until it was certain the force would sail, when they were driven direct to the ports of embarkation. This arrangement worked very satisfactorily and a similar plan is recommended on future occasions.

Area Security

(i) A representative of M.I.5 who visited Weymouth, Southampton, Portsmouth, Warsash, Stokes Bay, Shoreham, Brighton, Newhaven and Seaford between 11th and 21st August reported as follows:

(*a*) *Weymouth* – The presence of No. 4 Commando naturally aroused some interest and speculation, but there was no indication of any disclosure concerning an operation. The models and mosaics necessary for No. 4 Commando were securely housed.

(*b*) *Southampton and District* – When the Canadian force had been embarked on 18th August, two ratings from H.M.S. *Tormentor* were found on board without authority. They were placed under restraint until 19th August, and then returned to Warsash to be dealt with.

After the Canadians had been embarked, a grenade exploded and 22 men were injured and taken to hospital. Security arrangements made there were successful and no cases of leakage have been reported.

(*c*) *Portsmouth* – Troop movements and assemblies of craft caused comment and speculation, especially in Southsea, on 18th August.

Security of disembarkation at Portsmouth was not good. This failure was due to the fact that the Security Control Officer (S.C.O.) was not given the necessary facilities to carry out his duties. It is understood that this matter is being pursued by M.I.5.

(*d*) *Shoreham and Newhaven* – There was much indiscreet talk. Canadians of the Calgary Tank Regiment were held to say that their tanks had been waterproofed for wading, that some were already loaded in L.C.T., that Commando troops were also involved, etc.

(ii) A report from S.C.O., Newhaven, states:

Harbour Area – Throughout 18th August Security patrols were active and there was a strict supervision at all entrances to the harbour. Only Service personnel concerned with the operation and dockyard employees were allowed near the craft. There were no Security breaches in this connection.

After the operation a number of unauthorised reporters, including some Americans, tried to gain admittance to the port. Naval sentries and Field Security N.C.O.s were posted to reinforce the Harbour police, but these proved inadequate. An unauthorised correspondent managed to bluff his way past the sentries and into the harbour area. He was traced and left when requested to do so; it was found, however, that he had telephoned a story to London. The story was subsequently stopped.

Censorship Report

During the week ending 20th August, 1942, snap censorship was imposed on the following towns: Chatham, Chichester, Dartmouth, Dover, Exmouth, Folkestone, Gillingham, Great Yarmouth, Harwich, Hull, Littlehampton, Newhaven, Plymouth, Poole, Portland, Portsmouth, Ramsgate, Sheerness, Shoreham, Southampton, Sunderland, Teignmouth, Weymouth and the Isle of Wight.

Although stories of an expectant operation and of a Second Front have been seen in many letters very few were in any way specific. The 19th August was one of the dates sometimes mentioned, but it was no more prominent than several others and as far as the small percentage of mail examined goes, the secret was well kept.

The Security Lessons Learned

The Security lessons are as follows:

(*a*) The cancelling of leave presented its usual difficulty. There appears to be no solution short of giving no leave at all.

(b) Certain press representatives had access to wounded in hospitals. In future, hospitals will be warned not to allow this practice.

(c) In some cases, wooden bungs for filling up shell holes were loaded just before the operation. All ships should hold these permanently so as not to arouse any suspicion by last minute loading.

(d) "Most Secret" maps were given by Canadian Military Authorities to press representatives to help them in their duties. A warning against this practice will in future be put in notes for Force Commanders.

(e) The numbers engaged in this operation were too large to be handled on return by the Security authorities available. After an operation is under way the help of additional Field Security Personnel should be obtained.

(f) The only way to stop leakage due to obvious deduction would be to keep a permanent camp, where troops could be sealed for a fortnight or longer if necessary and embarked direct.

(g) Troops should be specially instructed in the importance of bringing back every possible item for M.I.19 investigation.

(h) It is of the utmost importance that all reports of security lapses are immediately reported to C.O.H.Q. to enable C.CO. to judge to what extent the operation may have been compromised.

Appendix II

SECURITY LAPSES AND ACTION TAKEN

SECURITY LAPSES AND ACTION TAKEN

(a) 5613511 Pte. H. Wills, of No. 3 Commando, visited Weymouth and discussed Commando training with friends in No. 4 Commando. He is alleged to have stated that his Commando was shortly going to carry out an operation in France and that the objective was some A/A guns. This case has been investigated by S.S. Bde., who are satisfied that Pte. Wills did not in fact give away such information.

(b) Lieutenant Henry Andreae, R.N.V.R., gave details of the Operation to a woman in Southampton on 15th August. The woman reported the incident and the matter was put in the hands of the N.O. i/c Southampton. C.-in-C. Portsmouth has reviewed the case and found it not sufficiently strong to ensure a conviction. Lieut. Andreae was given a severe warning.

(c) Lieutenant H.L. Fry of No. 3 Commando told two R.N.V.R. Lieutenants at Newhaven that a large scale operation was about to take place and gave some details concerning it. This information was circulated in the Naval Base and became widely known. Lieut. Fry was tried by court-martial, awarded a severe reprimand by the Army Commander 1st Army and returned to his unit.

(d) Lieutenant-Commander D.G. Mason, R.N.R., having been briefed, left his ship with the operation orders in is pocket and returned some hours overdue, being unable to recall exactly where he had been. He has now been invalided out of the Service.

(e) Two A.T.S. subalterns, billeted in the same house as the fiancée of a Signaller of 2nd Cdn. Div. Sigs. reported that the latter had told his fiancée that he was going on a raid.

(f) 2nd Canadian F.S. Sec. reported that at Seaford on the night of 15th or 16th August a Canadian soldier apprehended by the civil police told them, "You can't keep me here. I'm going on a raid on Dieppe Wednesday".

(*g*) 1st Canadian F.S. 2nd Sec. reported that during the change over of 1st and Canadian Divisions "I" Sec. of 48 Highlanders were told of forthcoming raid on Dieppe by "I" Sec. of R. Regt. C., who discussed the operation freely.

(*h*) 3rd Canadian F.S. Sec. reported that an N.C.O. of the Fusiliers Mont Royal visited a Brighton boarding house on 16th August, 1942, and told the landlady he was going on a raid and would not be back.

Note – It is understood that in the case of items (*e*) to (*h*) the necessary action was taken by Canadian Corps.

Appendix JJ

GERMAN STATE OF READINESS

Evidence from interrogation of German Prisoners captured at Dieppe:
(*a*) The captured Guard Report Book of 813 Army Coastal Defence Artillery Troop proves that the Guard was normal on the night of the 18th/19th August, and that there was nothing to report up to 0345/19.
(*b*) At 0130/19, personnel returning to the battery position undressed and went to sleep, despite the fact that this period of August was an "alert" period, in which they were supposed to sleep in their boots. Periods of alert when the weather and tides are favourable for attack are known to be the practice.
(*c*) At the Casino, the alarm was only given about 0500.
(*d*) German air reconnaissance on the night of 18th August, and the immediately preceding nights was, if anything, below normal.
(*e*) The only reinforcements, recently sent to Dieppe, consisted of a new draft for 302 Infantry Division of a low category.
(*f*) The only suspicious circumstances so far revealed are that on 16th August the defences of the Casino were reorganised, and that on 15th August all *Soldbücher* were called in, though this was not done at Varengeville and Poles were given theirs back. German P/W state, however, that the paybooks were withdrawn for vaccination purposes.
2. German unpreparedness for the raid is further shown by:
(*a*) The very late arrival on the scene of the German Air Force.
(*b*) The fact that a lightly escorted convoy was in the area.
(*c*) When the force approached the French coast, Pointe D'Ailly Light and Dieppe leading lights were burning.
The two facts in (*f*) above are trivial in comparison with the rest of the evidence. If a raid was really expected at Dieppe no serious steps were taken to prepare for it; even after the Naval brush in the Channel no forewarning seems to have reached private soldiers.

Appendix KK

ENEMY DEFENCES AND WEAPONS

General
The area of Dieppe was held by *Infanterie Regiment* 571, with two Battalions forward and one in reserve, to a depth of about seven miles. In general, the defences were sited in an *anti-raid* role as opposed to *anti-invasion* role, and the greater part of the fire power was concentrated to cover the available landing beaches. The II Battalion, holding the town itself, west of the river, occupied a position of about 1,500 yards deep, and the landward defences were sited to deal only with an attack from the rear by paratroops or land forces.

Details of located enemy weapons on the main beaches are shown in the map of the defences, and it will be noted how completely the beach is covered by enfilade fire from the west headland. Details of defences sited in the east headland are not available, but the enemy was able to cover not only the sea approaches to the harbour and the main beaches, but also the greater part of the main beach enfilade. Light machine guns along the promenade were sited with arcs of fire out to sea only, and not to sweep the beaches. The Infantry Sections were instructed to fire only at approaching or retreating craft, and the supporting arms alone, in the hands of specialists, had the task of defending the town against a landing.

Prisoners of war seemed to think that the defences on the front were mainly intended as a decoy to draw the fire of the landing parties while the main defence was to come from the cross-fire from the headlands.

It is of particular interest that in both east and west headlands some weapons were sited in artificial caves. On the east headland it is reported that some of these weapons came out to fire and were then pulled back into the caves. Fire from positions such as these is extremely difficult to locate, and it must be realized that their existence could not have been established prior to the operation by air photographs.

The greater part of the weapons on the main beaches were sited in pill-boxes, casemates and behind road blocks, the construction of which is described below. The enemy also made use of a number of shallow grenade pits, which were entered by means of crawl trenches. These were sited to cover wire obstacles or bottle-necks where assaulting troops would be likely to bunch. In particular this was noticed in the angles of the groynes, which were also covered by predicted mortar fire. Mortars were extensively used on all the beaches and in the village of Pourville. Their fire was extremely accurate and well co-ordinated with the machine-gun fire plan, covering areas that were defiladed from machine-gun and small arms fire. The rapidity and accuracy with which new targets were engaged indicate that mortar fire was controlled from Observation Posts. It is reported from all beaches that artillery shells and mortar bombs buried themselves in the sand and shingle before exploding, and consequently the danger area from an individual blast was not very great.

Weapons covering the main beaches included a very heavy proportion of anti-tank guns. Some of these were so sited as to be able only to engage landing craft approaching the beaches and not to cover the beach itself. A heavy flame-throwing equipment was allotted to each of the two forward Platoons of 7 Company holding "White" and "Red" beaches. One of these was sited behind the Casino, and there is a report that the one sited on "Red" beach was used against the men on the sea wall, but this has not been confirmed.

Coast Defence and Field Artillery
(*a*) *Varengeville 6-gun Coast Defence Battery* – The six 15 cm. Coast Defence guns were sited in sunk concrete emplacements, with the primary task of engaging seaward targets by observation from a concrete Observation Post on the cliffs to the north-west of the battery position. This Observation Post was in telephonic communication with other units, presumably at Dieppe. Predicted shoots were also laid on, one of which consisted of a sea barrage in front of Dieppe at about 8,600 yards range, and called for six rounds per gun to be fired. Flak defences consisted of two (possibly three) 2 cm. A.A. guns. The whole position, including the crews' billets, Quartermaster's Stores, etc., was surrounded by a double apron wire fence. Various defence posts within

this perimeter were manned by personnel drawn from the gun crews when required for defence against paratroops or ground forces.

(b) *Other Artillery Positions* – Details about the other battery positions in the Dieppe area are not known, but from available information it may be assumed that the 4-gun Coast Defence battery at Berneval was similar to the Varengeville battery. Field artillery sited south of Dieppe fired principally on the beaches and assault craft approaching the beach came under fire at a range of approximately 500 yards off shore. Mobile batteries were brought into action during the course of the operation but their exact locations were never established. In one case (approximately 0815 hours), three German Infantry guns were seen moving north and crossing the bridge at 209662.

Heavy and Light A.A. Defences

A.A. guns were sited mainly on the two headlands west and east of "White" and "Red" beaches, with the dual role of A.A. defence and enfilade fire on shipping and assault craft approaching the main beaches. It is certain that they also engaged the tanks as they landed on the beach. No details of calibre are available.

Fortifications, Emplacements and Obstacles

(a) *Pill-boxes* – One pill-box, containing machine-guns, was built of concrete about 6 ft. 6 in. high, with only 4 ft. showing above ground. The walls and roof were about 1½ ft. thick, and the door was estimated to be 2 ft. thick. This pill-box was circular, with an inside diameter of 10 ft., and had only one horizontal fire slit. Another pill-box, which contained a 4.7-cm. anti-tank gun, was of similar construction, but square instead of round. The walls and roof were estimated to be 3 ft. thick. At the east end of "Red" beach an obsolete French tank was embedded in concrete and armed with a 3.7-cm. anti-tank gun sited to fire along the beach. Most of the houses on the sea front had been fortified by masonry and/or concrete blocks.

(b) *Road-blocks* – Road-blocks were placed across all the entrances to the town from the promenade. Most of these closed the streets entirely, but in some cases a small gap was left. These road-blocks were about 8 ft. high and some 3 to 4 ft. thick, with a sloping back on which a fire step had been built. Anti-tank guns were sited behind most of these road-blocks to fire over them and directly onto the beaches. The roads on the outskirts of Dieppe were blocked in several successive places so that only one vehicle could pass at a time. Double apron wire fences ran into the fields from these road-blocks and in some cases trip wires were installed to the side of the road to a depth of about 14 ft.

(*c*) *Wire* – Defensive localities and the outer perimeter of the town of Dieppe were protected by double apron wire fences. Two rows of wire about 15 ft. apart covered the main beaches "White" and "Red". The first row nearest the sea consisted of triple dannert backed by a single apron fence. The second row was built on knife rest principle and was about 7 ft. deep. Reports from "Red" beach indicated that the concertina wire used was extremely heavy and sprang back into place when the tanks had crossed it. On the "Blue" and "Green" beaches wire was used to block all exits from the beach, and was invariably covered by mortar fire and from grenade pits.

Booby traps – Three cases of booby traps were reported:
- (i) At "Blue" beach trip wires were discovered on the top of the cliff, which was connected with explosive charges.
- (ii) At "Green" beach a pill-box was found deserted, and immediately prior to the withdrawal was exploded while it was being used as a shelter by some of our troops.
- (iii) At "Green" beach a number of tins were discovered on the sea wall purporting to contain tinned pineapple from Malaya and British Guiana. These were suspected to be booby traps and, for obvious reasons, no tins were touched or brought back.

State of Readiness

From prisoners' statements there appear to be three states of readiness on the French coast:
- (i) Normal state of preparedness.
- (ii) Highest state of readiness when all personnel sleep fully clothed at or near their posts.
- (iii) Extreme state of readiness when all posts are fully manned and weapons loaded, etc.

The highest state of readiness ((ii) above) is adopted during all periods when tidal and lunar conditions are particularly favourable for raids. Two such periods had been ordered since May – the first from the end of June to 25th July; the second (which coincided with the raid) from 1st August to night 19th/20th August.

Practice alarms had been held once a week since May.

Appendix LL

DEFENCES SUMMARISED

1233. The known defences at Dieppe were:

At 151673	S.W. of Varengeville a 6-gun battery. 150 yards N.W. of centre of battery, a single flak gun. 150 yards S.S.W. of centre of battery, a single flak gun.
At 171672	An unoccupied 4-emplacement battery position.
At 177680	An M/G post covering B.6 at Petit Ailly, and short trench system.
At 179678	Where a track leads S. from cliff top, a short trench system.
Between 192679 and 201681	Along Beach 5 at Pourville and on rising ground to the E., are seven M/G pill-boxes covering total distance of 1,000 yards.
At 202681	Close by most easterly pill-box, a searchlight.
At 199680	Pill-box enclosed by single wire, single M/G and short trench.
At 185678	Exit of Beach 5A covered by an M/G post, surrounded by single wire.
At 188678	Wire.
At 191674	A trench system, with an M/G post at each end, on E. side of minor road from Pourville to Le Hamelet.
At 189675	A short trench system.
At 197667	About 1,000 yards S.S.E. of Pourville, a trench system with an M/G post at S. Side.
At 208672	Possible searchlight.
At 203680	Constructional activity.
At 212683	R.D.F. station covered by 2-gun light flak battery – station and battery protected by separate system of single wire.
At 211678	An unoccupied emplacement, heavy flak position.
At 208674	Constructional activity within considerable trench system, which included six M/G pill-boxes and four single M/G posts.

At 218667	A 3-gun light flak battery with military huts close W. of it.
At 220665	4-gun battery.
At 220664	Just S. of above 4-gun battery position under construction.
At 218662	A trench system with three single M/Gs – another trench system with four M/Gs at the S., and two at the N., just S., of this, surrounding a building at 223659.
At 237652	An unoccupied 4-gun heavy flak position.
At 234661	An unoccupied 3-gun light flak position.
At 250646	4-gun battery protected on W. side by single wire.
At 239671	3-gun light flak position with searchlight 200 yards S. of it, and 600 yards W. of it; at 233669 unoccupied 4-gun battery position.
At 226672	*Gambetta* barracks with M/G posts on roof on W. side of road; at 225672 an M/G post.
At 222686	Beach 4, at Dieppe, single wire to W. jetty; six or seven pill-boxes and six covered M/G or A/Tk posts along the 1,700 yards of the beach.
At 243673	Wire along E side of buildings.
At 236688	3-gun unoccupied light flak position with searchlight 70 yards W. of it. N. of searchlight, on cliff behind *Quai de la Marne*, are two small trench systems with single M/Gs, and close N. of these at 235690 two single M/Gs.
At 238692	Three searchlights, Easternmost covered by two single M/Gs.
At 240693	Three searchlights, Easternmost covered by two single M/Gs.
At 245693	Three searchlights, Easternmost covered by two single M/Gs.
At 242693	2-gun light flak battery.
At 243694	4-gun heavy flak battery.
At 258687	4-gun battery; at 256685 a 3-gun light flak battery under construction. These two batteries in centre of large trench system, 1,200 yards (N. and S.) by 800 yards (E. and W.); on N. and N.W. sides three M/G pill-boxes and three single M/Gs. Pill-box under construction on N.E. side, single M/G at middle of E. side. Seven single M/Gs along S.E. and S. sides, 3 single M/Gs on W. side.
At 244675	Short trench system (N. and S.) with single M/G post at each end.
At 254691	550 yards due S. of beach a trench system (E. and W.), with three single M/G posts; 500 yards W. of this another short trench system with single M/G.

At 249688	A further short trench system (N. and S.), 900 yards S.S.W. of beach; it includes single M/G post.
At 257694	Road block S.E. of Puits.
	Many of the fortifications built in Dieppe-Pourville area were reported to have first-class underground shelters for guns' crews.
At 23691	A casemate of recent completion, size approximately 35 ft. by 20 ft.
At 198681	A casemate 16 ft. square appearing to face E. and N.
	A number of excavations, mostly rectangular, were in progress throughout area, from their siting possible foundations for future casemates. Particulars are as follows:
	(a) *Sea Front Area*
At 231689	In side of Boulevard de Verdun, just E. of exit Rue Parmentier.

Appendix MM

SECTIONS OF GERMAN DEFENCE PLANS

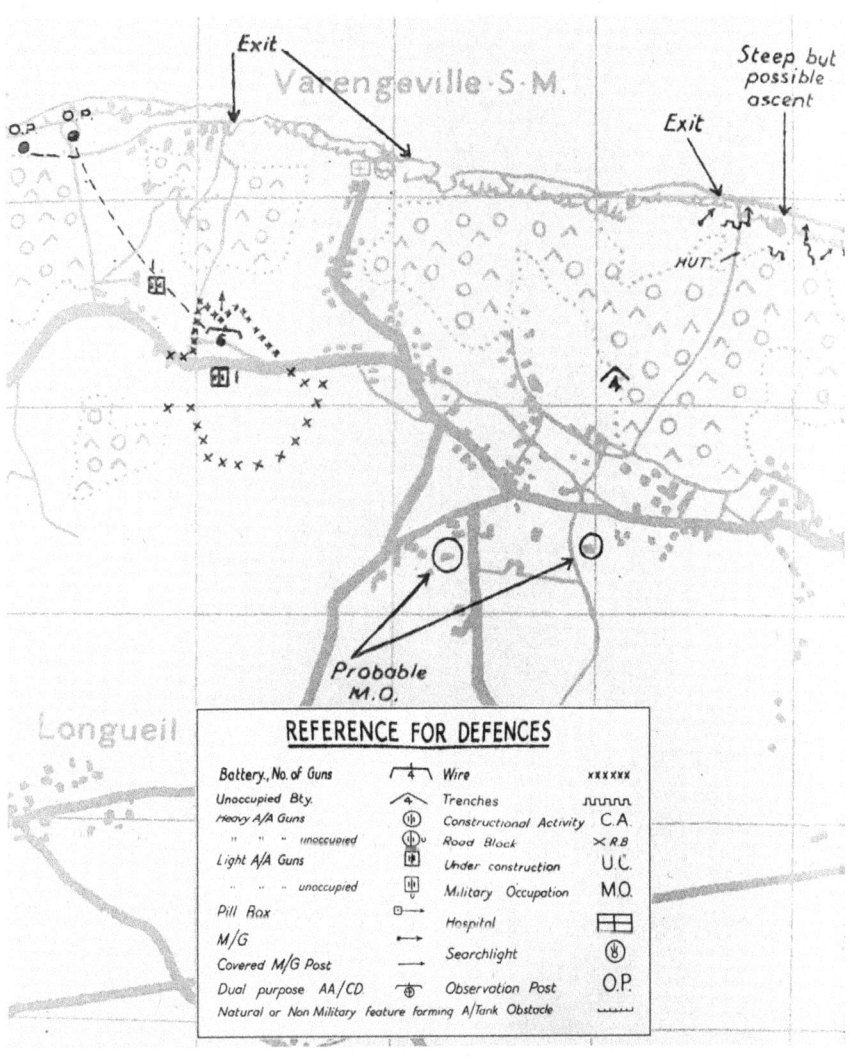

APPENDICES

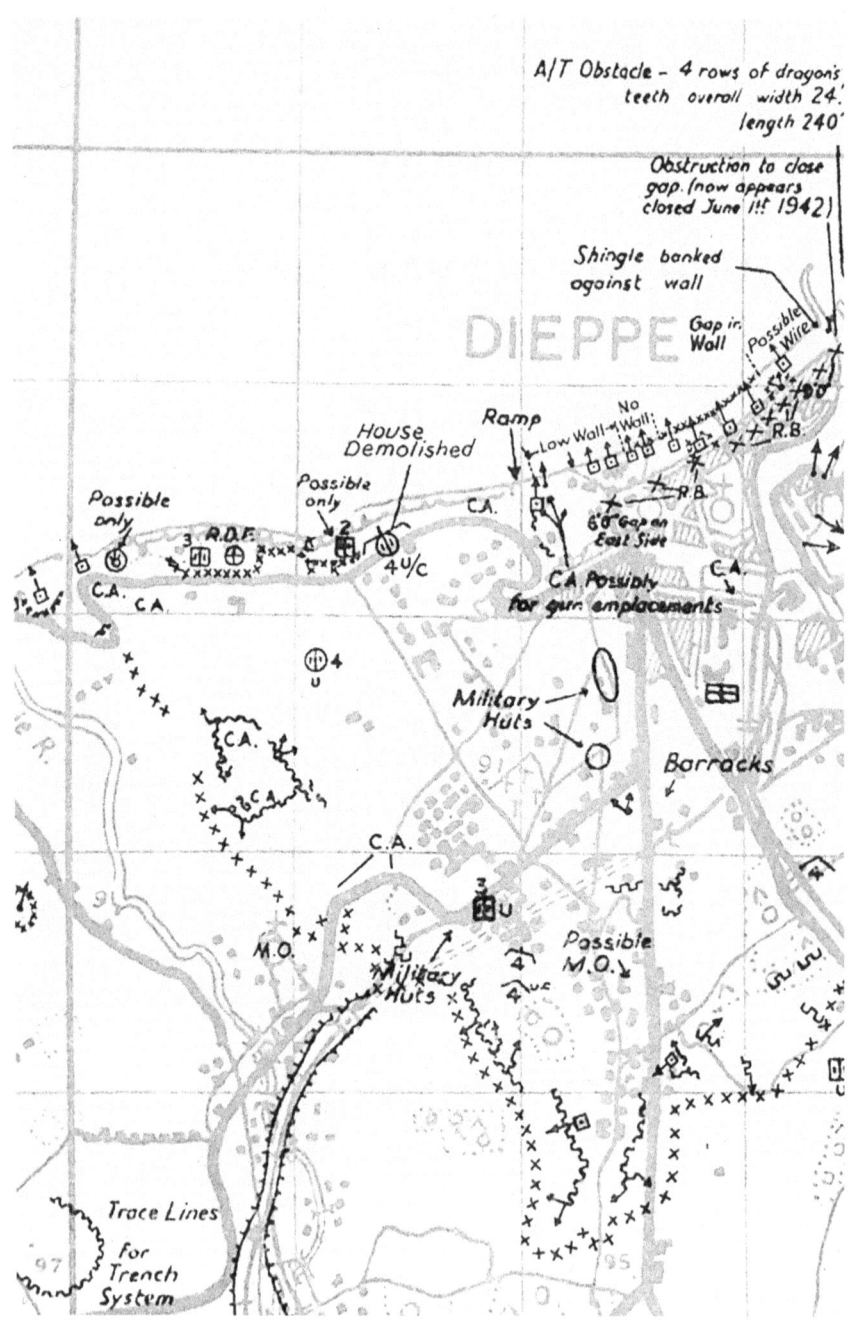

APPENDICES

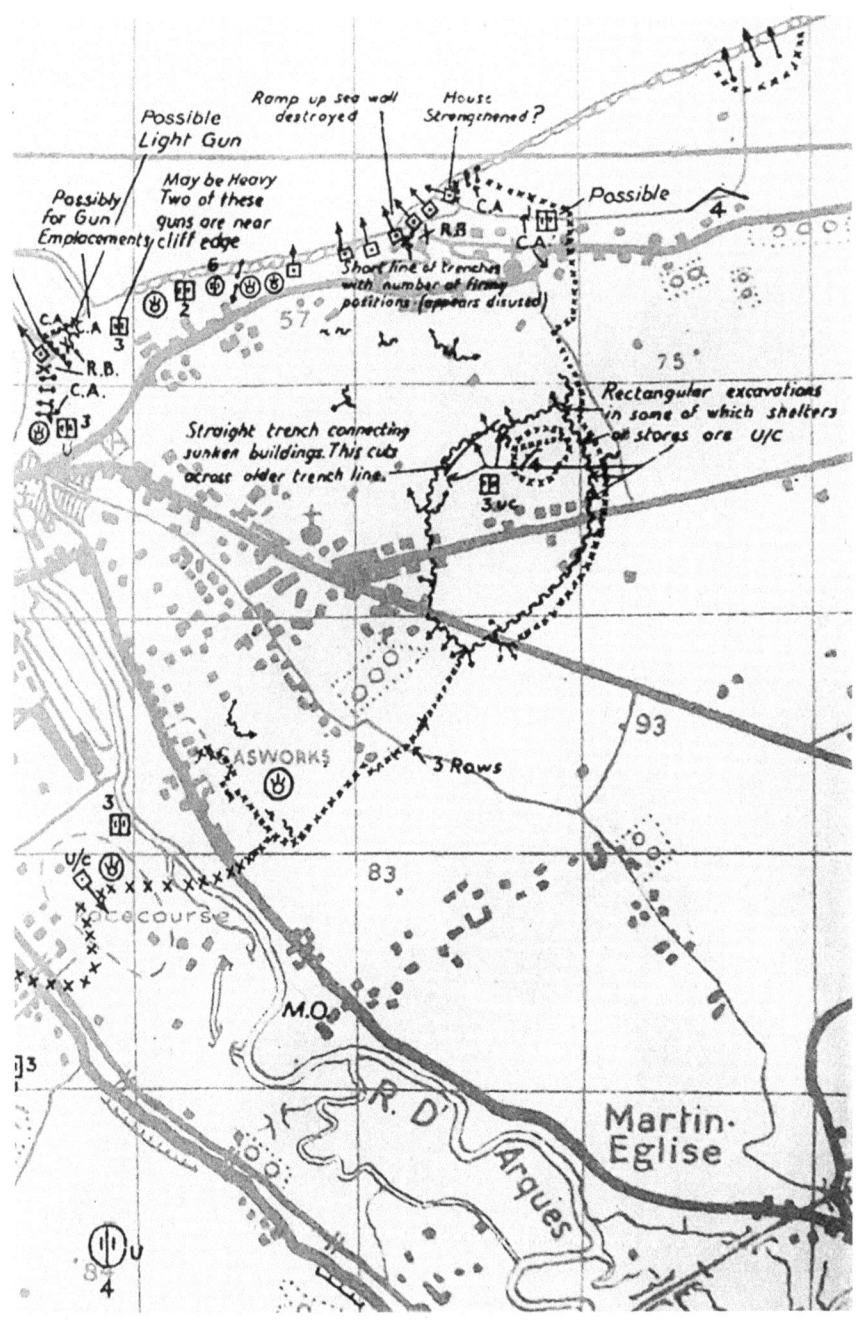

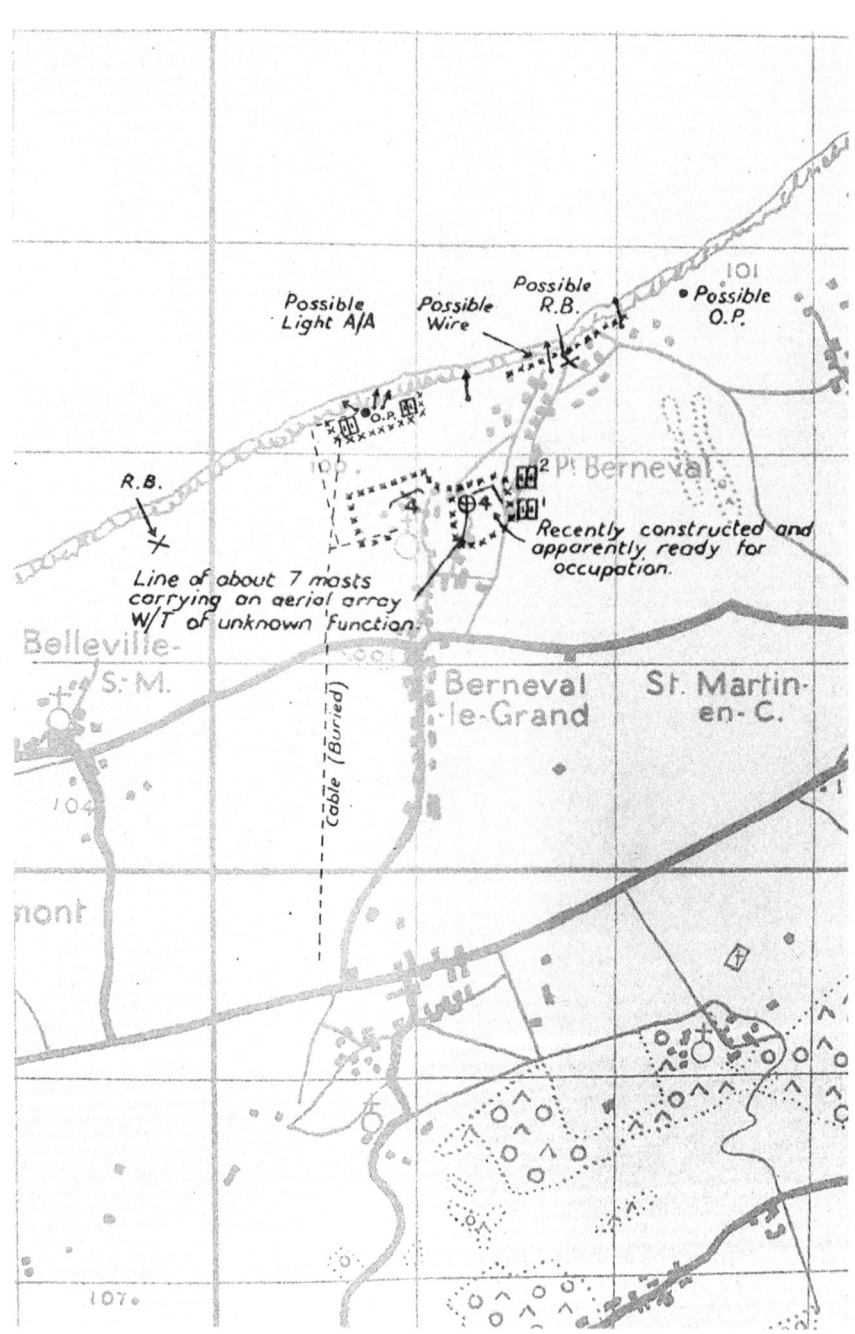

Notes and References

1. Casualties to capital ships and carriers had been particularly unfortunate. In the Mediterranean, the *Ark Royal* and *Barham* had been sunk in November 1941, and the *Valiant* and the *Queen Elizabeth* severely damaged by limpet mines in December; the *Prince of Wales* and *Repulse* were sunk that month off Malaya. Seven cruisers had been sunk in the last 6 months, and the *Dorsetshire*, *Cornwall* and carrier *Hermes* were lost early in April.
2. See Naval Staff History, Battle Summary No. 12.
3. B.R.1887. The Dieppe Raid Combined Report, 1942, p.1. This will be referred to as "B.R."
4. In point of fact the defences were stronger than was thought. There was a coastal battery at Arques La Bataille and two field batteries on each side of the town. In addition, there were eight 75m.m. guns in the town, emplaced so as to sweep the beaches. (Canadian Official History Vol. I, p. 54)
5. This date is taken from B.R. p. 2. It is probable that verbal discussions of which no record was kept had taken place at C.O.H.Q. during March.
6. The policy at this time was to stage a series of raids on an increasing scale (see p. 2.). Dieppe was the largest raid so far contemplated, and the first in which a considerable military force – not under C.C.O's control, as were the Commandos – was to be put ashore. It was these changed circumstances that led the Chiefs of Staff to make their approval of the military part of outline plans for large scale raids contingent on their being agreed by a senior officer of Home Forces from which the troops taking part were to be drawn.
7. B.R. p. 2.
8. B.R. pp. 2,3. The Canadian History gives the date as 11th May.
9. B.R. p. 1.
10. Admiral-of-the-Fleet Lord Mountbatten has explained that an important object of the raid was to test the possibility of capturing a fully equipped enemy occupied port in a condition sufficiently <u>intact and undamaged</u> to land and maintain the follow-up formations. This aspect of the operation may have had its influence on the decision to abandon the high-level bombing of Dieppe as originally planned (see Sec. 7) and on the scale of naval gunfire provided.
11. Adl. Baillie-Grohman would have liked a battleship to have been made available, but it was explained to him that one of the purposes of the raid was to provide a success – or what could be represented as a success – to hearten public opinion after the shocks it had endured in the last six months. Whatever happened, the operation could not have been represented as a success, had a battleship been lost by mine or otherwise in the confined waters off Dieppe.
12. B.R. p. 6. At this meeting Lieut.-General (now Field-Marshal) Montgomery who was then G.O.C., South-Eastern Command, took the chair.

NOTES AND REFERENCES

13. B.R. p. 6.
14. The B.R. does not state whether the question of using more powerful warships was considered. C.-in-C., Portsmouth (Admiral Sir William James) in his letter to the Admiralty, dated 6th September, 1942, stated that in his opinion "a ship with heavy guns and up-to-date control for bombardment might have made a very material difference to the course of the operation after the first landings."
    Naval Force Commander stated (Narrative, para 30). "A capital ship could have been operated during the first hours of daylight without undue risk and would probably have turned the tide of battle in our favour." The report of Rear-Admiral McGrigor's committee (in M. 051641/42) stated that a battleship could have been usefully employed immediately before the landing, but the committee was doubtful whether a capital ship would have been of much use after the troops had landed.
15. 21st-26th June, 4th-9th July, 20th-25th July, 3rd-8th August.
16. Information supplied by Admiral Baillie-Grohman.
17. Captain Hughes Hallett pointed out that with the troops already trained as they were, the raid could be mounted in such a way as to make it very difficult of detection in advance, for there was no need to concentrate the force beforehand. The various units could move direct from their stations to their ports of embarkation and embark there on the same evening on which they were to sail. Further dispersion before sailing was obtained by sending certain troops direct from England in their landing craft, instead of in L.S.I. for transhipment off the French coast, as previously planned.
18. Weather conditions permitting the landing of troops, tanks etc., from the Naval point of view were not necessarily suitable for paratroop operations. In point of fact on the day of the operation, the weather, though satisfactory from the naval point of view, would have made the employment of airborne troops impossible.
19. Constitutional questions were involved, the Canadian General Officers being responsible through Lt. General McNaughten, G.O.C.-in-C., 1st Canadian Army, to the Canadian Government. The matter is dealt with at length in the Canadian Official History, "Six Years of War", Vol. I Chapter X.
20. As events turned out, General Montgomery left the United Kingdom for the Middle East on 10th August, about a week before the raid on Dieppe took place.
    In his memoirs published in 1958, Field-Marshal Lord Montgomery, after alluding to his objection to the remounting of the operation on security grounds, criticises the revised plan for "Jubilee" on two counts, to which he states that he himself would not have agreed.
    a. The elimination of paratroops and replacement by Commandos. "Commando units, if thought necessary, should have been an addition to, and not a replacement of, the paratroops."
    b. The elimination of any preliminary bombing of the defences from the air. "The demoralisation of the enemy defence by preliminary bombing was essential (as was done in Normandy in 1944) just before the troops touched down on the beaches".
    As regards (a), the reason for the elimination of paratroops has been given in the foregoing. It is pertinent to remark that in the event the Commando on the western flank was completely successful in capturing the battery at Varengeville, and on the eastern flank, but for a fortuitous meeting with a German convoy when approaching the coast which resulted in a failure to land most of the troops, there is no reason to suppose that they would not have been equally successful. As it was, the 20 troops who got ashore considerably embarrassed the battery with rifle fire during the main landing.
    As regards (b) the decision to eliminate heavy air bombardment had been taken at a meeting as early as 5th June, at which General Montgomery presided of (B.R. p. 6: "Six Years of War", p. 336), for reasons which no doubt seemed adequate at the time.
    The Field-Marshal also remarks that there were too many authorities with a hand in it; "there was no one single operation Commander who was solely responsible for the operation from start to finish". With the C.C.O. – responsible, but without an entirely free

NOTES AND REFERENCES

hand, – C.-in-C., Home Forces, C.-in-C., 1st Canadian Army and their delegates, C.-in-C., Portsmouth, all, to a greater or less degree involved, besides the R.A.F. Commands, the set-up was certainly complicated. But it must not be forgotten that this was the first large scale combined operation of the kind, and to a large extent experimental.

21 Details of forces are given in Appendices A and B.
22 In point of fact the headquarters had been removed to Envermeu six miles further east. (Canadian History Vol. I, p.352).
23 Zone minus 1 Time (B.S.T.) is used throughout.
24 Nautical twilight (sun 12° below horizon) Commenced 0431. Civil twilight (sun 6° below horizon) 0515. Sunrise was at 0550.
25 B.R. p.10.
26 Before sailing the Naval Force Commander, after consulting C.C.O., placed on record the circumstances in which he intended to abandon the expedition viz., if a considerable number of ships carrying the troops were sunk on passage (B.R. p. 10 and M enclosure 2, par.23), and went on to state that "if a number of heavy bombers could have been provided to make low flying attacks on enemy batteries, his conclusion as to the losses he would accept would have been profoundly modified".
27 The problem arose of how to assemble the flotilla at Newhaven without arousing German suspicions. This was done by sending a flotilla not participating in the raid to Newhaven ten days in advance of the operation, embarking the tanks in pairs of tank landing craft for several nights before the operation and subsequently exchanging loaded craft for empty ones.
28 See the maps provided.
29 See the maps provided.
30 See the maps provided.
31 A number, however, were observed by our forces during their return.
32 18th August, moonset 2316. 19th August nautical twilight 0431.
33 For details of Groups see App. A1.
34 The Portsmouth Naval Staff had grave doubts as to whether it would be possible to pass the whole of the force through the gate of the boom within the forty-minute period that the timing of the operation required. As much as 4 or 5 hours was suggested, but actually it went according to schedule. Captain Hughes Hallett considered that this was among the most important lessons learned.
35 The passage through the swept channels depended on the use of "G" equipment (Navigational aid) in each ship leading a group. The equipment was lent by Bomber Command and worked by R.A.F. personnel. There were doubts about the efficacy of the equipment at the time, and the approach to a narrow channel accurately and without delay had been rehearsed night after night for 14 days before the operation; but in the event it was so successful that under the name "QH" it was subsequently fitted in practically every warship operating in coastal waters.
36 As footnote 35.
37 As footnote 35.
38 AS footnote 35.
39 Landing Ships Infantry.
40 As footnote 39.
41 As footnote 39.
42 As footnote 39.
43 As footnote 39.
44 As footnote 39.
45 As footnote 39.
46 As footnote 39.
47 As footnote 39.
48 See the maps provided.

NOTES AND REFERENCES

[49] German Report, para 1a
[50] M, App. 7, page 47. Extract of Report by Commander Wyburd. Commander Wyburd estimated that he was half a mile to the East of the approach course and six to seven miles from the coast.
[51] Estimates of the strength of the enemy vary; the above figure is taken from the German Report (App. G, para, 1a). Actually, the version of the report used, which is translated from the Italian, says that the convoy was escorted by three submarines. It is possible that the original German was "V. boote" = "Vorpostenboote," and that the Italians who readily confuse the letters U and V read "U. boote" = submarines. Alternatvely the Germans may have called them UJ boote (submarine chasers). The survivors from U.J. 1404 who were rescued by the *Brocklesby* said convoy consisted of eight small ships escorted by four escort vessels. (C.B. 4051/49).
[52] The *Brocklesby* says (M, App. 27, p. 101) "at 0348 sighted gunfire bearing 200°, 6 to 8 miles." N.F.C. says "weather, at 0348, wind force 3 from 160°, sea slight, visibility clear but very dark."
[53] UJ 1404 was armed with one 88-mm. gun and smaller weapons.
[54] B.R. p. 12, para 66.
[55] Report of C.O. of M.L. 346 in M, App. 8, p. 55. This probably means that there was such traffic congestion on all waves that no messages could be sent.
[56] Commander Wyburd in his narrative (M, App. 7, p. 50) says one enemy trawler was sunk for certain and probably two more. The German report mentions no losses among ships of convoy but says the convoy was dispersed North of Dieppe and that at 0745 a small part of it was off St. Valery en Caux. The report also says that three harbour look-out vessels were off Dieppe when the action began. These retired into harbour where one sank probably from a hit received during the battle. It must be remembered however, that this is essentially a military report.
[57] One of these arrived at Newhaven commanded by a sergeant of the Hampshires, all the Naval crew being casualties. He navigated the craft with an army prismatic compass.
[58] There are discrepancies in the different accounts of the movements of L.C.P. after the action. S.G.B. 5 returned to Newhaven with three L.C.P.; it must be assumed that two of these came from another group or else that they were two of the damaged craft. As report of C.O. of S.G.B. 5 is not included in the Appendix to M, it is impossible to be definite about this point. The report of C.O. of L.C.P. (L) 1 is also not included in M.
[59] H.M.S. *Garth* had obtained a contact at 0328 of some vessel some 24 miles to the westward.
[60] In the list of "important signals" (enclosure 5 of M) the two signals from C.-in-C., Portsmouth, are not mentioned, and it is not clear whether, or by what ships, the second signal was received. *Calpe's* signal log has not been seen.
[61] M, App. 22, p. 91.
[62] M, App. 21, p. 89.
[63] M, App. 21, p. 89.
[64] M, Enclosure No. 1, Naval Force Commander's Narrative, p. 1.
[65] Orders to destroyers, JNO (Jubilee Naval Orders) 3 in B.R., p. 66.
[66] Captain Hughes Hallett subsequently expressed the opinion that the Polish Commander Tyminiski of the *Slazak* failed to comprehend the operation orders; he himself would have preferred Lieut.-Commander Pumphrey of the *Brocklesby*, as Senior Officer of the destroyers. It was not until after the operation was over that Captain Hughes Hallett found that a secret order permitting a British officer to be placed in charge, regardless of seniority, in such circumstances, was actually in existence. This order was, however, issued to Commanders-in-Chief only – a good example of the dangers of excessive security.
[67] B.R. p. 52, para. 393.
[68] M, App. 4, p. 33.
[69] B.R. para. 66. The assault force for "Orange" beaches also sighted enemy vessels but successfully avoided them. See section 21.

70. M, Enclosure 1, p.1.
71. M, App. 7, pp. 47-51.
72. German Report, App. G, para. 2.
73. Lt.-Cdr. Goulding in M.G.B. 316, making for Blue beach about 0500, found the Dieppe Harbour lights on (M, Enclosure No. 3, Detailed Narrative, para. 28). Point D'Ailly Light was "burning at 0350" (lt.-Cdr. Mulleneux, idem, para. 9). Point D'Ailly was "an extremely conspicuous and useful mark" (N.C.F. in M, Enclosure No. 9).
74. German Report, para. 10.
75. High water 0405, rise 27 feet. Nautical twilight commenced 0431, sunrise 0550.
76. M, App. 8, p. 52. It is not clear whether this was directed at the escort or at the landing craft. Commander Wyburn's report speaks of touching "down without any opposition." App. 7, p. 49.
77. German Report, para. 10.
78. German Report, para. 60.
79. These vessels were probably the Dieppe patrol vessels mentioned in Chap. II, Sec. 14.
80. B.R. p. 16.
81. German Report paras. 30 and 10. The author of the Canadian History doubts the accuracy of this report and quotes the German 81st Corps' report of material losses sustained. This indicates the destruction of six 5.9 inch guns, but it does not follow that all of them belonged to "Hess" battery; two may have been destroyed in bombing attacks on the other batteries.
82. B.R. p. 17.
83. Conference on Landing Assaults Captain Hughes-Hallett's address, Vol. I, p. 21.
84. B.R. p. 84; provision, however, was made for such support if either landing got held up and a call for fire was received from the F.O.O. concerned.
85. See Sec. 12.
86. Some accounts say at 0507.
87. M, App. 3B, p. 24.
88. M, App. 18, p. 75.
89. L, Vol. I, p. 21.
90. Apparently over 50 of the troops never landed.
91. B.R. p. 18, says "it may well have been the enemy." It had been decided prior to the raid that as the troops would only be ashore for a short time, plain language could be used for operational signals after the attack had started. There is evidence that the Germans noticed this early and made use of it.
92. M, p. 45.
93. The Canadian History (P. 73) states that an error was made in landing the troops, nearly all of whom were put ashore to the west of the River Scie instead of being landed each side of the river mouth and attributes the failure to capture the high ground east of Pourville to the resultant delay. No naval report mentions that the troops were not landed in the right place.
94. M, p. 2. M, App. 16, p. 71. Some were even later; B.R. p. 20 has "ten minutes late at 0530."
95. The sea wall from which numerous groynes ran out towards the sea, was about 10 feet high, but the shingle had been washed up against it, and for most of its length the height above the beach varied from 2 to 4 feet. At five places there were steps leading to the beach.
96. B.R. p. 22, Lt.-Cdr. McMullen's report is given in App. To M.
97. Lord Beatty's orders were that the first three L.C.T. were to beach as soon as possible after, but on no account before, the L.C.A. This would have been at 0525. The next three L.C.T. were to beach at 0535 and were on time.
98. B.R. p. 23.
99. The Naval Planning Staff had repeatedly pressed for the preparation of special explosive tanks for this task.
100. M, App. 11, p. 63.

NOTES AND REFERENCES

[101] Canadian History p. 76.
[102] M, p. 11.
[103] B.R. p. 27.
[104] German Report, paras. 47 and 72.
[105] It seems probable that this claim was exaggerated. The total number of enemy aircraft destroyed during the operation was only 48. (See Section 44)
[106] Captain Hughes Hallett subsequently remarked that it was "remarkable that at no time during the entire operation was there any organised opposition from German naval forces."
[107] B.R.R. p. 139.
[108] L., Vol. I, p. 22.
[109] M, App. 19, p. 80.
[110] R.M. 10410/42, Capt. J.C. Manners' Report. M, App. 19, p. 80.
[111] B.R. p. 26. S.O. of Chasseurs however, says, (M, App. 19, p. 80): "Five of the landing craft had reached the beach and had been shot to pieces. The remaining two had been in and had been ordered back by Col. Phillipps." The S.O.'s. craft had been hit and temporarily disabled shortly before and his report may have been from hearsay, but he was sufficiently well informed of the situation to make a signal to N.F.C. The casualties, however, suffered by the Marines do not seem to correspond with the destruction of five craft.
[112] R.M. 10410/42. The final count of the Royal Marines' total casualties is 7 officers and 93 other ranks, of whom 4 officers and 27 other ranks lost their lives. This includes the Royal Marines serving in the L.C.F.
[113] See Sec. 39.
[114] C.B. p. 21.
[115] "With the help of the beach party these were quickly loaded and had just shoved off when there was a rush of military personnel towards the departing craft. In order to stop this I plunged into the sea and made for the nearest craft. I reached this and gave orders to go full speed astern in order to get clear, but the few extra men who had managed to scramble aboard, together with timely enemy fire, upset the trim of the craft and she sank. One of the remaining craft received a direct hit and sank." – (Extract from report of Lieutenant P. Ross R.N.V.R. White Beachmaster).
[116] M, App. 16, p. 72.
[117] H. and A. 1235/45.
[118] M, App. 16, p. 72.
[119] In B.R. 1887, p. 28 para. 243.
[120] The total number of L.C.A. engaged in the operation was 60. A few had been destroyed during the landing and 14 were employed at Green beach (see Section 36). About 40 were available to evacuate Red and White beaches.
[121] H. and A. 1235/45, M. 3146/45.
[122] The total number of Canadian troops who returned to England was 2078 of whom about 850 never landed at all. After careful investigation, the Canadian Army Historian finds it impossible to determine with complete certainty the number of men evacuated from the beaches. Though fairly reliable statistics are available for the men of each unit who returned to England, there is in most cases no basis for determining how many of these men had actually landed.

The figures finally arrived at are as follows:

Green Beach (Pourville)
Camerons of Canada	258
South Saskatchewan Reg.	<u>343</u>
	601

Red and White Beaches	
14th Army Tank Reg.	3
Royal Hamilton Lt. Infy.	192
Essex Scottish	41
Fusiliers Mont Royal	65
Royal Canadian Engineers	17
Miscellaneous (R. Can. Signals, Royal Marines, Rangler, French Commandos.)	<u>50</u>
	368
Blue Beach (Puits)	
Royal Regiment Canada	<u>6</u>
	6
Flank Beaches	
No. 4 Commando	227
No. 3 Commando	<u>20</u>
	247
Grand total	1222

[123] L. Vol. I. p. 23.
[124] Note, for fuller details, see B.R. 1887 p. 144, et seq.
[125] With him throughout the operation were the Chief of Combined Operations and the G.O.C., 1st Canadian Corps. They had before them on the naval, military and air plots, which were constantly kept up to date as signals came in over the very complete W/T and land line system of communications, a complete picture of the action. Except for a number of discussions on various points with the Royal Air Force Commander, the Chief of Combined Operations and the G.O.C., 1st Canadian Corps refrained from interfering with the course of the operation, which the Force Commanders clearly had in hand.
[126] B.R. p. 32.
[127] C.B., p. 164. "The cover and support afforded by No. 11 Group, R.A.F., were magnificent." M, para. 4.
[128] The Germans claim to have brought down 112 of our aircraft. German Report.
[129] B.R. pp. 33, 164.
[130] Information from Air Ministry Historical Branch.
[131] For Summary of "Lessons Learnt" see App. F.
[132] See pp. 41 (note), 68.
[133] The necessity for a permanent selected force was actually put on record by Captain Hughes Hallett and agreed to by the Chief of Combined Operations two days before the forces sailed for Operation "Jubilee".
[134] The instructions were accepted by Admiral Kirk U.S.N. and used for the Pacific landings; they were also adapted and used in the Mediterranean. Subsequently re-issued as "General Instruction for the conduct of Naval assault forces", they were issued in the great closing amphibious operations of the war.
[135] M. 3146/45.
[136] H. and A. 809/45.
[137] Including permanently missing, and those who died in captivity (mostly from wounds received in the raid).
[138] A considerable number of prisoners of war were wounded. Of these there is no record except for the Canadians, of whom there were 1306 unwounded, 568 wounded.
[139] Including 2nd Canadian Division, Commandos, Rangers and Royal Marine Commando.

NOTES AND REFERENCES

[140] Including permanently missing, and those who died in captivity (mostly from wounds received in the raid).

[141] A considerable number of prisoners of war were wounded. Of these there is no record except for the Canadians, of whom there were 1306 unwounded, 568 wounded.

[142] On p. 26 of B.R. tank losses are given as 28, but the accounts of the landing show that out of 30 tanks carried by the 10 L.C.T. all but one left the craft; 28 were landed and one was drowned. The Germans claimed to have captured 29 tanks (German report, para. 50.).

[143] The crews of L.C.F.(L) varied somewhat in the different craft but were about 2 naval officers and 15 ratings and 2 marine officers and 50 other ranks. In addition, some craft carried a medical officer. (Information from D.C.O.P.)

[144] From B.R. 1887. These lessons are considered in detail in B.R. 1887 and also in a pamphlet B.R. 1887(1) – "The Raid on Dieppe: Lessons".

[145] This lesson did not apply to tanks subsequently developed for special assault purposes e.g. "D.D" ("Swimming" Tanks), A.V.R.E. (tanks equipped for moving beach obstacles, manned by Royal Engineers). See N.S.H., Battle Summary No. 39, "Operation 'Neptune'."

[146] This cannot be correct. Escort vessels are evidently meant, see main text, Section 14, note.

[147] *See* Section 17.

[148] (sic) This no doubt means Admiral, France, *i.e.* German Naval C.-in-C., France.

[149] This was "Goebbels Battery".

[150] This was "Hess Battery".

[151] These were the nine L.S.I. returning home.

[152] This was a small convoy of small ships (C.W. 116) westbound from Southend to St. Helens. There were no large transports in it. There are several references to it in the German Report.

[153] See Note above, para. 11 (d).

[154] See Note above, para. 11 (d).

[155] As above.

[156] App. G. See Note, para. 11.

[157] This was "Hess" battery.

[158] See Note, para. 11.

[159] "Hess" Battery.

[160] Note. Presumably the armed trawler UJ 1404 is meant. There were no E-Boats present.

[161] See Note, para. 11 of this Appendix.

[162] No landing was attempted at this spot.

[163] Presumably for "expended".

Notes on Sources

1. B.R. 1887 issued by Combined Operations H.Q. and containing the combined report on the raid with many plans, diagrams and air photographs. This is referred to in the text as B.R. This report was issued under the signature of the Chief of Combined Operations 15th October 1942, just two months after the raid had taken place. The part of the report which deals with planning, preparation etc., may be taken as accurate, but the part which deals with the actual events of the raid, casualties etc., naturally requires amendment in the light of information not available when it was produced, e.g. reports of returned prisoners of war, German documents captured in 1945, etc. With these reservations the report should be studied if it is desired to go more deeply into the details of the operation.

2. M. 051641/42, Report from Naval Force Commander to C.-in-C., Portsmouth, dated 30th August, 1942, referred to throughout as M. This contains the detailed narrative of the Naval Force Commander (not included in B.R.) and his conclusions and recommendations. It also contains a number of reports from commanding officers of ships and landing craft and from senior officers of groups. Some of the reports are not complete, being extracts only from the original, and in a number of them, times are not given.

3. *Conference on Landing Assaults* (two volumes) issued by the United States Assault Training Centre, Etousa, and here referred to as L. Volume I contains an address given on 26th May, 1943, by Captain Hughes-Hallett on the Dieppe Raid, and an address by General Roberts, who was Military Force Commander at Dieppe.

4. N.I.D. 07886/44. Report by the German C.-in-C., West (Field-Marshal von Rundstedt) containing a report from G.O.C., 81st Army Corps, in whose area Dieppe lay, and also from G.O.C. 15th Army. This is referred to as the "German Report". It is an English translation of an Italian version of the German original. The text may have suffered in the double translation.

5. C.B. 4051(49). Interrogation of survivors of German Armed Trawler U.J. 1404.

6. The Royal Marines report (R.M.10410/42).

7. M. 3146/45. Report of Lt. P. Ross, R.N.V.R., Beachmaster, White Beach.

8. H. and A. 809/45. Award to Lt. D.T. Bibby, R.N.V.R., Beachmaster, Red Beach.

9. H. and A. 1235/45. Report of Commander G.T. Lambert, R.N.

NOTES ON SOURCES

10. *The Canadian Army*, 1939-45, by Colonel C.P. Stacey, Chapters 4 and 5.

11. *Six Years of War (Official History of the Canadian Army)* by Colonel C.P. Stacey, Vol. I, Chapters X, XI, XII.

12. *The Memoirs of Field-Marshal the Viscount Montgomery of Alamain*, K.G. (Collins, 1958).

13. Notes by Vice-Admiral J. Hughes-Hallett, February 1958.

14. Notes by Vice-Admiral T. Baillie-Grohman, June, 1957.